RACE AND RESISTANCE

RACE AND AMERICAN CULTURE
ARNOLD RAMPERSAD AND SHELLEY FISHER FISHKIN
GENERAL EDITORS

RACE & RESISTANCE

LITERATURE & POLITICS IN ASIAN AMERICA

VIET THANH NGUYEN

OXFORD
UNIVERSITY PRESS
2002

OXFORD
UNIVERSITY PRESS

Oxford   New York
Auckland   Bangkok   Buenos Aires   Cape Town   Chennai
Dar es Salaam   Delhi   Hong Kong   Istanbul   Karachi   Kolkata
Kuala Lumpur   Madrid   Melbourne   Mexico City   Mumbai   Nairobi
São Paulo   Shanghai   Singapore   Taipei   Tokyo   Toronto

with an associated company in Berlin

Published by Oxford University Press, Inc.
198 Madison Avenue, New York, New York 10016

www.oup.com

Oxford is a registered trademark of Oxford University Press

Library of Congress Cataloging-in-Publication Data
Nguyen, Viet Thanh
Race and resistance : literature and politics in Asian America / Viet Thanh Nguyen.
p. cm.
Includes bibliographical references and index.
ISBN 0-19-514699-9; 0-19-514700-6 (paper)
1. American literature—Asian American authors—History and criticism.
2. Asian Americans in literature.
I. Title.
PS153. A84 N48   2002
810.9'895—dc21   2001035851

9 8 7 6 5 4 3 2 1

Printed in the United States of America
on acid-free paper

PREFACE

Asian American literary critics are part of a larger class of Asian American intellectuals, broadly defined here to include academics, artists, activists, and political leaders. As an intellectual class, we share a certain set of assumptions about the object of our collective work, Asian America, and in *Race and Resistance*, I argue that this consensus can be seen through the work of Asian American literary critics, particularly in the theory of value that literary critics use to assess literature. These critics have been inclined to see Asian American literature as a body of texts that demonstrates opposition to, or accommodation with, the various kinds of oppression that Asian Americans have had to endure. Even as critics recognize that there are some, perhaps many, Asian American works that embody a politics of accommodation or a tendency toward accommodation, these critics are still predisposed to read for resistance, to either look for and place value upon those works that embody this type of politics or emphasize the propensity toward opposition that may be found in ambivalent texts. Likewise, on a larger scale, Asian American intellectuals as a whole have tended to see Asian America as a place of resistance and have not been capable of articulating a theoretical framework that can address Asian America's ideological diversity and contradictions. In order for Asian American intellectual work to be more effective, it must be able to recognize the existence of this diversity within Asian America's populations, and it must be able to anticipate the day when the current political consensus of Asian American intellectual work will end as this ideological heterogeneity makes itself manifest among the ranks of Asian American intellectuals themselves.

In this book I both follow the well-established and vital political tradition of Asian American literary criticism and go against it. Like the critics who have gone before me and laid the foundations for my work, I argue that the literature we read and the criticism we write are deeply political, but I also draw attention to the fact that the political significance critics have found in the literature may stem as much from the critics' own biases and priorities as from what may be found in the evidence offered by the texts themselves. This critical predisposition on the part of Asian American studies is a result of its origins in the political upheavals of the late 1960s. This era and its attendant struggles shaped Asian American studies' vision of itself as a local site for opposition within academia and the world of intellectual work. Examining Asian American literature published from 1899 to 1999, I demonstrate that the critical tendency to read for resistance or accommodation actually misreads the literature in certain cases, first through a polarization of the options available to the authors and second through an idealization of the political and ethical value that can be attributed to resistance or accommodation. I contest the dominant theory of value by closely reading Asian American literature's deep concern with representing the Asian American body. These representations of the body are the most consistent trace of political consciousness in the literature, because authors engage with the dialectic of oppression, resistance, accommodation, and absorption centered on Asian American bodies by deploying their own characters' bodies as symbolic of a larger Asian American "body politic," the collective Asian American community. These authors use flexible textual and political strategies that defy easy categorization into either resistance or accommodation, and they represent a wide range of diverse ideological opinions. The difference between the ideals of Asian American literary criticism and the actual ideological heterogeneity of the authors and texts is symptomatic of the difference between Asian American intellectuals and their object of concern, Asian America.

This divergence between theory and object, between the intellectual perception of Asian America and its actual multiplicity, constitutes a crisis of representation for Asian American studies and Asian American intellectuals as they seek to study, organize, and lead Asian America. In order for Asian American studies and Asian American intellectuals to address this crisis of representation, I argue that we need to reevaluate some of our rigid theoretical assumptions about politics, race, and social change.

Le Cao, for her humor and kindness. I count myself incredibly fortunate to have found in Lan Duong a soul mate with whom I have been able to share and experience many things. She has been a source of constant good cheer and affection, and her intellectual and emotional presence in my life has made me a better person and a better scholar. My parents, Joseph Nguyen Ngoc Thanh and Linda Kim Nguyen, who always wanted me to be a doctor, nevertheless graciously stood by me as I studied literature and pursued a different kind of doctorate. They have asked me many times since I graduated when I would finally be finished with my book, and I am happy to say, here it is. This book is dedicated to them, as a small acknowledgment of their struggles in raising my brother and me, and helping us in our endeavors.

Los Angeles
March 2001   V. T. N.

CONTENTS

RACE AND RESISTANCE

INTRODUCTION

A Crisis of Representation

This book, like many other works of Asian American literary criticism that preceded it, is about literature and politics. For better or worse, Asian American literary critics have generally approached Asian American literature as being symptomatic of ongoing historical concerns for Asian Americans—to read the literature, then, enables the critic to form political theses about the state of Asian America. I follow in this tradition because I believe literature matters, and in this book I insist that Asian American literature literally embodies the contradictions, conflicts, and potential future options of Asian American culture. I also argue that the way critics have tended to read this literature, as cultural works that demonstrate resistance or accommodation to the racist, sexist, and capitalist exploitation of Asian immigrants and Asian Americans, may be as much a reflection of the critics' professional histories, political priorities, and institutional locations as what may be found in historically framed close readings of the works themselves. Furthermore, the relationship of critics to literature parallels the relationship of Asian American intellectuals generally to Asian America. In other words, the theory of value that critics use to approach literature—what critics consider as the important things they should look for, encourage, and propagate—is shared by Asian American intellectuals as a whole as they seek to study, represent, and lead Asian America.

In many of the works that I examine in this book, resistance and accommodation are actually limited, polarizing options that do not sufficiently demonstrate the *flexible strategies* often chosen by authors and characters to navigate their political and ethical situations. This book negotiates between the flexibility and diversity of the texts on the one hand and the more rigid discourses of American racism and Asian American literary criticism that shape the reception and interpretation of the literature on the other hand. The ultimate irony in contemporary Asian American literary criticism is that a key flexible strategy used by Asian American literary criticism to enable its institutional survival in the university is often disavowed by Asian American literary criticism when it comes to evaluating the authors and characters of the literature. This strategy is one that Yen Le Espiritu calls "panethnic entrepreneurship" (*Asian American Panethnicity* 166). Panethnic entrepreneurs literally capitalize upon their panethnic, or racial, identity. While we can see the post-1968 founding of Asian American literary criticism, and of Asian American studies in general, as a shift of Marxist-inspired political struggle from the "community" to the academy and from "real" politics to textual politics, the contemporary institutionalization and growth of Asian American literary criticism and Asian American studies is now equally beholden to the strategy of panethnic entrepreneurship, trading in the commodity of race.

Panethnic entrepreneurship is a product of the dialectical relationship between a capitalism that exploits race and the democratic struggles that have fought for greater racial and economic equality. This dialectic has transformed race and racial identity into focal points of organization and struggle, but it has also transformed race and racial identity into commodities. This dialectic and its result in panethnic entrepreneurship for Asian Americans can be traced to the nineteenth century, with the arrival of Chinese immigrants and their economic exploitation by American capital. The subsequent strategies that Chinese American authors such as Onoto Watanna and Sui Sin Far deployed included a deliberate blurring of the ethnic lines that separated European, Chinese, and Japanese Americans. These experiments with ethnic identity were not, however, articulated through a post–civil rights understanding about the potential of racial identity, or panethnicity, as a mode of political resistance. The emergence of a unique Asian American identity after 1968 was dependent upon such an understanding, but it also coincided with the maturation of a global capitalism that had the ability to turn even resistance into a commodity. In this contemporary moment of global capitalism, our modern version of panethnic entrepreneurship is a flexible strategy of pragmatic political struggle that blurs the clear-cut, idealized distinction between resistance and accommodation that is the foundation of a self-defined Asian American identity stemming from the 1968 campus and community struggles.

As people who have participated in these struggles or as inheritors of the legacy of these struggles, Asian American critics do not generally read literature or look to the historical past in order to uncover examples of panethnic entrepreneurship and its effectiveness. The entire concept of panethnic entrepreneurship, with its basis in race as a product or function of economic capital and its connotations of "selling out," is antithetical to Asian American academia specifically and to Asian American intellectuals generally. The Asian American intellectual class, defined here as inclusive of academics, artists, activists, and nonacademic critics, is a part of the realm of cultural production that finds its basis in what Pierre Bourdieu calls the economic world reversed (*Cultural Production* 29). In this reversed world, it is not economic capital, that is, money and its investment, that matters as much as *symbolic* capital, other things besides money that we invest with value and which eventually generate an economic return. For the Asian American intellectual class, it is racial identity as a mode of resistance to capitalist exploitation that accrues symbolic rather than economic capital. In simple terms, we as academics or intellectuals make very little economic capital, *relative* to something like the world of corporations, but this is partially a function of our investment in the idea of Asian America as a place of resistance to capitalist exploitation. In the case of Asian American studies specifically, while it is obviously a worthy political and intellectual endeavor in many ways, it is also an enterprise of panethnic entrepreneurship within academia, reaping the particular and peculiar rewards of academia by using the symbolic capital of race and resistance.[1]

In writing this book, I aim to read Asian American literature *for* its flexible strategies that concern struggle, survival, and possible assimilation, which means often reading *against* the rigid assumptions of a newly institutionalized Asian American literary criticism that disavows panethnic entrepreneurship. In a similar vein, Jinqi Ling argues that Asian American literary critics often overlook the fact that Asian American literary texts engage in a process of "negotiation" (*Narrating Nationalisms* 11), whereby "these texts' ideological tendencies and formal characteristics, as well as the specific forms of their social imagination, were shaped not by any single determinant but rather by the complex interplay between authorial design, available social space, and accessible cultural resources" (30). Ling attributes the tendency of contemporary Asian American literary criticism to misread early Asian American literary texts as being ideologically or textually simple to the criticism's poststructuralist sympathies. Expanding upon Ling, I propose here that the problem of misreading is much graver, and stems from an ideological rigidity in the criticism itself. I argue that the criticism tends to read for signs of resistance or accommodation because critics are reacting to the demands of American racism, which have historically treated Asian Americans as the bad subject to be punished or expelled or as the model minority to be included or exploited for complicity. At the same time, the criticism does not recognize how such a critical predisposition resonates with the commodification of race and the practices of panethnic entrepreneurship within the academy. Such a lack of recognition may indeed be a function of disavowing uncomfortable contradictions. The critical misreading of the texts that results becomes emblematic of the more significant misreading that Asian American intellectuals are engaged in when it comes to Asian America as a whole.

To support these contentions about the political unconscious of Asian American critical practice, I read Asian American literature for its representations of the body, because these representations collectively constitute the most consistent form of political consciousness in the literature. They are commentaries upon the troubled place of Asian Americans in the American body politic and upon the nature of an Asian American body politic as well. For Asian American writers, a deep interest in representing the body, through a variety of fashions and over a range of time and situations, is almost always evident in the literature. This is not surprising given the way that dominant American society has historically used derogatory, bodily centered representations of Asians and Asian Americans in order to facilitate capitalist exploitation and foment racial hatred. Asian American writers, as a result, have turned to the representation of the body as a method of exploring and possibly countering the consequences of such exploitation and hatred. Their literature contains a history of representations of the body that develops in relation to the changing status of the Asian American body politic in the United States during the past century. As this status changes, so do the representations of the body, resulting in the domination of particular kinds of bodies in the literature at different historical moments. These changing bodies constitute a rhetoric of the body that has existed since the 1899 publication of Onoto Watanna's *Miss Numè of Japan*, the first novel written by an Asian American, and extends to 1999, with the publication of Lois-Ann Yamanaka's *Heads by Harry*, the last novel I consider in this book. As we shall see, by its very nature the Asian American body politic is defined not only by race and class—the traditional intellectual lenses of Asian American studies—but also, simultaneously, by gender and sexuality, to such an extent that Asian American writers, male and female, often articulate their concerns about race and class *through* gender and sexuality. As Rachel Lee argues, "Gender and sexuality remain instrumental to the ways in which Asian American writers conceive of and write about 'America'" (*The Americas* 3).

The fact that the Asian American body is composed simultaneously through race, class, gender, and sexuality has become an accepted truism of Asian American critical practice, exemplified in Lisa Lowe's justly famous characterization of the Asian American body politic as being marked by "heterogeneity, hybridity, multiplicity" (*Immigrant Acts* 60). For the most part, however, Asian American critics have been concerned with the *demographic* heterogeneity of the Asian American body politic and not with its *ideological* heterogeneity, the concern of this book. (Ideological heterogeneity should not be mistaken, of course, for *class* heterogeneity, which most Asian American intellectuals are willing to acknowledge.) While American racism's focus on the body has meant that the representation of the body remains as a trace of political consciousness in almost all Asian American literary works, this does not mean that there is a predetermined ideological orientation to the works or that an ideological consensus can be found in them. In contrast, Asian American critics tend to see texts as demonstrating either resistance or accommodation to American racism. Not willing to read for ideological heterogeneity, the critics betray their own ideological rigidity. The primary consequence of such rigidity is that critics tend to evaluate resistance as positive and accommodation as negative, without questioning the reductiveness of such evaluations. Part of this critical consensus stems from the fact that although this century-long span of 1899 to 1999 has witnessed significant changes for the roles and perceptions of Asian Americans, it has also witnessed a noticeable and important *lack* of change that concerns the *basic* political representations of Asian Americans. In the past and in the present, dominant American society has tended to cast Asian Americans in one of two ways: as an inevitably foreign threat (the "bad subject") or as an exemplary example of domestic integration—the "model minority." Given this bifurcated representation of Asian Americans, we might assume that resistance and accommodation, bifurcated responses, are the most commonplace categories of action for Asian Americans. It is my argument, of course, that this is not the case, and the flexible strategies exhibited by Asian American authors and literary characters are testimony to the ways Asian Americans in general pick and choose their tactics of struggle, survival, and possible assimilation. The fact that Asian American studies specifically, and Asian American intellectuals in general, prioritize resistance and condemn accommodation stems from the moment of 1968, when Asian American intellectuals self-consciously formed "Asian America."

The year 1968 is historically convenient and memorable but not quite adequate in encompassing previous or subsequent efforts to unify diverse Asian ethnicities into one political and cultural bloc. Nevertheless, I proceed from this time because it forms a landmark in the self-definition of the most influential portion of the Asian American intellectual class, who identify this year as critical because it allows for a unification of political potential over cultural diversity. In short, 1968 forms a clear moment of *self-articulation* on the part of Asian American intellectuals that concerns the constitution of an Asian American body politic as a diverse but unified group engaged in a struggle for racial equality. The belief in racial equality, or specifically the idea that race should not be used to exploit people politically and economically, is probably the *only* safe description of any political consensus in Asian America today.[2] While one can conjecture that the mainstream Asian American intellectual class generally favors proactive methods and ideologies for creating a situation of both racial and economic equality, it is unclear if there is a consensus regarding what those methods and ideologies are and what is meant by "equal-ity." In addition, as the visibility of Asian Americans on the American political landscape has increased in the past thirty years, the political and intellectual leadership of Asian America has been challenged in practice by the diversity of its constituents, initiating a *crisis of representation* in the Asian American body politic that has not yet been fully recognized by the leadership but has exploded in incidents such as the controversy over Lois-Ann Yamanaka's novel *Blu's Hanging*.

In 1998 the Association for Asian American Studies decided to award its annual prize for literary merit to *Blu's Hanging*, immediately igniting a firestorm that almost destroyed the Association. *Blu's Hanging* is a novel that centers on a local Japanese family living in Hawaii's multiethnic, class-stratified society. Part of the novel depicts the molestation and rape of a local Japanese boy, Blu, by a young man of mixed Filipino and Japanese ancestry, Uncle Paulo, who also has incestuous sexual relations with his pubescent nieces. The cycle of violence and victimization initiated by Uncle Paulo continues with the nieces, who not only take sadistic pleasure in torturing and killing cats but also are ac-tually responsible for Blu's sexual initiation, prior to his molestation and rape. Before and during the Association's annual meeting, Yamanaka's novel became the target of concerted protests by Filipinos and their supporters over allega-tions that concerned the book's racist depictions of Filipinos. The Association was divided between the supporters of these allegations and those who argued that the protests were attempts at censorship.[3] During the annual meeting, as the Association's membership discussed revoking the award (which they even-tually did), the Association's board of directors resigned en masse—with one exception—for fear of assuming personal legal responsibility over the renun-ciation of the award, since the Association was neither incorporated nor insured.

Blu's Hanging clearly demonstrates the importance of the body and its representation in both literature and politics. The representation of the body be-comes immediately apparent when we remember that the controversy is fo-cused on a sexual crime that occurs in a novel generally concerned with the problems of female adolescence and sexual consciousness in a class- and ethnic-conflicted setting. It is this crime centered on the body that leads to the contro-versy over the nature of the Asian American body politic itself. One aspect of this controversy concerns the ethnic diversity of Asian America and how it might contradict a unified Asian American political front. The problem of ethnic diversity among Asian Americans, considered in isolation, may lead us to turn to a pluralist ideology of interest-group negotiation, resolved by the motto *e pluribus unum*, as a solution. The controversy ignited by Yamanaka's novel, however, signifies a graver problem than ethnic diversity for Asian America. That greater problem is *ideological* diversity, and it threatens the ability of Asian America to represent itself in a unified fashion. The particular way in which this crisis of representation over ideological diversity takes place in the controversy centers on the following question: should the Association be com-

mitted to a model of equitable political representation for all its constituent ethnicities, or should it be committed to a model of free speech and artistic freedom? These choices, while crudely articulated here, nevertheless characterize
the positions adopted by the opposing sides in the controversy.

One of the ironies in the controversy was that Asian American intellectuals, artists included, have rarely found it problematic to speak out against anti-
Asian racism in American art, most memorably in protests directed against the
Broadway musical *Miss Saigon*.[4] Yet, in the Yamanaka controversy, we find Yamanaka's defenders, including many artists, returning to the same language of
artistic freedom deployed by *Miss Saigon*'s producers. The case of *Miss Saigon*
demonstrates that anti-Asian racism makes us all Asian, rather than singularly
ethnic, and that Asian America as a category or identity is effective in a *defensive* posture. In contrast, from the perspective of Yamanaka's defenders, the
issue of possible prejudice becomes purely a problem for Filipinos and cultural
philistines who do not understand literary technique and artistic freedom. In
other words, when prejudice is intraethnic rather than racial, the ability of
Asian America to articulate a cohesive identity is fractured. Asian America,
born from a dialectic of racism and antiracism, may not in the end be very effective in presenting an *offensive* posture in order to address issues beyond racial
discrimination. We can understand the implications of the Yamanaka controversy when we consider the larger issue of Asian American demographics and
what it entails politically. As Asian America has witnessed the growth of its
power in the past thirty years due to a rising population and increased political
organization, it has also witnessed the growth of a demographically diverse
population that is also ideologically diverse due to its wide range of origins and
points of entry into American society.

In the past and to some extent in the present, Asian American intellectual
and political leadership could count on the threat of racism to unify the Asian
American population. This racism often expressed itself through capitalist exploitation or working-class rivalry. Therefore, antiracist positions advanced by
the leadership often had anticapitalist connotations. In the contemporary moment, however, American and global capitalism is succeeding in the *reification*
of Asian American culture, despite the best efforts of Asian American intellectuals. Reification transforms human relationships into the relationships between things, originally made by humans but now seemingly independent (and
"imagined as originally independent" [Bottomore 462]).[5] Thus the contemporary Asian American identity that has allowed Asian Americans to participate
in American politics—frequently as an anticapitalist force—has now also become a thing, a commodity, to be marketed and consumed. While Asian American political identity has enabled political resistance against racism and capitalist exploitation, Asian American cultural identity in the present moment
furthers the aims of capitalism because Asian American cultural identity—an
Asian American *lifestyle*—is both a commodity and a market at the same time.[6]

As a consequence, Asian American intellectuals who have traditionally opposed reification and the way capitalism has historically used racial differences to exploit Asian American populations must now confront Asian American populations that find in this racialized capitalism a positive form of cultural exploitation. Asian American intellectuals have not seriously explored *either* the reality that Asian American identity is a commodity *or* the positive possibilities that such commodification enables. In other words, if Asian American intellectuals were to investigate the commodification of Asian American identity, they may be predictable in doing so by examining *only* its negative consequences. Yet it may be the case that in the next few decades some of the most important Asian Americans, in terms of transforming American perceptions of Asian Americans, will not only be Asian American intellectuals but also Asian Americans who are capitalists or who are unabashed panethnic entrepreneurs. An example of the former is the Internet and high-tech entrepreneur, who is destroying the stereotype of the Asian American as technician and middle manager; examples of the latter are the creators of *A. Magazine*, which combines a liberal political and cultural slant with a slick marketing of fashion, technology, culture, and lifestyle to upwardly mobile, highly educated, cosmopolitan young Asian Americans. Regardless of what one thinks of the *kinds* of achievements these Asian Americans are making or whether it is worthwhile to reform American capitalism to be inclusive of Asian Americans, it is inarguable that such achievements have a radical and material impact on Asian American culture. These achievements enable greater political and cultural participation in American society for many Asian Americans—including Asian American intellectuals.

This transformation of racialized capitalism, from a totally negative exploitation of race through the mid–twentieth century to its partially positive exploitation today, finds its roots in the intersection of racialized capitalism with American pluralist democracy. In order to obtain political voice and economic equality, Asian Americans found themselves forced to participate in a pluralist political system that privileges representation by large political interests, one of the most noticeable being, after the civil rights movement, racially defined groups. Political representation through race, taking the form of multiculturalism, has transformed minority racial identities from being stigmatized to celebrated, at least on the level of the *representative* (if not necessarily the *represented*). This celebration of race in the form of pluralist political and cultural representation has also meant that racial identity has become a cultural icon and commodity, in variable ways for different racial populations. For Asian Americans, this transformation of race into a cultural icon and commodity in the marketplace of multiculturalism is embodied in the model minority. The model minority is an identity that is testimony to the Asian American ability to be good citizen, productive worker, reliable consumer, and member of a niche lifestyle suitable for capitalist exploitation. The model minority is the vehicle of entry for a racial population not only into American capitalism but also into American politics—indeed, the two go hand in hand.

For Asian America, therefore, a significant tension exists between an attraction to the marketplace of multiculturalism, represented by the model minority, and a distrust of or outright resistance to capitalism, represented by the mainstream of the Asian American intellectual class. This ideological conflict within Asian America is a problem for the Asian American communities and signifies that Asian America is and will be in a state of flux that is part of the process of racial formation. Racial formation in the United States has saturated racial identities with political meanings, although that does not mean that the Asian American body politic is inherently oppositional to a political order based upon racial differentiation, class stratification, and the contradictory tensions between democracy and capitalism. Racial formation is an aspect of *hegemony* in the United States. Hegemony is the political process by which the dominant class of a society extracts the political consensus of subordinate classes whose interests may be contradicted by that dominant class. As an aspect of hegemony, then, contemporary racial identities involve some type of consensus to the dominant political order. Therefore, Asian America is not simply or only a mode of opposition to this order. It also participates in political struggles over the meaning of citizenship and subjectivity within the American body politic, assuming a variety of possible positions that range from opposition and contestation to acquiescence and consensus with the dominant body politic.

Asian American intellectuals, however, have been most interested in representing themselves and the object of their study—Asian America—as sites of political and cultural contestation against forms of racial and class hierarchy integral to American society.[7] We have not been as interested in critiquing how we ourselves may be obscuring differences of power within Asian America or the limitations to our own theory and practice that ensue from an ideological belief that Asian America is *only* a place of ethnic consensus and resistance to an inherently exploitative or destructive capitalism. It is my belief that for Asian American intellectual work to grow in vitality not only must it continue the vital task of criticizing American society's methods of racial and class domination, but it must also engage in a self-critique that results in an understanding of Asian America's limits.[8] I am not alone in this belief, for there is also a significant, if minor, strand of thought among Asian American intellectuals that articulates a similar concern about these limits. Interestingly, many—although far from all—of these intellectuals are of Filipino and South Asian descent, suggesting that the theoretical concerns they and I have about the theoretical and political consensus within Asian American intellectual work is at least partially a product of a sense of intellectual and ethnic exclusion from an Asian American coalition whose concerns and priorities have been shaped by the historical domination of intellectuals who come primarily, although not exclusively, from Japanese and Chinese American backgrounds.[9] It is important for me to acknowledge, however, that when I speak of Asian American intellectuals in this fashion, I do so in complete recognition of how the work of an earlier generation has enabled my own. The list of artists and academics I am indebted to is

lengthy, and their work is cited throughout this book as a gesture to the foundations they have built and upon which this work is constructed. Their commitment to a model of intellectual work as political contestation, which has directly
contributed to the formation of Asian America and the creation of Asian American studies, has made my own critique possible.

What I propose in my critique is that the challenge for Asian American
intellectuals is to reconsider conventional assumptions that concern race and
its formation without at the same time engaging in a reactionary "retreat from
race," simply because racial identity is a contradiction.[10] Asian America as an
identity and focal point for alliances and cultural formation has proven to be
useful and productive in many ways, allowing for the articulation of genuine
dissent with the racial and class politics of the United States. It has also allowed,
arguably, the formation of an exciting, hybrid culture that is first and fore-
most Asian American, rather than ethnically specific. While it is critical for us
to acknowledge that Asian America is an outcome of radical social movements
that were opposed to capitalism and its excesses, we must not forget that in the
contemporary moment Asian America is also useful to capital through racial
formation. Through race in its contemporary form, the state is able to identify
populations and select representatives for a pluralist system of government
that is committed to propagating capitalism, which in its turn transforms Asian
American identity into both a lifestyle commodity and a market for that commodity. Asian American identity and American capitalism are thus engaged
in a dialectical relationship of mutual transformation. For Asian American academics, this intersection of race and capitalism is manifest in our own disavowed practice as panethnic entrepreneurs; while entrepreneurial practice
allows us to further our existence within the academy, the disavowal of such
a practice fundamentally shapes our theoretical views, predisposing us to an
ideological rigidity that we ourselves do not practice professionally and that
is difficult to see in the Asian American historical and literary past. In the relationship between Asian American literature and Asian American literary criticism, we thus witness a tension between flexibility and rigidity, a tension that
also marks this book as it traces that relationship. Another important moment of tension and contradiction for Asian American intellectuals and their
relationship to both Asian America and the American nation is marked by pluralism. Pluralism is a hallmark of American nation and culture that Asian
American intellectuals often like to assail because it is a form of political organization that represents a vast group of constituencies under a singular
identity that is inadequate in terms of fully addressing the cultural, political,
and class heterogeneity of American populations. Ironically, as Susan Koshy
demonstrates, even as Asian American intellectuals reject American pluralism,
they implicitly endorse it for Asian America as a necessary strategy that enables
Asian American political agency, unifying a diverse set of ethnicities under a
singular racial label (315–317). This pluralist Asian America then forms both
the horizon of intellectual consensus for Asian American intellectuals and the

critical limit to our ability to think through the problem of race, gender, and capital.

RACIAL FORMATION AND THE BODY POLITIC

I have spoken repeatedly of the Asian American intellectual class and its consensus regarding the role of Asian Americans in the American body politic, as if this class is homogeneous, especially in relation to a diverse Asian America. I will argue that unlike Asian America as a whole, the contemporary Asian American intellectual class—what I have referred to as the *mainstream* class—does indeed exhibit a much higher degree of ideological homogeneity. It can at least be characterized as being left-of-center, with the wide range of possibilities from liberal to Marxist that is implied, and it can at least be characterized as being invested in the value of an Asian American identity. This last point is particularly important to establish, because it separates the class I am talking about from those intellectuals *who only happen to be Asian American* but either do not recognize the importance of such a classification or disagree with that classification to begin with. An example of such an intellectual would be the neoconservative Dinesh D'Souza; since many neoconservatives are already inclined to reject racial classification and identity, they are already not, by definition, part of a self-identified Asian American intellectual class. Another example of such intellectuals—if we include political leaders among such a classification—is the Chinese American parents who have sued to end affirmative action in Bay Area high schools like Lowell. Their political efforts are a precursor of what will come; the moment when these Chinese American parents, or others like them, start articulating their struggle as an Asian American one will be a critical point in the articulation of an Asian American neoconservatism that will force the intellectual and political leadership of Asian America to recognize a challenge to its consensus. There are already such people as Asian American neoconservatives, of course, who embrace both neoconservative ideology and Asian American identity, but they exist as an emergent group whose exceptional status *at the present moment* proves the rule of Asian American intellectual consensus. Furthermore, what is particularly provocative about the prospect of Asian American neoconservative political leadership is their potential ability to lay claim to the mantle of what Antonio Gramsci calls the "organic intellectual"—the intellectual of the people, a position to which mainstream Asian American intellectuals now generally aspire.[11]

In this next section, I will focus specifically on an important subset of this mainstream class, Asian American academics, who have presented the most cogent theories that concern the formation of Asian America and its political function. The theories presented by Asian American academics and the actual practice of Asian American communities are oftentimes contradictory, as we can see in the case of academics and their community in the university. Within the academy, it is not only the case that the theories Asian American studies deploys to analyze its object (re)create that object in important ways, but they also serve to (re)create Asian American studies itself, as David Li argues:

> [Asian American knowledge production] cannot take place without the (re)production of capital and capitalistic social relations; neither can it be indifferent to the academy's system of (e)valuation. . . . We may say that Asian American studies as a political instrument of radical social transformation has been successful only to the extent that it has constituted itself as an academic discipline and has thus ensured a limited intellectual and racial representation within the academy. (201)[12]

Thus the dilemma that Asian American studies faces is that its oppositional theories are the currency that enables its institutionalization and survival. In the context of Asian American literary criticism in particular, Sau-ling C. Wong also notes that Asian American literature is an "emergent and evolving textual coalition whose interests it is the business of a professional coalition of Asian American critics to promote" (*Reading Asian American Literature* 9). Therefore, while Asian American literary critics have striven to be at the forefront of political consciousness in Asian American studies, they are also invested in the visibility and value of Asian American literature as the proof of their own professional usefulness to the academy and the English department. While Asian American studies is not unique in this professionalization, what is significant is the *contradiction* between the radical intellectual goals of Asian American studies and its institutional location.[13] Furthermore, what is important about acknowledging that Asian American studies is a *business* is the implications that this has for understanding the theoretical practice of Asian American studies, built simultaneously upon the critique of racist capitalism and the disavowal of its own capitalist practice. The idealism that characterizes such a disavowal is then embedded in the critics' view of the past and their object of study; therefore, this study follows Rey Chow's call for an "ethics after idealism."

For Asian American intellectuals, an ethics of intellectual inquiry and political practice that rejects the idealization of both racial identity and political resistance is necessary in order to confront the dilemma of confrontation and institutionalization that marks the trajectory of racial formation and the shaping of racial communities, as argued in the influential work of Michael Omi and Howard Winant.[14] This trajectory follows an arc that moves from a moment of unstable equilibrium between races to a contestation by a racial minority against racial exclusion or oppression, followed by the accommodation and inclusion of the minority's concerns on the part of the state, leading to a period of unstable equilibrium between the state and the minority. The last moment of unstable equilibrium ended with the crisis brought about by the civil rights movement, a crisis finally brought under control by the state in the 1970s, shifting the United States to a new period of unstable equilibrium in which we are still living. In this state of equilibrium, racial difference is no longer *principally* policed by violent coercion (although that is still used) but is instead primarily maintained and negotiated through the consent of racial minorities. Omi and Winant borrow the term "hegemony" from Antonio Gramsci in order to characterize the post–civil rights era and argue that "hegemony operates by including its subjects, incorporating its opposition" (Omi and Winant 68). Part of that incorporation is the bureaucratization of race through civil rights, the census, and affirmative action. While race existed as a bureaucratic, political category before 1964, it also became, subsequent to 1964, a method of charting inequality and state-mandated opportunity. Asian Americans became increasingly aware of their identity as a racial group, both as defined by the state and in self-defined methods.[15] Asian American studies is one of those self-defined methods, and the contemporary state of Asian American studies in this moment of unstable equilibrium is marked by both pragmatism, where its radical views have been domesticated in the name of institutional survival and respectability, and reaction, where the actions of past Asian Americans are evaluated through the lenses of either resistance or accommodation, the bifurcated responses to American racism's desire to either suppress or incorporate Asian Americans.

Contemporary Asian America, as a product of racial formation that is embraced by the state, also reproduces some of the state's features, which is inevitable under the process of political consensus that characterizes the contemporary moment. What is *not inevitable*, however, is the disavowal of that reproduction on the part of Asian American intellectuals. This disavowal is an ironic example of an "articulate silence" deployed by Asian American intellectuals and can be witnessed in their adoption of the panethnic strategy in order to attain a greater degree of political influence in the United States' pluralist system of representation.[16] Pluralism as a system premised upon a hierarchy of representatives and those they represent favors interest groups and spokespersons or organizations, and panethnicity gathers the heterogeneous communities of immigrants and citizens of Asian descent into one identifiable body. The system of pluralistic representation in the Asian American context has promoted the leadership of middle-class professionals for panethnic groups, so that as Yen Le Espiritu writes, "Pan-Asian ethnicity has come to signify the 'bourgeois' politics of the professionals, lobbyists, and politicians" (*Asian American Panethnicity* 53).[17] Asian America, therefore, is capable of exercising the same rhetoric of pluralism that the American state does, promising equality but practicing hierarchy when it comes to dealing with various Asian ethnic groups with conflicting interests.[18] This translates into the Asian American panethnic coalition being built upon an alliance of politically unequal partners—those who represent and those who are represented. Given the history of Asian immigration, with different ethnic groups arriving at different times with different advantages or disadvantages, this has meant that older, more established ethnic groups such as the Chinese and Japanese have produced more of the leadership of the community. They have also had the opportunity to establish a higher level of economic success on the average, and casual observers may draw a correlation between economic success and particular ethnic identities, so that economic inequality within Asian America has often seemed to be a function of ethnic difference.[19] Ethnic difference in and of itself, however, does not constitute a serious problem for a panethnic coalition, because, as Espiritu notes throughout *Asian American Panethnicity*, panethnic coalitions can exist comfortably with such difference. The critical factor in helping to determine unity or disunity in a panethnic coalition is class homogeneity or the lack thereof.

The fact that the middle class has an investment in pluralism signifies that pluralism allows them economic and political access and that it contributes to the stability of the nation and its overall economic health by alleviating racial conflict through ethnic inclusion. In the pluralist model, the cultural inclusion of a minority within the nation is a difficult but attainable goal, achievable over time. This premise undergirds multiculturalism, which becomes what Slavoj Zizek calls the "cultural logic of multinational capitalism."[20] To the extent that Asian America replicates the pluralistic principle of multiculturalism in a capitalist society, it, too, consents to what Paul Ong, Edna Bonacich, and Lucie Cheng argue is the most basic principle or "goal of the state": "to protect and enhance profit" (7).[21] Within a pluralist Asian America that repeats the rhetoric of the state, mutable ethnic differences can be overcome to achieve a cohesive Asian American identity that facilitates political and economic representation by the ethnic middle class. In the interests of such representation, proponents of Asian American identity may suppress other contradictory issues. Peter Kwong argues that as a result of this suppression, Asian American panethnicity is a "reactive one" whose "union is merely a pragmatic alliance" of different groups; "proponents of Asian panethnicity, understandably, want to stress the collective attributes to reinforce this unity and avoid issues, such as class, that might be divisive" (76).[22]

A refusal on the part of Asian American studies to investigate such divisions and internal differences accelerates the dialectical relationship between race and capitalism, whereby racial identity is initially demonized by dominant society at least partially in order to facilitate economic exploitation, asserted as a strategy of political survival by the subordinate group and then ironically transformed into an idealized commodity. This commodification has already taken place to some extent, as we can see that within academia Asian American culture is something that academics not only study but also trade in as a form of symbolic capital. For Bourdieu, "'Symbolic capital' is to be understood as economic or political capital that is disavowed, misrecognized and thereby recognized, hence legitimate, a 'credit' which, under certain conditions, and always in the long run, guarantees 'economic' profits" (*Cultural Production* 75). These profits result even though, ironically, Asian American academic work is generally geared toward criticism of the dominant order. Late capitalism—in this case embodied in the university—is capable of accommodating even rebellion, transforming acts of cultural and political resistance into commodities. Distinguishing economic from symbolic capital enables us to recognize the subtle process of rebellion and reward that is a part of bourgeois society and its efforts to domesticate dissent through commodifying it.[23] Acknowledging the significance of symbolic capital for Asian America on our part is important because it demonstrates the contradictory location of Asian American intellectual work—contradictory because it is both antagonistic to and in some cases rewarded by capitalism.[24]

For Asian American culture, one particular object invested with both symbolic and economic capital is the body. In this book, I use the term "body politic" to describe the vast formal entity that arises in the literature when authors use the bodies of their narrators or characters to represent Asian Americans and their collective relationship to both nation and capital.[25] Thus bodies in Asian American literature are never just individually significant but point instead to the intersecting relationships of race, class, gender, and sexuality that ascribe meaning and substance to the very idea of an *Asian American* body in the first place (versus the normative, unmarked body of dominant American culture). These intersecting relationships mark the Asian American body as not just *a* cultural product but *"the* cultural product" (Grosz 23).[26] I would also add that the Asian American body is a historical product, and the condensation of culture and history in the Asian American body makes it a critical place to conduct any inquiry into the formation of Asian America. The Asian American body politic as a term, a formal entity, speaks to the fact that merely invoking the identity "Asian American" erases the distinction between the individual and the collective, gesturing instead to the United States' long history of treating Asian Americans as an indistinguishable group rather than as an aggregate of individuals—hence inevitably politicizing them and their bodies. This treatment of Asian Americans as a racial other proceeded in two stages, according to David Li, who characterizes the distinction between the earlier period of exclusion and marginalization and the contemporary moment as a shift from "Oriental alienation" to "Asian abjection," in which Asian Americans are regarded initially as inassimilable aliens and then, subsequent to World War II, as legally acceptable but culturally inassimilable foreigners.[27] Usually these relationships were ones of sexual, economic, and physical threat or servitude on the part of Asians, with threat and servitude being the two sides of the same essential stereotype concerning the "Oriental."[28] It is through this rhetoric of demonization, marginalization, and exclusion that Asian Americans are created as a separate and dangerous body politic within the United States—as a cancerous entity within the American body politic.[29] Asian American culture is characterized by this constant tension between American racism's efforts to construct Asians as a singular body and the Asian American response that there are instead multiple ones. American racism's effort to create a singular Asian American body also works in conjunction with American political economy's contradictory effort to deny the existence of *white* bodies and enforce, instead, a legal reliance upon abstract and bodiless persons.[30] This "rhetoric of bodily denial" (Sánchez-Eppler 140) serves to create an unmarked subject of the law who is in practice masculine and white while also creating its other, a marked subject whose differences are rendered visible and corporeal. The creation of the Asian marked subject serves to unify the definition of the American citizen "against the Asian immigrant, legally, economically, and culturally" (Lowe, *Immigrant Acts* 4), sanctioning the unity of an American body politic through the formation of a racial other.

In response, Asian ethnic groups cohered as their own bodies politic, unifying and organizing around their scant ethnic numbers until mass mobilization and consciousness by these ethnic groups was made possible in the late 1960s. Asian America was thus created from the damage inflicted upon Asian immigrants and their descendants by racial discourse in the United States, a discourse that also articulated itself through the demands of heterosexual patriarchy and class exploitation. For the new Asian Americans to proclaim their unique identity as an American population was also for them to lay claim to the humanity of their individual bodies and to the legitimacy of their collective political body. The Asian American body politic is composed of both this vast array of individual bodies and the collective body they form together. This collective body, shaped through both the negative, exclusionary and objectifying pressure of American racism and the positive will of political agency on the part of these negatively identified populations, allows the aggregate of individuals to articulate their voice and be heard within the American political system. At the same time as collective racial identity allows participation in political pluralism, it also ironically allows its own commodification in the post-1968 moment. Racial identity as commodity supplements the self that has been damaged by racial difference and discrimination, overt or covert in its manifestations.[31] In such a scenario, the act of consumption serves to supplement the self, with the commodity being an "object of desire" that represents "something lacking" (Falk 131). In this case, what is lacking for people of color as a result of racism is a sense of a whole identity. There are implications, of course, for Asian American identity as we know it today if anti-Asian racism subsides or changes—namely, that Asian American identity may no longer be necessary or at least no longer as compelling for political mobilization.

The efforts to mobilize an Asian American movement around a rehabilitated body constitute a body project on the part of some panethnic entrepreneurs, who seek to turn the body from being negatively marked by a history of racist signification to being positively marked and marketable in the arena of multiethnic identification and consumption.[32] While the critics who have dealt with the body as a project have focused their attention upon methods such as plastic surgery, exercise, and fashion, race as a form of signification through racial formation is also a method for transforming the body symbolically.[33] Certainly the contemporary concept of Asian America is a product of the efforts of intellectuals to symbolically rework the body that was stigmatized by American racial discourse as alien and threatening. The cultural (re)signification of the body is thus an important component of body projects in general and racially formed bodies in particular, and within the realm of literature-as-culture the body has been of great significance. Peter Brooks claims that beginning in the eighteenth century, "modern narratives appear to produce a semioticization of the body, which is matched by a somatization of story: a claim that the body must be a source and a locus of meanings, and that stories cannot be told without making the body a prime vehicle of narrative signification" (*Body Work* xii). With race, the semioticization of the body and somatization of story achieves a particular meaning, as we can see in the well-documented depictions of Asians and Asian Americans by Europeans and European Americans.[34] In Asian American literature and arguably in other forms of Asian American culture, there is also an intense focus upon the methods of semioticization and somatization. Asian American literature attempts to resignify the body, inherently assuming its status as a politicized body, and makes the body itself a "prime vehicle of narrative signification" that produces different meanings at different historical periods. The history of the Asian American body politic in Asian American literature is an uneven one, exhibiting traces of the contradictory policies of the United States toward Asian immigrants and Asia. This history is also an ideologically unpredictable one, rife as it is with explicit examples of ethnic and panethnic entrepreneurship and the deployment of flexible strategies that resist easy categorization into either resistance or accommodation.

Furthermore, what we find in the literature is not a teleological development of the body but instead the development of multiple versions of bodily signification that exist simultaneously, particularly with the increasing demographic diversification of Asian America. While a recognition of such multiplicity may be a cause of celebration for some in Asian America, it is a crisis of representation for others. The crisis in the Asian American body politic—both the collective one and the individual one—is part of a larger social crisis. The proliferation of discussions that concern the nature, constitution, and interpretation of the body indicates this larger social crisis, because "when we see a culture self-consciously defining bodies, it is already in trouble" (Hyde 11). The destabilization of the body is an indicator of our changing perceptions concerning the natural state of the body, as advances in medical science and social mores and changes in various kinds of cultural and political definitions of the body allow people increased control over the appearance, production, reception, and interpretation of their bodies.[35] Not surprisingly, the destabilization of the body has led to vigorous attempts to restabilize it, and in the realm of race, racial advocates have struggled to propose a unified and cohesive definition of the racial body politic. Asian America has endeavored to develop a consensus about the nature of its body politic, and the panethnic consensus it has achieved in recent years has been for the most part one that resonates with the pluralist consensus already found in American culture. It is not the resonance with pluralism that should necessarily bother us, of course, since it is to some extent inevitable, but the contradiction that this poses with the actual diversity of Asian America's constituents.

POLITICAL CONSENSUS AND DETERRITORIALIZATION

Mari Matsuda's argument in *Where Is Your Body?* illustrates this contradictory attempt at defining a unified Asian American body politic and hence furthering its ability to exercise political power through consensus. Matsuda argues that in the contemporary period we have witnessed the rise of the "Asian American Racial Bourgeoisie." Matsuda is profoundly disturbed by the phenomenon of a racial bourgeoisie descended from the revolutionary origins of Asian America, and she notes, in language only slightly less provocative than Frank Chin's that concerns "real" and "fake" Asians, that "not everyone with an Asian surname is in fact Asian within the meaning of our constructed coalition. To speak plainly, there are some people of Asian descent we might not embrace as representing our community, even if they were elected to Congress. If Asian-American [*sic*] identity is constructed, and constructed in part by a history of activism, then issues do define us" (177).[36] Matsuda's position reveals the contradiction that constitutes Asian America, torn between its imposed construction as an abject racial identity and its self-construction as radical political identity. Both constructions imply a type of acceptable identity, delimited in the former instance by social notions of race and in the latter instance by political notions of ideological legitimacy. Antiracism compels what Espiritu calls a "reactive solidarity" among Asian Americans to protect themselves against violence, but that solidarity of identity and ideology breaks down in the contemporary period of increasing assimilation and lessening violence—at least for the middle class that constitutes Asian American panethnic leadership. Unless Asian Americans agree to the highly unlikely possibility of formally policing their identity, the political and cultural reality for Asian America is a new era of internal conflicts that stem from the recently recognized reality of Asian America becoming what Susan Koshy calls a deterritorialized ethnicity.

A territorialized ethnicity is one that is invested in the territory of the nation, the attendant language of nationalist identification and assimilation, and the commodification of racial identity that is now a part of U.S. late capitalism's acceptance of multiculturalism. Asian American intellectuals are ambivalent about the ideology of the territorialized ethnicity, embodied in the model minority, which they see as a mode of "false consciousness" that misrecognizes the ideological position of Asian Americans in American society.[37] At the same time, Asian Americans as a territorialized ethnicity are at least unified in their political focus upon assimilation and overcoming the obstacles of racism and exclusion, and Asian American intellectuals stand relatively unified behind such a focus. The deterritorialization of ethnicity, in contrast, is emblematic of even more complicated ideological conflicts that Asian America faces. Koshy argues that the deterritorialization of ethnicity stems from the changing nature of Asian immigration and identification, which increasingly is no longer defined in the traditional model of pluralism and assimilation that undergirds Asian American literary criticism and American ethnic literary criticism embodied in the work of scholars such as Werner Sollors. The assimilationist paradigm of descent and consent in Sollors's work and the imperative to claim an American identity found in many accounts of Asian American literature are no longer necessarily the dominant motivations of new immigrant populations. For them, "ethnicity metamorphoses at multiple sites of transit, return, and arrival in the movement between and within nations; it can no longer be defined through the negotiation between origin and destination" (Koshy 338). Without the compelling narrative of assimilation and political resistance against exclusion, the possibilities for uniting Asian America over its heterogeneous constitution rapidly begin to fracture.[38]

This fracturing is especially evident in the case of global capitalism and its impact upon the divided formation of Asian American constituencies. This division is between those who can profitably exploit the mobility of capital in global capitalism (the transnational capitalist subject who delights in travel) and those who are exploited by such mobility—the migrant, poor, or undocumented laborer whose mobility is not so much voluntary as compelled by circumstance and necessity. Aihwa Ong has termed the transnational capitalist subject a model of "flexible citizenship" who engages with the mobility of capitalism willingly. Ong argues, counter to some usual assumptions, that for these transnational subjects "flexibility, migration, and relocations, instead of being coerced or resisted, have become practices to strive for rather than stability" (*Flexible Citizenship* 51). Flexibility enables economic survival, the ability to maximize the individual's opportunities in a world of mobile capital and corporations. The issue of free choice and its definition becomes critical in dividing this class of flexible citizenship from its other, compulsorily mobile aliens. Within Asian America, both deterritorialized populations are found, people who are mobile by choice through the exploitation of their capital and people who are mobile by circumstance through the exploitation of their labor. Often, although not always, this division correlates with a domestic division between the model minority and their opposites, the "bad subjects" of the American body politic.[39] Asian American intellectuals, who generally align themselves with transnational labor and the nonmodel minority, form the population of bad subjects by choice.

In some cases, the flexible citizens from Asia, transplanted to America, "make whiteness a more problematic concept in the era of globalization," a racial transformation with contradictory effects, including those upon the model minority (Ong, *Flexible Citizenship* 109). As a significant new component of the model minority, these flexible citizens participate in the transformation of the meaning of whiteness in its symbolic register. Through their arrival with wealth, Ong argues, Asian immigrant capitalists weaken the dominance of traditional whiteness (defined through European descent), which is dependent upon pluralism and gradual assimilation. In this model of traditional whiteness, nonwhite immigrants are supposed to gradually work their way up the socioeconomic ladder and move more closely to approximating whiteness with the passage of generations. The sudden appearance of wealthy Asians displaces this assumption that traditional whiteness is associated with wealth and that both whiteness and wealth are to be earned over the passage of time. By putting traditional whiteness into crisis, the new Asian capital also puts Asian America as a whole—not just the model minority—into crisis in its efforts to claim a domestic authenticity that does not threaten whites. Asian Americans may fear guilt by racial association with these wealthy new Asian immigrants and may also fear guilt by association with cheap and possibly undocumented migrant labor.[40] Together, the dangers of Asian foreign labor and capital are reprised in the dominant American imagination as a return of the "yellow peril." The perennial status of Asian Americans as foreigners haunts Asian American efforts to retain a place in the American body politic and compels the nationalist, assimilatory drive of Asian Americans even more vigorously. The conflict over (de)territorialization signifies the consequences of the ideological choices that Asian America makes between nationalist and global identities. While a nationalist identity entails difficulties in confronting the racial problematic of multiculturalism and racially defined American identity, it allows the opportunity for a cohesive political identity with clearly articulated goals. Globalization in contrast allows a challenge to racially defined American identities but also promotes the mobility of capital, which offers contradictory socioeconomic opportunities for different Asian ethnic and class populations.

These differences of possibility under global capitalism are not expressed purely economically but also in terms of ethnic and cultural divisions that threaten to fracture Asian America internally. These fractures are not due so much to an Old World legacy of conflicts between nations of origin but to contemporary conflicts over equitable political and economic representation within Asian America. A contestatory ideological position for Asian American intellectuals, which focuses on domestic inequality within an international frame that concerns historical American imperialism and the ongoing impact of global capitalism, seeks to be inclusive of all Asian American ethnic groups and their vastly different histories. This position contrasts with multiculturalism's version of Asian America that reproduces the rhetoric of pluralism and undercuts the importance of equitable economic representation—however that can be defined. This position faces difficulties in accounting for the vastly different histories of Asian Americans, which position Asian American ethnic groups unequally in the contest over resources and representation. Multiculturalism's seemingly clear benefit for Asian Americans is that it has displaced the black-white dualism of American race relations, introducing instead racial multiplicity and the possibility of an Asian American position in American politics and culture. A good case can be made, however, for the fact that polarization still exercises a strong, if symbolic, influence in the American imagination and will continue to do so in the future. That polarization aligns race and class, so that black and white are symbolic signifiers of exclusion and inclusion. Multiculturalism does not fundamentally change the economic terms of equality and inequality in the United States but instead proposes the equivalent of a racial face-lift on the American body politic, as many critics have already established.[41] In the continuing polarization of American society around the symbolic oppositions of white and black, Asian America will, in the near future at least, be divided domestically between the model minority and the bad subject. This domestic division is matched by an overlapping global division between flexible citizens and compulsorily mobile aliens, with domestic citizens caught ambivalently in between. At the juncture of these voluntary and compulsory identifications stands the mainstream Asian American intellectual class, which must combine a theoretical agenda that is oppositional to global capitalism and domestic race/class stratification with a valid assessment of the multiple and contradictory practices of Asian Americans in general. Not surprisingly, these practices reveal that Asian America is an often willing and enthusiastic participant in global capitalism, racial domination, and class stratification.

ASIAN AMERICAN BODIES POLITIC

Within Asian American literature, we find a history of representations of the body that provide evidence for the speculations in the previous section. In the rest of the book, I hope to provide an account of how these representations of the body constitute a form of political consciousness about the Asian American body politic that is an important source of influence on the rest of Asian American intellectual thought. The book itself is marked by a tension between, on the one hand, the plurality of bodies and the flexibility of authorial strategies found in the texts and, on the other, the relative rigidity of Asian American theoretical assumptions that has been stressed in this introduction. This is because Asian American studies has generally found itself engaged in a dialectic with American racism, whereby that racism's compulsion to represent Asian Americans as either dangerous (the bad subject) or docile (the model minority) has compelled an equal and opposite reaction on the part of critics, who vociferously reject the model minority stereotype but end up prioritizing and idealizing Asian America as a bad subject that is dangerous because it is politically resistant and oppositional. While Asian American literature has worked under the shadow of the same racism, it has been more ambivalent about the appropriate response, demonstrated in the flexibility that almost all the texts included in this book show as they fluctuate between resistance and accommodation, avoiding, for the most part, evaluating resistance or accommodation either positively or negatively, as Asian American critics are wont to do.[42] At the same time, this plurality and flexibility does not exist absolutely; it must be read, received, interpreted, marketed, purchased, and, in general, "used" ideologically by readers and critics who are members of not only a literary public but also a wider American public permeated by racial attitudes and global capitalism. Therefore, this plurality and flexibility demonstrated historically is, in the *contemporary* moment, overwritten by the commodification of Asian American culture, the transformation of Asian American identity into a fairly homogeneous product for consumption that reaffirms the ideological location of Asian Americans in American culture for other Americans and supplements an Asian American lifestyle for Asian American consumers.

Asian American intellectuals have yet to confront this problem of commodification, which is a feature of the unstable equilibrium that Omi and Winant argue characterizes race relations today; rather, Asian American intellectuals implicitly disavow that they are implicated in the problem of commodification, and the theoretical consequences are manifest in their reliance upon a discourse of the bad subject (a discourse that I shall treat in my conclusion). A recognition of such complicity would entail an acknowledgment that Asian American identity may no longer be adequate in pursuing the *long-term* radical political goals that are the generally (if vaguely) professed consensus of Asian American intellectuals but probably is adequate in pursuing the *short-term* goals of a middle-class-based project of nationalist assimilation into a capitalist society. While Asian American identity is, in short, not completely determined by capitalism and capitalism itself is not totalizing, the possibilities of social and political change offered by Asian American identity are limited, precisely because that change is now routed through a commodified identity. As a consequence, it could be argued that if contemporary capitalism has succeeded in transforming Asian American identity into a commodity, despite Asian America's diversity, then the Asian American intellectual tendency toward an equally flattening, bifurcated response—resistance or accommodation—may be adequate. This is not true, however, primarily because such a response denies the possibility that change, however limited, can be enacted through the commodity. Such a response prefers an idealized vision of radical change less compromised by capitalism. This idealized vision, again, is a disavowal of the less than idealized position of Asian American academics and many other intellectuals who themselves choose to enact change institutionally. By bringing these issues up, I seek not to be merely negative but instead to point out the limits of Asian America and, within those limits, what types of change can be enacted. Those limits are, in summary, the implicit pluralism found in contemporary constructions of Asian American identity, the commodification of that racial identity, the ideological heterogeneity of a diverse Asian American population, and the willingness of a considerable portion of that population to participate in and perpetuate such commodification and the social and economic practices that lead to it. By recognizing these limits and by encouraging a move to dissensus rather than consensus, we can deliberately bring ourselves into a moment of crisis, disrupting the equilibrium of racial identity and its commodification that we have begun to take for granted. By doing so, we can more clearly articulate our political goals and move toward other constructions of political identity that would be more useful in furthering these goals.

In chapter 1, turning toward the origins of Asian American literature at the end of the last century, we can recognize that even then, at another moment of equilibrium when the situation of Asian Americans was much more dire than today, there was a lack of consensus regarding the cultural and political options faced by Asian Americans. The situation of the Eaton sisters, the first Asian American writers, serves as a kind of parable about these options and their consequences. Edith and Winnifred, half-Chinese and half-English, wrote under the pen names Sui Sin Far and Onoto Watanna, respectively, and lived and worked in Canada and the United States. Edith assumed a Chinese authorial persona and Winnifred a Japanese one. Their respective strategies, personas, and reception offer us two enduring cultural positions that are still the basis of Asian American cultural work today and will be in the near future. Sui Sin Far's confrontational persona explicitly contested inequalities of race, class, and gender and was clearly aligned with the Asian American as bad subject, embodied in the lives of Chinese immigrants, particularly women and children. Onoto Watanna's persona focused on the lives of Asians, in this case Japanese women, as quaint foreigners who occasionally ventured into the United States, where they were capable of assimilation (in small numbers) with whites. In the Eatons' work, we can see that Asian American literature has always been concerned with not just racial identity but gender and sexuality as well; the Eaton sisters, as do all the writers I consider, stage the relationship of the Asian American body politic to the American body politic through concerns about gender and sexuality. Thus the term "body politic" becomes useful in this book because it indicates the political importance of all facets of the body, not just its racialized dimension.

For both the Eaton sisters, then, the body politic belonged to women and children as much as it did to men, and stories of families and romances were critical to depicting this body politic. The Eatons' differences in identity, however, are equally important to discuss. Onoto Watanna passed as both Japanese and white, depending on occasion, and her survival and popularity, in contrast to her sister's demise and obscurity, remain as lessons in the costs and benefits of particular strategies oriented around the body politic, which assumed a hybrid form in the Eaton sisters' personal lives and literary work. In the Eaton sisters' choices, we may see an uncanny resemblance to the choices offered to contemporary Asian American authors: accommodation to the fetishization of a domesticated ethnic identity and resistance through assuming the threatening guise of an oppositional racial identity. Constructing their choices in this fashion, however, already presupposes a value assumption that concerns the political and ethical meaning of accommodation and resistance. It is not only the stories of the Eaton sisters that are important in discussing early representations of the body politic, therefore, but also critical, contemporary interpretations of their work that are implicitly based on assumptions about the contemporary Asian American body politic, projected retrospectively. Our concerns about racial identity and class politics in the contemporary moment, in other words, can shape our reconstruction of our past and intellectual lineage as one of subversion and resistance against racial and class domination. The contemporary criticism of the Eaton sisters exhibits a tendency that is common to Asian American studies, valuing subversion and resistance or examining the past for signs of subversion and resistance in unlikely places. Thus it is important to acknowledge that a figure such as Onoto Watanna deserves to be recovered not because she may be resistant but because she may be *compliant*. Compliancy and accommodation are flexible strategies that were *and remain* important political choices for Asian Americans that are overlooked by assumptions about Asian American identity as being inherently, or desirably, oppositional.

In chapter 2, the issues of resistance and accommodation in a moment of equilibrium marked by violent racial domination continue with the depression-era and post–World War II work of Carlos Bulosan and John Okada. In their books, *America Is in the Heart* and *No-No Boy*, respectively, the Asian American body politic is explicitly a masculine, wounded one struggling with the damage inflicted by American racism, which distorts the sexuality and gender identity of Asian American men. Through their use of irony, Bulosan and Okada demonstrate an awareness of the hypocrisies of American society, especially around race, and the limits of confrontation with such hypocrisies in the pre–civil rights era. Their protagonists, however, are trapped within those limits of what is allowable in the public discourse of American democracy; in this discourse, even if one believes that the United States is responsible for crimes against racial minorities, one also believes that American democracy and American culture provide the resolution and the healing for such crimes. This discourse of American exceptionalism works hand in hand with U.S. self-representation during World War II and the Cold War, when the United States presents itself to its constituents and the world as the defender of freedom and democracy. Only by stepping outside the boundaries of the United States in his little-known novel *The Cry and the Dedication* can Bulosan imagine another set of possiblities than that offered by American nationalism. Set in the Philippines amid the Communist-led Huk rebellion of the 1950s, *The Cry and the Dedication* rejects the discourse of American nationalism and exceptionalism, presenting a Filipino manhood restored by violent revolution. The open call to revolution against oppressive Filipino elites and the American neocolonialist enterprise in the Philippines marks *The Cry and the Dedication* as a novel ahead of its time during the 1950s. Ignored and forgotten until now, *The Cry and the Dedication* is a foreshadowing of the more confrontational 1960s.

In the 1960s, the state of equilibrium in U.S. racial relations was brought to crisis by the civil rights movement and its offspring, the racial empowerment movements. The work of Frank Chin and Gus Lee constitutes a second act to the discourse of Asian American masculinity initiated by Bulosan and Okada. Publishing after the 1968 watermark of Asian American consciousness, Chin and Lee argue that masculinity and American identity can be reclaimed through violence. The violence proposed by Chin and Lee is an attempt to meet the masculine, dominant American body politic, mythologically defined through frontier violence, on its own terms. Chin and Lee's work, although published from the 1970s through the 1990s, is born out of experiences prior to 1968 and transformed by the events of that year. As a result, their fiction belongs to the first phase, broadly defined, of Asian American literature that is produced in or from the era of alienation and is, to some extent, the climax of that period (1882–1943/1965).[43] In this climax, the alienation from American society that characterizes Asian American experience as a product of violent racial domination is gradually terminated. Asian Americans gain more political rights and more political and cultural visibility—in short, they increase their ability to lay claim to an American identity from which they had been excluded. In the age of alienation, therefore, the work of the Eaton sisters, Bulosan, Okada, Chin, and Lee—with the remarkable exception of *The Cry and the Dedication*—shares a similar territorial framework oriented around the nation, the cohesiveness of national identities, and the possibilities of or limitations to assimilation into an American national identity.

The new phase of racial equilibrium that ensues in the 1970s is marked by both this continuing territorial effort to solidify the claim to an American national identity and the beginnings of a postnational, deterritorialized identity. In the literature of the age of alienation, for example, while there are clear concerns with Asia in the work of the authors I consider, Asia usually functions as either the beginning of immigration or a place that is clearly delineated from the United States. In the literature that is published after the 1970s, the role of Asia in immigration, economy, and war, as represented in literary works, becomes much more important. This is a product, at least partially, of the radical changes brought about by the new immigration law of 1965, which allowed into the United States a much more diverse range of Asian immigrants, who carried with them the memory of their homelands and their experiences there. Even as post-1970s literature records these homeland experiences, it also serves a function in the new era of equilibrium, by consolidating—or by being forced to consolidate—a renewed sense of American exceptionalism after the failure of the Vietnam War, this time in the age of global capitalism. One of the most important representations of the Asian American body politic in the post–Vietnam War period is that of the victim. Historically, the role of the victim is one of the few "sympathetic" representations of Asians and Asian Americans in dominant American discourse. Subsequent to the Vietnam War, the representation of the victim assumes particular importance as a mode of rendering Asians visible. The autobiographical writings of Le Ly Hayslip exemplify this representation of the Asian American body politic as a victimized one. Her work is also important in its rejection of national identity, illustrating instead a body and identity located in mobility between nations and categories. Through representing herself as a victim of the ideological conflict between capitalism and communism, Hayslip both criticizes American hypocrisies and placates American sensibilities through a rehabilitated humanism. Her efforts lead her American readership to a sense of reconciliation with the traumatic past and enable the U.S. economy to resume business as usual through its search for new markets and new labor, this time in Vietnam.

The discourse of victimization and the status of the Vietnam War in the American imagination allow Vietnamese voices to attain a certain limited stature in American discourse. In contrast to Vietnam, the Philippines occupies the antithetical place in the American imagination. Whereas Vietnam has been highly visible, the Philippines has been relatively ignored, not even granted the acknowledgment of being a victim of American imperialism. It is the fact of the Philippines' obscurity in relation to its prominent role in the development of American imperialism that makes it critical. Ninotchka Rosca and Jessica Hagedorn, American-based writers, set their novels outside the United States, in the Philippines themselves, and deploy queer bodies as metaphoric signifiers of the relationship between the Philippines and the United States. The Philippines are, so to speak, "in the closet" when it comes to American history. While Rosca examines the culturally specific traditions of transvestites in the Philippines, Hagedorn looks at the practices of modernized, Westernized urban gay men in Manila; in both cases, transvestites and gay men become involved in the revolution against state dictatorship. In these novels, then, queer sexual practices, whether they are "traditional" or "Western," become allegories for struggle against a neocolonial dictatorship (sponsored by the United States) that also assumes a heterosexual, patriarchal cast. These novels seek to criticize the invisibility of Filipinos in the United States and American history, an invisibility that consolidates the American mythology of democratic exceptionalism and further stabilizes American equilibrium. This condition of equilibrium is concerned not only with racial relations but with international relations of economics and politics as well; to the extent that the United States considers itself the defender of the free, capitalist world, it must also believe in a domestic rhetoric of pluralist inclusion and equality, where racial inequality is an aberration rather than a structural flaw.

Hayslip, Rosca, and Hagedorn all pose challenges to the dominant nationalist, assimilationist model of Asian American literature, found in both fiction and criticism and premised upon the ideology of American pluralism. The characters and subjects in these works are transnational, not deeply concerned with the sovereignty of nations as ultimate horizons of possibility for their identifications, and not focused upon the necessity of claiming American identity. They also are produced from nations whose historic relationships to the United States have been characterized by both a deep mutual antagonism and a one-sided patronization by the United States. These characters and subjects thus introduce the history of American imperialism into Asian American studies. The victim and the queer are two particular representations used by American imperialism—and domestic racism—to depict its objects of domination. The victim appeals to a lingering sense of American guilt, while the queer is suitable only for the closet. These two forms of the Asian American body politic are a direct function of American intervention overseas and immigration reforms at home that have transformed the size and diversity of Asian America, allowing for new and contradictory variations of the Asian American body politic in its relationship to the American body politic.

In the conclusion, I argue that the basic pattern of contradiction in terms of how Asian America relates to the American body politic is exemplified in the binary choices of identification that dominant American discourse offers to Asian Americans, which Asian Americans have adapted to some extent: the model minority and the bad subject. As the term suggests, the model minority is living testimony to the possibilities of assimilation and upward mobility that America holds out to immigrants and racial minorities. The model minority serves a particular ideological purpose in America's self-representation as a land of opportunity, disciplining *non*model minorities whose lack of success would therefore seem to be due to their own meager desires, skills, or resources, rather than being due to racial discrimination or class oppression. Asian American intellectuals who have written on the model minority unanimously agree on its pernicious ideological uses and create in opposition what I call a discourse of the bad subject, which both appropriates the dominant representation of Asian Americans as a dangerous and subversive population and idealizes Asian America as a site of political opposition and resistance. In the conclusion, I trouble this binary of model minority and bad subject by examining the processes of generalization and idealization that the discourse of the bad subject engages in, processes that are embodied in Cynthia Kadohata's novel *In the Heart of the Valley of Love*. Theresa Cha's *Dictee* and its relationship with a companion volume, Elaine H. Kim and Norma Alarcón's *Writing Self, Writing Nation*, illustrate a more complex enactment of the discourse of the bad subject. Despite the sophisticated tools and brilliant insights of the critics of *Writing Self, Writing Nation*, *Dictee* manages to exceed their interpretations through both its representation of identity as fluid and its own inflexibility as a text, which results in a resistance to critical exegesis. Fluidity and inflexibility, leading to resistance, are the emblems of Asian America's relationship to its intellectuals. Finally, I read Lois-Ann Yamanaka's novels, not as examples of Asian American literature but as examples of a local literature of Hawai'i that has been claimed by Asian Americans. Given this context, I read her depictions of the local community as an analogy for the continental Asian American community and argue that the world Yamanaka depicts, where Asian identity is taken for granted, allowing for the possiblity of interethnic and interclass strife among Asian populations, is the future of Asian America.

If this world of strife is a possibility for Asian America, then perhaps the viability of Asian America as a political category with a clear ideological orientation is doomed. This is a critical issue that Asian American intellectuals must confront, the end of Asian American reality as they now see it. By considering the possibilities raised by this issue we can define the practice and potential of the contemporary Asian American body politic. While the future of Asian America is unpredictable in its detail and while projections may constitute arrogance, they are also necessary to some extent as we think about the potential consequences of our contemporary assumptions and strategies about Asian American community and politics.[44] At the contemporary moment, Asian America seems to be struggling to define an autonomous identity separate from the polar oppositions of blackness and whiteness; as David Palumbo-Liu puts it, "The nature of Asian American social subjectivity now vacillates between whiteness and color" (5). While such an autonomous identity may more accurately reflect the racial composition of the United States, therefore enabling a more effective analysis of social, political, and economic relations, it also reflects the contemporary understanding of racial formation and the racial state, which has helped to create and certainly perpetuate these racial identifications that are far from "natural." Within the terms of racial formation and the racial state, in other words, the struggle for Asian American autonomy is legitimate and indeed useful, but they are also the terms that Asian America frequently takes for granted as its intellectual and political horizon.

As an added consideration, we should also not ignore the possibility that the idea of autonomy may ultimately be ineffective in addressing the persisting symbolic division of the nation into black and white. While the creation of an autonomous Asian American identity will inevitably heighten the importance of multiculturalism in recognizing American diversity, this does not necessarily mean that the historically marginalized status of blackness and the historically privileged status of whiteness will not continue to serve as symbolic embodiments of failure and achievement for Americans, especially immigrants. As Herbert Gans argues provocatively, while the past and contemporary states of American racial and economic relations have been symbolically divided between white and nonwhite, the future may entail the continuing division of the nation into black and nonblack; in the case of Asian Americans specifically, Palumbo-Liu argues in a similar fashion that Asian Americans may be "negatively articulated" with whites, that is, against blacks (4).[45] An autonomous Asian American identity then furthers the Asian American claim to legitimacy in the nation by denying affiliations with blackness; it is a position that troubles founding notions of Asian American identity, and it is a position that Asian American intellectuals may not be able to prevent Asian America from assuming as its dominant—if not sole—mode of representation.

More problematic, and equally probable, is the internal division of Asian America, despite its own diversity, between the symbolic poles of black and nonblack, into bad subject and model minority, a division enacted not only by dominant society but also by Asian American intellectuals. This is a division that is important both to Asian American self-perception—because Asian Americans are capable of constructing ethnic hierarchies and practicing discrimination—

and to the perception of Asian Americans by the general American public. Asian America seems to believe that an American recognition of its claim to autonomy means that there will be a corollary increase in American racial sophistication concerning the real diversity of the nation, and that sophistication entails sympathy to economic and political inequality. The equally possible corollary to sophistication, however, is the ability on the part of other Americans to distinguish between those Asian Americans who are assimilable and those who are not. In reaction, Asian American intellectuals may seek to do what Mari Matsuda and Frank Chin advocate in their differing ways: to divide the Asian American population in an ideological fashion, into the "real" Asian Americans and the fake ones, the bad subjects and the model minorities. We may fall into what Judith Butler, in *Bodies That Matter*, describes as "the despair evident in some forms of identity politics . . . marked by the elevation and regulation of identity positions *as* a primary political policy" (117). In this scenario, with so much at stake, Asian Americans must make ethical choices that concern their alliances and alignments, as well as their identity and its consequences. Ironically, as we shall see in the next chapter, Asian America has not advanced as greatly as it has imagined in the past hundred years concerning these ethical choices and political commitments. Indeed, the ethical, moral, and political choices contemporary Asian Americans face bear an all too familiar resemblance to those that confronted the first pioneers of Asian American identity at the end of the last century.

ON THE ORIGINS OF ASIAN AMERICAN LITERATURE

The Eaton Sisters and the Hybrid Body

In Asian American literature, critics have often pointed to Edith Eaton, also known as Sui Sin Far, as an originator of Asian American literature written in English. In recent years, however, there has been at least one other choice offered for such an honor: Edith's younger sister, Winnifred, also known as Onoto Watanna.[1] The critics who have written literary accounts of the Eatons have often invested the sisters' life choices with a moral and ethical significance that reflects the political convictions of Asian American intellectuals since the 1960s. It is easy to see why when we consider the histories of the sisters. While they were half-Chinese and half-English, raised in Canada and professionally active in the United States, only Edith identified herself publicly as Chinese.[2] In 1896, she began publishing stories and articles that featured the lives of Chinese Americans. Her career climaxed with the publication in 1912 of her one book, an obscure collection of short stories about Chinese American life titled *Mrs. Spring Fragrance*; she passed away in 1914.[3] Winnifred chose a Japanese public identity, wrote a series of popular romance novels set in Japan, became a Hollywood scenarist, and enjoyed a long life. The moral and ethical quality of their choices becomes heightened by the consequences they faced at a time when being Chinese was literally criminal. To identify with the Chinese as Edith did—that is, to identify with one's actual heritage rather than a fictional one—can then be construed as a heroic act, against which the choices of Winnifred seem opportunistic.

It should not be surprising, then, that in the Asian American critical imagination Edith remains as the logical choice of a literary predecessor, given the similarity between her political choices and those of the post-1968 generation of Asian American intellectuals, who generally see themselves as bad subjects. Asian American intellectuals who looked toward the past understandably were interested in finding predecessors who shared their values and their political identification. For literary critics, this meant a search for writers who were "authentic," meaning that the literature they wrote was more "truthful" in regard to the experiences of Asian Americans than the stereotypical, often racist representations of Asian Americans in popular culture and historical discourse.[4] In the perspective of contemporary readers, Onoto Watanna's novels of Japan, in contrast to her sister's writings, may seem to reinforce stereotypical expectations of Asians as exotic and foreign. The author herself may seem to be inauthentic, claiming a Japanese identity to which she had no cultural connection. Tomo Hattori characterizes the contemporary critical representation of Edith and Winnifred Eaton as a discourse of the "good" sister versus the "bad" sister, respectively ("Model Minority Discourse" 229). He goes on to argue that "the recovery of Winnifred Eaton from her characterization as the 'bad,' opportunistic, and complicit minority sister is a sincere ethical project. . . . [But] the recovery of an Asian American subject is useless if it does not acknowledge that Asian American culture may be the site of the internalized extension of dominant cultural projects and their psychic forms" (230–231). If we look at the recent reconsideration of Onoto Watanna's work, what we discover is that it is not a reconsideration of the reasons that she was ignored, overlooked, or devalued by Asian American literary critics in the first place. It is, instead, a judgment of her work as possessing the typical traits of subversion and resistance—the work of the bad subject—that Asian American literary criticism has always valued.

As Hattori does in his article, I seek to question rather than reaffirm the values of Asian American literary criticism through comparing the lives and works of the Eaton sisters. The options of the bad subject and the model minority that are offered by American racism toward Asian Americans and generally accepted by Asian American intellectuals are inadequate in terms of evaluating the flexible political strategies of Asian Americans, past or present. The current recovery of Onoto Watanna's work exhibits both an idealization of resistance and of the bad subject and is a misreading of the political significance of her life and work for our contemporary moment. It is not necessary for Asian

American intellectuals to argue that Onoto Watanna was a rebel or misunderstood in order to find her work valuable. Instead, we can argue just as effectively, and perhaps more accurately, that her *compliancy* with dominant society's attitudes toward Asians constitutes a viable and important political gesture in its own right and still does in our contemporary moment. For us to dismiss the model minority or those who tend toward accommodation with dominant society does not erase their enduring historical presence or the consequences of their choices in shaping Asian American culture. As Hattori puts it, "Winnifred Eaton marks the secret sense that Asian American studies has been making since its inception—as an apparatus that has capitalized and continues to capitalize on the symbolic stock of minority culture. The time has come to give her the respect she deserves as the unashamed pioneer of Asian American culture as a model minority discourse" (245).

At the same time that we should question the positive and negative values we habitually attribute to the bad subject and the model minority, we should also question the very rigidity of such a polarized set of options in the first place. Both sisters actually practiced political and textual strategies that are, in short, *flexible*, bridging resistance and accommodation, the bad subject and the model minority, as appropriate to their contexts. Their flexible strategies centered on articulating race through gender and sexuality and vice versa. While Sui Sin Far challenged racial domination, she often did so through conceding to gender restrictions and patriarchal expectations. Meanwhile, as Onoto Watanna's most recent critics have argued, she often defied these same gender restrictions and expectations, a gesture that is supposed to ameliorate her accommodation to the racial demands of the day. Both of these writers have been unjustly served by the tendency in Asian American studies to idealize resistance and accommodation as good and bad and to see political decisions and textual strategies in one category or the other. Defying idealism allows us to see that the political and ethical choices made by *both* the Eaton sisters are viable and that these choices *remain* as valid options for Asian American intellectuals and other panethnic entrepreneurs today.

The sisters also remain important as models of hybrid racial identity and what that signifies for the Asian American body politic. Their mixed-race status complicates the imaginary nature of a post-1968 Asian American community predicated upon contemporary conceptions of racially pure identities propagated by the state and racial interest groups. Whereas the contemporary state of the American nation is a movement—perhaps inevitable but also perhaps not total—toward further racial hybridization, Asian American intellectuals and ethnic entrepreneurs are deeply invested in stable categories of racial identification. As I argue in the introduction, there is also a corollary to be drawn between the commitment to racial stability and the commitment to ideological rigidity—the commitment of preference on the part of Asian American intellectual work to those who uphold Asian American identity as an identity oriented toward political contestation with a dominant society bent on racial discrimination. Those Asian Americans who are not so oriented are anomalies in Asian

American intellectual discourse, as was the case with Onoto Watanna, until she could be recovered in a way that made sense to the discourse, that is, recast as politically resistant. This discourse of Asian American identity is therefore often incapable of addressing the nature of political choices available to earlier, pre-1968 Asian Americans, as well as the complications of racial hybridity then and now. For example, Winnifred Eaton's choice of a Japanese identity is a complicated one that is embedded in the contradictions of racial discourse at the turn of the century. Asians as a whole were despised in the United States due to racist perceptions that attributed racial difference to immutable, biological distinctions, but at the same time American racial discourse could draw distinctions between Asian nationalities, constructing a hierarchy of superiority with Japanese over Chinese, due to the legacy of the Japanese victory over the Russians in the Russo-Japanese War of 1904–1905. While Winnifred's choice is beneficial in this context, it nevertheless creates the figure of Onoto Watanna as a Japanese at a time when this identification still entailed some personal cost— and personal profit, in Winnifred's case.

Instead of only regarding Onoto Watanna/Winnifred Eaton as the less scrupulous of the two sisters, we should understand that by rewriting her ancestry as Japanese, Winnifred actually chooses hybridity with its limitations and possibilities, unlike the other Eaton siblings who simply passed as white. Sui Sin Far and Onoto Watanna thus exemplify the fact that acknowledging hybridity inevitably meant racial identification rather than social license to be white and "free," even though the consequences for each were quite different. For *both* the Eaton sisters, acknowledging hybridity means being included, albeit in substantively different ways, in the Asian American body politic as it evolved at the turn of the century, a stage that included difficult-to-maintain distinctions between Asia and Asian America.[5] The fact that different national and ethnic identifications within the Asian American identity produced different social representation by other Americans is not too different from the contemporary situation of *differential racialization* and *internal differentiation*. Through differential racialization, American racial discourse distinguishes— when necessary and contingent—between Asian Americans of the model minority, generally those from capitalist, democratic, technologically advanced Asian nations, and Asian Americans of the "yellow peril," generally those from communist, dictatorial, and poor nations.[6] Through internal differentiation, Asian Americans themselves make hierarchical distinctions between Asian ethnic groups.[7] These politically fraught and contradictory situations that demanded racial similarity *and* national/ethnic differentiation produced in the sisters' work techniques characterized by tricksterism and irony, particularly as they are deployed in relationship to the phenomenon of deliberate racial passing and its close second, the successful assimilation of a minority into whiteness.[8] In this chapter, I explore the specific meanings of these techniques in relationship to the categorical obsessions of both our own era and the era in which the sisters lived.

THE UNITED STATES IN A COLONIAL CONTEXT

The Eaton sisters lived and wrote at a time marked by particular social circumscription for and contradictory perceptions of the Chinese in North America. Around the turn of the century, an obscure writer named Olive Percival described the Chinese ghetto of San Francicso in travelogue terms that still resonate today: "It is the Chinese Quarter, familiarly called Chinatown. Here, in the narrow, sunless streets of Our Cathay, are the picturesqueness of the Far East and its wealth of pure, rich colors; here also are its squalor and odor" (50). Percival's perception of Chinatown as a site characterized by both exotic beauty and horrendous filth, remaining essentially a part of China itself, is part of a tradition of American orientalism and xenophobia directed toward the Chinese. In 1877, the California Senate issued a report on the Chinese, which describes them this way:

> Morally, the [Chinese are] the most debased people on the face of the earth. Forms of vice, which in other countries are barely named, are in China so common that they excite no comment among the natives. They constitute the surface level, and below them are deeps and deeps of depravity so shocking and horrible that their character cannot even be hinted. . . . *Their touch is pollution*, and harsh as this opinion may seem, *justice to our own race demands that they should not be allowed to settle on our soil.* (quoted in Moy, 35)

Chinese immigrants provide a clear example of a domestic minority that is also a colonized minority, imported by the dominant population for labor and segregated in housing and employment, excluded from political participation and enfranchisement, and relegated to exceptional treatment under the law.[9] The model of internal colonialism that developed during the late 1960s and early 1970s, while possibly ill-suited to describe the conditions of racialized minorities during that time, proves useful in understanding the conditions of nineteenth-century Chinatown specifically and Chinese urban and rural ghettos across the nation in general.[10]

Chinatowns at the turn of the century certainly bore some features that resembled colonies, at least in popular depictions of them as essentially foreign, exotic, and dangerous and, most important, separate as a geographical and cultural zone. Ronald Takaki states that "[as] a ghetto, Chinatown confirmed views of the Chinese as unhealthy, unassimilable, and undesirable immigrants, yet this same negative imagery opened the way to the development of Chinatown as a tourist center—a 'quaint' and 'mysterious' section of the city, a 'foreign colony' in America" (*Strangers* 246–247). James S. Moy further demonstrates how the Chinese were moved from invisibility to contained visibility in the field of American representation, through the segregated urban formation of Chinatown:

> While earlier representations in cartoons and photographs sought to absent the Chinese by displacing them into an imaginary Orient, many photographs from the turn of the century attempted to document populations confined in Chinatown. . . . By 1885 the containment field for the Chinese in San Francisco consisted of approximately ten city blocks. . . . The overall map of San Francisco appears as a white city in which Chinese-occupied cells stand out, like a cancer inhabiting the body of white America. (65)

The Chinese were seen, then, not as assimilable but as perpetual "natives" on the equivalent of a reservation where time itself was suspended.[11]

Labor exploitation, social exclusion, and genocide also characterize the situation of the Chinese, who must be examined in relation to other racial minorities of the time.[12] Takaki, for example, has demonstrated the particular role of the Chinese immigrants in the United States of the mid– to late nineteenth century:

> While the Chinese were "Negroized," they were also assigned qualities which distinguished them from blacks in important ways. They were viewed as "intelligent," not "ignorant and brutish" like blacks; they would make "dexterous cotton pickers, never bungling ones." "Quiet" and "peaceful," they were not given to "excessive hilarity"; they made "excellent houseservants," occasionally "sullen but never stupid." (*Iron Cages* 219)

Within the gendered-racialized economy, the Chinese male laborer, because of his perceived intelligence and asexual docility, occupied a rung slightly higher than the black worker but below the white worker. However, the Chinese laborer proved threatening because of his intelligence and his ability to imitate skilled white workers in the handling of machines and tools and the carrying out of complicated tasks. Even as Chinese labor was being exploited by American industry, the same industry helped demonize the laborers in an effective attempt to create a scapegoat for white American working-class frustrations. The Exclusion Act of 1882 prevented the further immigration of Chinese laborers, and with the end of railroad construction and surging nationwide racial violence and exclusionism, Chinese workers found themselves restricted to urban ghettos and agricultural work. Of the few women who were allowed to enter the United States, most became forcibly indentured prostitutes; although their percentage declined after 1870, the image of the Chinese woman as prostitute would linger.[13]

Geographically, cartographically, culturally and temporally, then, the Chinese at the turn of the century were fixed on the American spatial-temporal field of representation. The Chinese were also fixed on a gender-sex binary, being depicted as desexed males or oversexed females, and on a moral binary, being depicted as either "good" or "bad" in relation to white American concerns, but being nevertheless alien.[14] Against this fixity, Sui Sin Far and Onoto Watanna would explore the possibilities of hybridity, possibilities generated from their recognition that the boundaries that ostensibly separated the local from the global, the minority from the colonial, and the domestic from the foreign were quite porous. Both of them question the boundaries between the racial and gendered self and other in different ways.

AUTOBIOGRAPHY AND ETHNOGRAPHY

In both sisters' works, autobiography and ethnography become critical as genres that are related for the colonized and minority subject who, under the pressures of the racialized and sexualized gaze of colonial and majority authority, always sees herself through her own eyes and through that authority's eyes simultaneously. Sui Sin Far's predicament at the intersection of autobiography and ethnography is exemplified in her essay "Leaves from the Mental Portfolio of an Eurasian," a brief, episodic, and autobiographical piece that highlights particular moments of her life, especially as they concern her racial and gender identity. The essay foreshadows our late-twentieth-century concerns over issues of authority, objectivity, representation, and knowledge that are found in these genres. James Clifford summarizes these issues when he asks: "Who has the authority to speak for a group's identity or authenticity? . . . How do self and other clash and converse in the encounters of ethnography, travel, modern interethnic relations?" (*Predicament of Culture* 8). Through the genres of autobiography and ethnography, the Eaton sisters struggle to claim an authoritative voice for their respective ethnic communities and identities, and in so doing, they make ethical and political choices that concern their personas, styles, and subjects, all of which entail material consequences.

The problem of voice and its correlates—the validity of an author's gestures at aesthetic and political representation—is central to Sui Sin Far's work, crystallizing around the degree of authenticity that can be attributed to her characterizations of Chinese American life. To a large degree, the argument that Sui Sin Far's representations of Chinese American life are authentic is dependent upon her body and its perceptions by others.[15] As Charles Lummis, one of her editors, notes:

> To others the alien Celestial is at best mere "literary material"; in these stories he (or she) is a human being. . . . For all her father, [Sui Sin Far] is evidently her mother's daughter—a Chinawoman transplanted and graduated. And her work has a poignant intuition for her people that makes it good to all who understand that literature is, after all, something more than words. . . . For, like woman, literature must have a heart. (336)

For Lummis, Sui Sin Far's hybridity is nevertheless evidence of her essential Chinese identity. This bodily dimension of Sui Sin Far's racial identity, the inescapable taint of racial ancestry, is complemented by her other bodily dimension as "woman," who is characterized by "heart" rather than mind. Sui Sin Far must represent through and against these conceptions of her bodily confirmed authenticity, by taking advantage of how others perceive her body as a type of physical evidence but also by attempting to subvert that evidence.

Lummis portrays Sui Sin Far as what she certainly thought of herself as, an advocate for the Chinese in America, a cultural mediator or translator, and— even though she herself may not have used the word—an ethnographer who was simultaneously inside and outside of the community she was depicting. She was both the native informant and the participant-observer, and was aware of what it meant to be both the object of a gaze as well as the subject who was conducting that gaze. As an autobiographer, Sui Sin Far occupied a similarly conflicted position. She was not, in any sense, a "proper" autobiographer, according to Georges Gusdorf's limited definitions of the classical autobiography.[16] Gusdorf first postulates that autobiography is a culture-specific phenomenon that "expresses a concern peculiar to Western man, a concern that has been of good use in his systematic conquest of the universe and that he has communicated to men of other cultures" (29). Autobiography is in this case, like classical anthropology, an expression of imperial desire and a genre that is itself a colonizing tool.[17] Gusdorf also argues that "the autobiographer strains toward a complete and coherent expression of his entire destiny" (35). This notion of autobiography argues for a representation that can be all-encompassing and "authentic" but is also predicated upon obscured privileges of gender and class, not to mention race: that is, classical autobiography is premised upon having the leisure, education, and opportunity to reflect upon and reconstruct one's life. Wholeness then becomes the property not of truthful reconstruction but of privileged reconstruction.

Ethnography and autobiography work in complementary ways to reinforce the developmental narrative that grounds European imperial history. If autobiography in its classical construction produces a unified, public subject of the West, ethnography constructs that subject's other. Both classical autobiography and ethnography are predicated on the idea of a wholeness that can be represented faithfully; in the case of autobiography it is the masculine subject who represents himself, and in the case of ethnography it is the racial other who is represented by the colonizing author. Partial or fragmented identities only exist as the signs of representations produced by an immature or less civilized people, whether they are women or the colonized. Sui Sin Far's autobiographical essay "Leaves from the Mental Portfolio of an Eurasian" cannot even be called an autobiography in the classical sense, not simply because of its length but because of its fragmentary form and the particular, incomplete narrative it chooses to tell. As an example of a certain kind of autobiographical writing, "Leaves" has much in common with a large body of such writing by women, which is characterized by obliqueness, ellipticallity, irregularity, nonlinearity, and fragmentation (Jelinek 15–19). Women's autobiographical writings tend to avoid the public space of economic and political achievements that culminates in the creation of a masculine "autonomous selfhood" (Smith, *Poetics* 9). These women's writings are historically caught in a dilemma that concerns gender and the act of writing. According to Sidonie Smith, because "traditional autobiography has functioned as one of those forms and languages that sustain sexual difference, the woman who writes autobiography is doubly estranged when she enters the autobiographical contract" (*Poetics* 49), in terms of both her marginal social status in patriarchal society and the act of speech itself. Before the later twentieth century, the female autobiographical writer speaks primarily to an audience composed of men and faces a reader who functions as a representative of patriarchal society, a situation exacerbated by race for women writers of color.[18] Sui Sin Far thus writes as a minority and colonized woman in the context of a masculine and imperial genre, and the discontinuous and self-conscious nature of her essay is an expression of the constraints that she faced.

As Traise Yamamoto argues, however, discontinuity and fragmentation in narrative form do not necessarily imply a limited or corrupted mode of autobiographical representation. Instead, they may exhibit a formal attempt by Asian American female autobiographers to claim more complicated, multiple selfhoods that are as valid as the "autonomous selfhood" of conventional, masculine autobiographies (107–117). These autobiographies of successful men usually treat the coming into maturity of the author as an allegory for the nation as well, such that personal and national identities in the autobiography are metonymic in relation. In contrast, "Leaves" concludes in the following fashion: "After all I have no nationality and am not anxious to claim any. Individuality is more important than nationality" (123). While this conclusion seems to elicit from the reader an identification with the narrator, as one individual with another, the essay offers at least two alternatives to this. First, Sui Sin Far's denial of national identity in favor of individual identity is offset by a self-proclaimed racial identity throughout the narrative, exemplified in her adopted name and actions.[19] Second, individuality in the American ethnic context is often associated with an assimilationist narrative of cultural self-effacement and economic progress, a narrative that is utterly absent in "Leaves."[20] By "individuality," then, Sui Sin Far is not referring to the abstract, atomized type of individuality favored by American capitalism but instead an antiracist form of identity that is resistant to a capitalism that exploits racial differences.

"Leaves" demonstrates this antiracist resistance through its primary focus on the moments of difference the narrator experiences from others, especially when her body becomes visible to herself, its difference becoming manifest through the gaze of others. In an early memory of a party, she remembers how she is singled out from the other children "for the purpose of inspection. I do not return to [my play]. For the rest of the evening I hide myself behind a hall door and refuse to show myself until it is time to go home" (112). These early moments of stark visibility and shame become the roots for an eventual self-discovery that will foreshadow the identity narratives of other Asian Americans later in the century.[21] More important, it is the young Sui Sin Far's first exposure to a gaze that might be called anthropological—"Very interesting little creature!" the observing patriarch says of her—and its limitations. She is aware in her shame that she, the object of the gaze, always exceeds her eventual "representation" by the cultural other. As James Clifford and George E. Marcus put it, "The historical predicament of ethnography [is] the fact that it is always caught up in the invention, not the representation, of cultures" (2). The difficulty then posed for any mediator between cultures is this deployment of an ethnographic representation that is actually an invention or a fiction. This problem of using ethnographic representation is especially acute for those who have already been subjected to it and are the self-conscious objects of its invention.

Sui Sin Far, for example, comes to self-pride at a moment that is typical of the colonized subject's confliction when she learns about her "self" and her history through books presumably written by Western orientalists:

> Whenever I have the opportunity I steal away to the library and read every book I can find on China and the Chinese. I learn that China is the oldest civilized nation on the face of the earth and a few other things. At eighteen years of age what troubles me most is not that I am what I am, but that others are ignorant of my superiority. I am small, but my feelings are big—and great is my vanity. ("Leaves" 116)

The ethnographic gaze of the West is evident in both the domestic and foreign representations of herself and China as other within the United States. Sui Sin Far could turn either to the orientalist archive of knowledge about China or to the explicitly racist or sentimentalist archive of knowledge about Chinese in America. The inevitable result, as Tejaswini Niranjana notes in the context of British colonization in India, was that "post-colonials would seek their unrecoverable past in the translations and histories constituting colonial discourse. The subaltern, too, exists only 'in translation,' always already cathected by colonial domination" (43). The status of self-knowledge and hence self-representation therefore becomes problematic even for the cultural insider/native informant, when he or she realizes that absolute separations between cultures are difficult, if not impossible, to maintain.[22] Sui Sin Far expresses a recognition of the impurity of cultural identities when she states that "my mother's race is as prejudiced as my father's" (117). Instead of depending upon essentialist notions of cultural identity as a reflexive reaction to racism, Sui Sin Far demonstrates that prejudice and racism are behaviors that do not inherently proceed from identity. Instead, they are practices grounded in context and circumstance, capable of being used by any culture or race. Subsequently in her work, racial identity itself is destabilized as an essential property or pure identity.

The act of passing becomes critical in assessing this unstable nature of race. When Sui Sin Far goes to a West Indian island, what she notices is not the exotic splendor or the picturesque natives but her links to the oppressed blacks who serve on the island. "Occasionally," she writes, "an Englishman will warn me against the 'brown boys' of the island, little dreaming that I too am of the 'brown people' of the earth" (119). The Englishman's fear of miscegenation stems partially from a fear of what will result: unrecognizable, unclassifiable anomalies such as Sui Sin Far herself, who ironically is visible to the "brown boys" as simply another white woman. Onoto Watanna's work also utilizes ethnography and autobiography in order to deflect the gaze that objectified Sui Sin Far; in particular, Onoto Watanna, through passing, becomes the subject of the gaze. In her anonymously published autobiographical novel *Me: A Book of Remembrance*, Winnifred Eaton, through the persona of her narrator, Nora, assists her passing by diverting the racial and masculine gaze of her primary reading audience away from herself as an object to a convenient other, the black man.[23] The conventional autobiographical genre that Eaton adapts is primarily, as Sidonie Smith argues, a public, masculine, and white space ("Resisting the Gaze"). In this space, the female autobiography is a transgression read and witnessed by a primarily white male audience. As a consequence, the female writer is subject to the judgmental gaze of the reading audience, in an analogous fashion to the racial subjection of blacks and other people of color through the white gaze. This gendered and racialized gaze also has a sexual dimension, as Smith argues when she states that the female transgression through writing threatens to align the author with a monstrousness that symbolizes her rejection of her "proper" place in the domestic, private sphere. By leaving that disembodied private sphere where female sexuality is harnessed and hidden for the sake of the family, women become "embodied" and, with this, become bearers of the implicit sexual desires of the body ("Resisting the Gaze" 83). According to Smith, the female autobiographer "both asserts her authority to engage in self-interpretation and attempts to protect herself from the cultural fictions of female passions and contaminated sexual desires," usually through adopting masculine traits or asserting even more strongly the persona of an ideal woman (55).

In order to assert a masculine and a feminine identity, then, Winnifred tells Nora's story through both an adaptation of the conventional rags-to-riches story of the American bildungsroman, and the female romance of trial, tribulation, and virtue. Nora is simultaneously an ideal woman who seeks the love of one (wealthy) man, while fending off the advances of lesser others, and a "new woman" who, like a man, blazes her own path to writerly success and economic independence.[24] The monstrousness that might be hers through an appropriation of masculine privilege is displaced onto the figure of the black male, who serves to absorb both her racial and her sexual transgressions. Blackness appears when Nora, like both Eaton sisters, sets off as a novice reporter to Jamaica, where she finds herself in a racial situation completely unlike what she was used to in Canada. Her first sighting of the black population of Jamaica is tinged with "excitement and fear" (Eaton 20), which rapidly turns to utter horror when she is approached by a black man, from whom she runs "crying out wildly" (21), despite the fact that she disavows any possibility of "race prejudice" (41). Subsequently, she is assigned to report on the parliament of Jamaica, which features an influential man of color named Mr. Burbank, who proceeds to propose marriage to her and kiss her. In the naive Nora's mind, kissing assumes an enormous importance as she says, "I want to be in love with the first man who kisses me" (49); Burbank's proposal and kiss constitute a violation that is akin to pedophilic rape, as she describes it:

> If some one had struck me hard and suddenly upon the head, I could not have experienced a greater shock than the words of that negro gave me. . . . I was so hurt, so terribly wounded, that I remember I gasped out a single sob of rage. . . . Suddenly I felt myself seized in a pair of powerful arms. A face came against my own, and lips were pressed hard upon mine. I screamed like one gone mad. . . . that great *animal* who had kissed me. . . . I knew it was something I could tell no one. It loomed up in my child's imagination as something filthy. (54–56)

Much later, when she informs Roger Hamilton, the love of her life, of this incident, he says, "Down South, we lynch a nigger for less than that" (75), upon which Nora has no comment. The incident with Burbank and the general attitude that Nora holds in regard to race serve a critical function in relation to both Nora and Winnifred's racial identification. Even though both Nora and Winnifred acknowledge their mixed-race heritage, Nora's identity, and through her Winnifred's, is recast through Nora's act of assuming the position of the white woman vis-à-vis blacks.[25] Black male sexuality assumes the status of what Frantz Fanon calls a "fact of blackness" that inherently threatens white female sexuality (*Black Skin* 109).

Burbank becomes the visual spectacle that literally overshadows Nora/ Winnifred's own potentially racialized self. While Nora's "darkness marked and crushed me, I who loved blondness like the sun" (Eaton 166), Burbank is sketched grotesquely as "a man somewhat dudishly attired in white duck. . . . His face was almost pure black. His nose was large and somewhat hooked. I have subsequently learned that he was partly Hebrew. He had an enormous mouth and teeth thickly set with gold. . . . I do not know why, but as I looked down into that ingratiating face, I was filled with a sudden panic of almost instinctive fear" (40). The instinctive fear, according to Fanon, rises from the fact that for whites "the Negro is a phobogenic object, a stimulus to anxiety" (151) due to the racist perception of black sexuality; "the sexual potency of the Negro is hallucinating" (157) and the "phobia is to be found on an instinctual, biological level" (160) due to the fact that the "Negro is the genital" in white perception (180). Nora appeals also to the white perception that "both [the Negro and the Jew] stand for Evil" (Fanon, 180).[26] While in Fanon's analysis the white gaze objectifies the racial other and fractures that other's sense of self, an experience replicated in the autobiographical memories of both Eaton sisters, the same gaze reconsolidates the self of the white subject. By placing herself on the side of the objectifying white gaze, Nora (and hence Winnifred) distances herself from the racial other and reverses the racial and sexual gaze that threatens her as a monstrous object—a woman who writes, intruding onto masculine space, and a racial hybrid, who embodies the taboo of miscegenation. Specifically situating herself as being naturally prone to the phobic sexual anxiety of the white female self, Nora further emphasizes not only her whiteness but her proper femininity as well, reinscribing herself as a legitimate female author for white male readers.

Nora, writing from the perspective of an already-successful author reminiscing about her youthful self, does allow herself two caveats about her life and career choices. In one caveat, she acknowledges Sui Sin Far by saying: "I thought of other sisters. . . . the eldest, a girl with more real talent than I—who had been a pitiful invalid all her days. She is dead now, that dear big sister of mine, and a monument marks her grave in commemoration of work she did for my mother's country" (194). In her other caveat, Nora says: "My success was founded upon a cheap and popular device. . . . Oh, I had sold my birthright for a mess of pottage!" (154). The selling of the birthright is both an allusion to the biblical story of Esau and an uncredited quotation from James Weldon Johnson's *The Autobiography of an Ex-Colored Man* (154), published in 1912, three years before the publication of *Me*. The allusion to Johnson's book constitutes another of Nora/Winnifred's oblique confessions about her racial heritage.[27] Johnson's book is the story of a black man who passes for white, effectively becoming an "ex-colored man." Nora/Winnifred is herself an "ex-colored woman" who has successfully passed, and *Me* is the muted but still audible record of the price—and profit—of such a passing.

CATEGORY CRISIS AND COLONIAL AMBIVALENCE

Within the rest of Onoto Watanna's work, her body of popular fiction set in Japan or concerning the Japanese in America, we find additional traces of the ambivalence concerning race, gender, class, and sexuality that pervades *Me*. According to Amy Ling, Onoto Watanna's novels of Japan are romances that feature the "same narrative structure and form" (*Between Worlds* 49) and include recurrent plot devices.[28] Her novels are interesting in that they often feature miscegenation as a theme and always feature headstrong heroines who, Ling points out, are like Winnifred Eaton herself: "bohemian," "sturdy survivors" who find "modest ways to invert the power structure" but who are also compromised by that power structure (52). In Eaton's fiction, Eve Oishi finds "coded arguments for the autonomy of the 'new woman,' a creature living between racially segregated worlds and between the choices of career and domesticity. . . . The racialized narratives of her Japanese fiction are actually the coded negotiations of her uncertain class status and struggle to establish an independent and successful career" (xxvi). These heroines are also half-castes or outcasts from proper society (xxvii–xxix). Thus Eaton's novels can be read as oblique allegories of her own experiences as a racial hybrid and independent woman author. While these novels do not constitute acts of transgression as some of her revisionist critics claim, they do constitute a more sophisticated and self-conscious body of work than her early critics allowed.[29]

One of the textual strategies that both Onoto Watanna and Sui Sin Far deploy in order to produce these oblique critiques of the American racial and gender order is the portrayal of what Marjorie Garber calls a category crisis:

> The apparently spontaneous or unexpected or supplementary presence of a transvestite figure in a text . . . that does not seem, thematically, to be primarily concerned with gender difference or blurred gender indicates a *category crisis elsewhere,* an irresolvable conflict or epistemological crux that destabilizes comfortable binarity, and displaces the resulting discomfort onto a figure that already inhabits, indeed incarnates, the margin. . . . Category crises can and do mark displacements from the axis of *class* as well as from *race* onto the axis of gender. (17)

While the transvestite appears in only some, rather than all, of the sisters' works, it is arguable that racial "passing" in general can also signify a category crisis.[30] These displacements from class and race onto gender, in Garber's original terms, and from race onto class and gender, in my appropriation, function to allow indirect criticism in a context of majority and colonial rule that actively discourages direct criticism of its regime. This is because racism and colonization are as much about gender as they are about race and nationality in the service of economic domination. Racism and colonization utilize metaphors of binarized and heterosexualized genders, deploy these metaphors to describe a gendered distribution of values and virtues, exploit a feminized division of labor, and create women as objects over which white men and men of color fight. The stability and correlation of gender and sexual identities is, in short, as necessary as the stability of racial and class identity to the perpetuation of colonial/majority rule. Through category crises, the Eaton sisters can displace some of the racial constrictions that they faced onto stories about class and gender discrimination.

In the case of Onoto Watanna, the displacement that is characteristic of category crises also has a national dimension, from the United States onto Japan. Her Japanese novels take place immediately before and after the Meiji Restoration of the mid–nineteenth century that transformed Japan from an isolated feudal society to an imperial, industrial power. The changing social mores of such a time allow her to feature men and women struggling with changing definitions of social class and gender roles. Class, caste, or racial differences often obstruct the romances between these men and women, and the successful resolutions of these socially marginalized relationships can be read as oblique commentaries on Onoto Watanna's own racial status and the perils it posed to romantic liaisons and upward mobility. The cultural context of setting her novels in Japan also allow her to transgress mildly some of the United States' own mores that concern racial relations and hierarchies; for example, she critiques the racial prejudice of whites in Japan, painting unflattering portraits of them.

The importance of the cultural setting in Japan and the freedom it allows is realized when Onoto Watanna depicts what happens to a Japanese girl who comes to America in *Sunny-San*. The girl, Sunny, is three-quarters white and is rescued from a life of prostitution in Japan by American high school boys on vacation, who informally adopt her but then must leave. Their thoughtless heroism returns to haunt them when they discover a few years later that Sunny is coming to America; before seeing her, they are deeply concerned about the fact that she is a foreigner who "didn't belong and . . . never could belong" (*Sunny-San* 114). When she actually appears, however, she stuns them by looking completely Western simply because of a change in wardrobe: the narrator notes that "it is astonishing how we are affected by mere clothes. . . . She had simply achieved the look of one who belonged" (117–118). Circumstances force Sunny to leave their protection and seek employment. During her search, she befriends an Irish girl who is racist in attitude but accepting in practice, believing in the fact that "you can *grow* into an American if you want to" (231). Sunny does discover racism, however, being fired from a job because of her race. The book is oblique in this matter, saying only that "nasty as the true reason was [for her firing], there is no occasion to set forth the details here" (235).

Published in 1922, *Sunny-San* demonstrates that an American context greatly limits the author's ability to critique American racism and discrimination and illustrates the terms of assimilation for people of color. The critique of American racial attitudes found in Onoto Watanna's novels set in Japan is absent, and the existence of American racism is avoided as an unpleasant subject, depicted only as a deviation from the ethnic assimilation advocated by the Irish.[31] Sunny's eventual fate—discovering that her long-lost father is actually an American senator—marks the possibility of assimilation as the equivalent to a fairy tale. The happy ending of *Sunny-San* is thus an *impossible* ending, one reserved for children in a country where one must ironically *grow* to become an American; such a contradiction seals the fate of the Japanese in the United States as a perpetually marginalized population.[32] What the novel does critique is the notion of race as biological and contradictory American racial attitudes toward culture. The American boys perceive Sunny, who is so named because of her white complexion, as *irredeemably* Japanese in the Japanese cultural setting, despite her three-quarters-white racial heritage. Her *transformation* into an acceptable immigrant is occasioned only by a change in clothing and a greater proficiency in English. Thus it is culture more than biology that determines racial identification in the novel, and culture itself is demonstrated to be highly malleable despite racial attitudes.[33]

In this and most of Onoto Watanna's novels, the representation of Japanese culture for an American audience is implicitly an act of ethnography, disguised or rendered entertaining and written from the perspective of a cultural mediator who is part Western and part Japanese. In her first novel, however, the ethnographic component is explicit and demonstrated through the explicit racial and sexual gaze that the novel constructs.[34] The novel, *Miss Numè of Japan* (1899), includes a series of photographs that feature two types of Japanese women: gentlewomen, embodied in Miss Numè (see figure 1.1), and geishas (see figure 1.2). The photographs serve no explicit purpose in the book, except to illustrate scenes of domestic Japanese life or scenes from the novel— the women playing games, writing letters, or simply posing for the camera. In terms of plot, the photographs are interruptions to the text, which does not refer to them (although the photographs do sometimes refer to the text). In terms of narrative, however, the photographic interruptions serve to create an implicit relationship between reader and writer, an ethnographic pact that situ- ates them outside of Japan and the cultural situations and people being de- scribed. It is no accident that the objects of this gaze are two types of Japanese women who collectively embody the contradictory aspects of Japanese female sexuality that alternately repel and draw white men.

The plot of the novel revolves around the intersecting cross-cultural ro- mances of Miss Numè with Arthur Sinclair, the American consul in Japan, and Sinclair's fiancée, Cleo, with Numè's betrothed, Orito. Sinclair, who before meet- ing Numè has found Japanese women to be repulsive, discovers in her someone who is a "strange, foreign, half-wild beauty" but who also possesses "sweetness, innocence and purity of heart" (*Miss Numè* 145; all text citations are from the 1999 edition). Numè's combination of sexuality and childishness, emphasized by her cultural naiveté concerning Americans, her moments of childlike wisdom, and especially her strange Japanese accent when speaking English, is contrasted with Cleo's calculating, coquettish nature.[35] Cleo's dishonesty in toying with Orito's affections leads Orito to break off his engagement with Numè, estab-

NUMÈ - SAN.

FIGURE 1.1.   From *Miss Numè of Japan*, 1899 edition

KOTO, KIRISHIMA, AND MATSU.

FIGURE 1.2.   From *Miss Numè of Japan,* 1899 edition

lished since childhood. When he discovers that Cleo does not return his affection, he commits suicide, an event that causes his father and Numè's father to commit suicide as well. Cleo belatedly realizes she did love Orito, and after suffering through a period of bereavement, which includes watching Sinclair and Numè get married, she gets married as well, to her cousin Tom. The chastened Cleo's fate is to become very much like Orito—betrothed to a childhood companion.

The conservatism that many critics have found in Onoto Watanna's works is evident in the contrast between Cleo, the American new woman, and Numè, the Japanese woman who is both traditional and transgressive. The novel's representation of Cleo as a chastened coquette is in effect a return of the ethnographic white gaze from the Japanese perspective. Her fate demonstrates the dangers posed by the incipient feminism of the new woman in the West. In contrast, Numè is represented in an ambivalent fashion. In the traditional representation, she is an embodiment of Japanese femininity and sexual difference, an object of the ethnographic gaze from the perspective of the West. In the transgressive representation, she is someone who rebels against both American and Japanese cultural constraints in order to marry Sinclair. While Numè remains a complicated figure in this regard, the potential female transgression she embodies is displaced onto the foreign site of Japan, where its existence for the reader may be overridden by a variety of orientalist conventions, configured most prominently in the ethnographic photographs. Historically, since the middle of the nineteenth century, the figure of the Japanese woman has been feminized and infantilized in the Western imagination, where she has served as a "metonym for Japanese national, racial and cultural identity . . . [becoming] the embodied site of both difference and desire" (Yamamoto 5); "once the threat of difference has been defused, it is the site of desire" (Yamamoto 38). In this regard, the ethnographic pictures of Numè and her friends, grounded in domestic settings, subdue the threatening potential of difference and reassert the authority of Western patriarchy in its ability to objectify the Japanese woman. Ethnography ultimately subdues transgression in this and other Onoto Watanna novels, and especially as it intersects with autobiographical conventions. In *The Wooing of Wistaria*, for example, Onoto Watanna is depicted in the frontispiece wearing a Japanese kimono (see figure 1.3), and in *Miss Numè of Japan* (1899) she also appears in the frontispiece, framed by a Japanese fan. These photographs serve to rewrite her cultural inheritance from China to Japan, serving the ambivalent purpose of both acknowledging her difference from a primarily white audience and defusing that difference at the same time through an emphasis upon Onoto Watanna as a cultural translator.[36] Onoto Watanna positions herself through these photographs as both object and subject of the Western gaze on Japan, but the ethnographic thrust of the novels emphasizes this subjective dimension much more strongly. This subjective identity allows her to write *Me* in 1915, having constructed a persona that is acceptable to the American public. The fact that the autobiographical novel is written in anonymity, however, indicates that racial difference and its threat to both the audience and Onoto Watanna have not been defused, only deferred.

The ambivalent intersection of ethnography and autobiography through the figure of cultural translation also manifests itself in the fiction of Sui Sin Far, although more pointedly than in her sister's work. The most interesting character, if also the most atypical, in the collection *Mrs. Spring Fragrance* is Mrs. Spring Fragrance herself, who occupies within the two stories in which she is featured the same space of cultural translation and mediation that Sui Sin Far herself occupied as author and advocate. In "Mrs. Spring Fragrance," the title character acts as a matchmaker between two Chinese American youths who love each other but are betrothed to others. In "The Inferior Woman," Mrs. Spring Fragrance is again a matchmaker, this time between two white young adults who are separated by class distinctions. At the simplest level, Mrs. Spring Fragrance and her husband, a self-made merchant, are the rebuttals to racist American characterizations of the Chinese as asexual/oversexed, dirty, poor, uncivilized, and so on. This racist simplicity often results in an equally simple, reflexive desire on the part of the minority-bourgeois for assimilation, who clamor for *equally* proper representation within the dominant society's *given* terms of representation. Mrs. Spring Fragrance, however, is a mimic who, in Homi Bhabha's terms, produces ambivalence in the colonizing subject through the act of mimicking him. According to Bhabha, colonizing discourse has already produced "another knowledge" of itself—the knowledge that colonial subjugation is radically at odds with the discourse of liberty and equality that is dangled before the colonized subject (86). The mimic, therefore, destabilizes the

ONOTO WATANNA
[Fac-simile of author's autograph in Japanese.]

FIGURE 1.3. From the frontispiece of *The Wooing of Wistaria,* 1902. This item is reproduced by permission of The Huntington Library, San Marino, California, call number RB 420411.

colonizing subject through her aspirations to assimilate, premised upon this contradictory other knowledge.

In this vein of mimicry, the stories that feature the Spring Fragrances are marked by the near-erasure of their bodies and any substantive differences from the white Americans among whom they live. Mrs. Spring Fragrance is described as "Americanized" and, more important, as being "just like an American woman" (*Mrs. Spring Fragrance* 14). "Just like" is the key phrase for Bhabha, because what is ambivalent about colonizing discourse is the fact that those who are "just like" the colonizer can never become the "same." The colonized subject is *"almost the same but not quite"* (Bhabha 86), *"almost the same but not white"* (89). Assimilation in the colonial context is, in other words, an asymptote, predicated upon never achieving anything more than a likeness, an approximation to the original. Indeed, Mrs. Spring Fragrance is distinguished by both her command of the English language and her simultaneous misuse of it. Mr. Spring Fragrance testifies to her mastery when he says, "'There are no more American words for her learning.' And everyone who knew Mrs. Spring Fragrance agreed with Mr. Spring Fragrance" (*Mrs. Spring Fragrance* 1). Later, however, she confidently misidentifies Tennyson as an American when she says, "Is there not a beautiful American poem written by a noble American named Tennyson, which says: ' 'Tis better to have loved and lost / Than never to have loved at all'?" Even as she moves comfortably and charmingly in her pleasantly bourgeois social circle, there is still a touch of the foreign to Mrs. Spring Fragrance, but this foreign quality allows her to parody, however unconsciously, the social mores of white American society.[37] At times, however, Mrs. Spring Fragrance's critique is self-conscious and deliberate, and she exploits her cultural difference in a subtle fashion that will not alienate the whites of her elite class. Given social etiquette, then, one can make a case for her as someone who is actively mimicking or mocking her social position and the hypocrisies around her. Bhabha defines the native mimic's effect this way: "The ambivalence of colonial authority repeatedly turns from *mimicry*—a difference that is almost nothing but not quite—to *menace*—a difference that is almost total but not quite. And in that other scene of colonial power, where history turns to farce and presence to 'a part' can be seen the twin figures of narcissism and paranoia that repeat furiously, uncontrollably" (91). The paranoia of colonial/majority authority manifests itself in the popular representation of the Chinese in America as depraved and alien, in short, *menacing*. The narcissism of that authority is evident in the condescension displayed toward the Chinese as being good imitators.

The mimic's instability—her ability to move between the roles of Chinese representative and user of American English discourse—further complicates the authority of colonial/majority discourse by mimicry's "partial," incomplete nature. According to Bhabha, the mimic subverts the gaze of authority that observes her lack by returning that gaze. This reversal is a "process by which the look of surveillance returns as the displacing gaze of the disciplined, where the observer becomes the observed and 'partial' representation rearticulates the whole notion of *identity* and alienates it from its essence" (Bhabha 89). In other words, the "narcissism" of colonial/majority authority—its desire to see itself in its colonized subjects—is subverted by the uncomfortable realization that the colonized subject's own lack of wholeness may be the "true" condition of identity, which is always partial, always displaced from an idea of origin and authenticity. Mrs. Spring Fragrance returns the gaze of authority and ethnography when she decides to write a book about Americans:

> Many American women wrote books. Why should not a Chinese? She would write a book about Americans for her Chinese women friends. The American people were so interesting and mysterious. Something of pride and pleasure crept into Mrs. Spring Fragrance's heart as she pictured Fei and Sie and Mai Gwi Far listening to Lae-Choo reading her illuminating paragraphs. (*Mrs. Spring Fragrance* 22)

"What an original idea!" exclaims one of her white American friends upon being told of the project. Through the mildly comic portrayal of Mrs. Spring Fragrance's adaptation of ethnography, the passage satirizes, by implication, Western ethnography's rendering of China and critiques ethnography's power in producing (doubtful) knowledge and (doubtful) self-knowledge.

In the story "The Inferior Woman," it is the white matrons who will learn about themselves through the translation of Mrs. Spring Fragrance. Mrs. Carman, one of the wealthy matrons, does not wish her son to marry Alice Winthrop, a working-class girl and the "inferior woman" of the title; instead, she desires that he marry Miss Evebrook, the "superior woman" of birth, wealth, education, and feminist sympathies. Mrs. Spring Fragrance proceeds to undertake the task of the ethnographer by eavesdropping on Mrs. and Miss Evebrook and transcribing their conversation. Miss Evebrook admires Alice for her achievements: "Women such as I, who are called the Superior Women of America, are nothing but schoolgirls in comparison" (*Mrs. Spring Fragrance* 36). When the Evebrooks discover Mrs. Spring Fragrance's presence, she offers to "translate for your correction" (something that nineteenth-century ethnographers certainly did not do) and promises to translate also for Mrs. Carman. Of course, the end result is that Mrs. Spring Fragrance teaches Mrs. Carman a lesson in feminist ethics: "You are so good as to admire my husband because he is what the Americans call 'a man who has made himself.' Why then do you not admire the Inferior Woman who is a woman who has made herself?" (*Mrs. Spring Fragrance* 43).[38] This class and feminist critique also encodes as a given the idea that a self-made man could be Chinese as well as white. The Chinese immigrants, in ethnic and social status, are portrayed as a norm around which the ostensible conflicts of feminism and class are staged, and Mrs. Spring Fragrance is central to the action as both observer/transcriber as well as translator/mediator. Sui Sin Far, by having Mrs. Spring Fragrance assume the role of the ethnographer who represents, questions the racial construction of identity that normally consigns the white self to the powerful role of observer, transcriber, and translator and the racial other to the role of the object to be observed and taught.

What happens after this reversal takes place—after the "partial" presence takes the place of the ostensibly "whole" presence—is left unanswered and displaced onto a foregrounded discussion over class and gender, when Mrs. Spring Fragrance utters these concluding lines: "Ah, the Superior Woman! Radiantly beautiful, and gifted with the divine right of learning! I love well the Inferior Woman; but, O Great Man, when we have a daughter, may Heaven ordain that she walk in the groove of the Superior Woman" (*Mrs. Spring Fragrance* 47). In "Mrs. Spring Fragrance" and "The Inferior Woman," sexuality and feminism are foregrounded because they are coded within a dominant, white discourse of suffragism, which if not absolutely socially acceptable is more acceptable than overt attacks on the racial order. This ambivalence in Sui Sin Far's work—the fluctuation between total and partial criticism—demonstrates the limits to mimicry. Sui Sin Far shows these limits through her ironic depiction of Mrs. Spring Fragrance's occasional obliviousness to political circumstance, as in this letter she writes to her husband in the collection's title story:

> The subject [of the lecture] was "America, the Protector of China!" It was most exhilarating, and the effect of so much expression of benevolence leads me to beg of you *to forget to remember* that the barber charges you one dollar for a shave while he humbly submits to the American man a bill of fifteen cents. And *murmur no more* because your honored elder brother, on a visit to this country, is detained under the roof-tree of this great Government instead of under your own humble roof. Console him with the reflection that he is protected under the wing of the Eagle, the Emblem of Liberty. What is the loss of ten hundred years or ten thousand times ten dollars compared with the happiness of knowing oneself so securely sheltered? (8–9; emphasis added)

"To forget to remember" recalls Benedict Anderson's assertion that nations as imagined communities are formed from a simultaneous process of remembering the mythical origins of the nation as well as forgetting the fact that those origins are quite recent and deeply historical. Mrs. Spring Fragrance's injunction does something of the same sort, calling for Mr. Spring Fragrance to participate in the American nationalist project by assimilating, remembering discrimination and exclusion but forgetting that they are more than just nuisances. Irony, which Annette White-Parks has shown to be one of Sui Sin Far's primary tactics, comes into play through the fact that the reader will remember—or, more important, learn—what Mrs. Spring Fragrance asks her husband to forget.

Mrs. Spring Fragrance, as an author and mediator herself, approximates Sui Sin Far's position in American society, as someone who is not quite white. Mrs. Spring Fragrance's gentle critiques of American society are a self-conscious parody of Sui Sin Far's own critiques, which are much more pointed concerning racial discrimination in the rest of the collection but which are not necessarily read that way by American audiences—if they are read at all. The rest of the collection enacts a Mrs. Spring Fragrance–like maneuver, but in reverse. While Mrs. Spring Fragrance denies racial discrimination but focuses on gender inequality, these stories explore racial discrimination but affirm patriarchal norms of family life for Chinese American women. Sui Sin Far follows such a flexible strategy of resisting racism and accommodating to patriarchy in a clear bid to restore to Chinese Americans what had been denied to them through immigration laws, a family life that would hopefully render them human in the eyes of American society. This Chinese American family life shares similar features with patriarchal visions of American family life, with women ensconced in homes, catering to husbands, and sacrificing their lives when necessary for the sake of others—all things that Sui Sin Far never did and denies in "Leaves from the Mental Portfolio of an Eurasian." While Mrs. Spring Fragrance is unironic concerning her own inconsistencies, Sui Sin Far, through her use of Mrs. Spring Fragrance as an authorial parody, demonstrates that she is quite aware of the concessions she is making to white people in the name of being almost like them, but not quite.

AN "ETHICS AFTER IDEALISM"

Earlier critics of Sui Sin Far read her irony as a socialized limitation, in which "she is a product of her time" (Dong and Hom 165).[39] The dismissal of Onoto Watanna's work followed along similar lines. These earlier attempts to place the sisters within a historical context were based on an implicit condescension toward the sisters, locating them at the early—and implicitly immature—end of a narrative and political development of the Asian American body politic. The critical insinuation is that if they are products of their times, then we, the critics, are products of a more sophisticated era of racial awareness and political consciousness that has created a more mature version of the Asian American body politic. Asian American literary critics place great importance upon racial awareness and political consciousness; racial awareness becomes a sign of political consciousness, and political consciousness becomes a positive literary value, a requirement a text must exhibit before it can be entered into the Asian American literary canon.[40] Asian American critics are preoccupied with determining whether the political consciousness of these texts evidences opposition or opportunism in relation to racial domination. Onoto Watanna's work seems to exhibit racial awareness only to exploit it by misrepresenting it, being inauthentic and claiming an ethnic identity that is not the author's own. Initially, then, Asian American literary critics dismissed Onoto Watanna as an opportunist who wrote formulaic romances that pandered to orientalist American taste. The more recent attempts to salvage Onoto Watanna by reevaluating her textual strategies as coded critiques of racial, gender, and class domination would seem

to be a corrective to the earlier, more simplified readings of her work. Nevertheless, these more recent criticisms are conducted with the same set of preoccupations concerning resistance or accommodation that drove the work of the earlier
critics.

In this more recent body of criticism, for example, Onoto Watanna's work
supposedly subverts "conventional frontiers of ethnicity and authenticity," constituting a "more radical version of the poetics of passing" than that enacted by
Sui Sin Far (Matsukawa 123). It is arguable, however, that Onoto Watanna's
work does neither of these things. Her act of passing as Japanese does not destabilize American racial assumptions; instead, it affirms the fact that American
racial perception could not distinguish, despite its own professions, between
Asians of different nationalities. Likewise, her writings were popular partially
due to the fact that they did not substantively challenge American assumptions
about the Orient, and the writings do not undermine "authenticity" for the
same reason that her passing does not undermine racial categories. If dominant
classes and dominant values are not threatened—as evidenced in the great rewards bestowed upon Onoto Watanna's writings and the lack of any readerly
recognition of danger in her work—then subversion is not by definition being
practiced. To argue for or against Onoto Watanna's work as oppositional or opportunist misses the point, however, because either argument simply affirms
the validity of the assumptions that Asian American literary critics have made
concerning what is valuable in Asian American literature. Reading Onoto
Watanna's work as either resistant or accommodationist is in the end mislead-
ing, because those options only matter in an idealist conception of political practice and racial authenticity. We could as easily argue, as I have stated earlier and
as I have sought to prove, that her work is valuable *because* it is compliant and
opportunistic, not in spite of being compliant and opportunistic. Her work
is emblematic of a flexible political strategy still available to and still popular
with contemporary Asian Americans, including Asian American literary critics
who refuse to acknowledge that they practice such a strategy. This strategy consists of primarily accommodating dominant society's expectations but also resisting in muted or minor ways. In the end, we need to recognize that the accommodation and resistance practiced by the sisters in varying measures and
combinations are rational choices that political subjects make. These choices are
productive and destructive in different ways. While the subjects who make
these choices may justify them with moral or ethical arguments of political pro-
priety, our own critical position in evaluating them and determining our own
choices should be dictated by an "ethics after idealism" that is both empathetic
and pragmatic. Asian American history is replete with moments where accommodation and resistance have commanded split allegiances among the Asian
American population—the internment of Japanese Americans, the Cold War,
the Vietnam War, and affirmative action, to name some of the most memorable.
In terms of retrospectively examining Asian American history, it is clear that

the consensual choices some Asian Americans have made have had productive consequences, such as the decision of Japanese Americans to fight with the U.S. Army in World War II.

If Sui Sin Far and Onoto Watanna represent varying degrees of accommodation and resistance, the critical act of retrospectively judging them from the position of idealism means imposing ideological rigidity onto our interpretations of culture and the past, which has serious implications given that these interpretations are used to structure our present. The genealogy that we construct based upon the sisters as originators may tell us more about our own desires and self-images than about the historical situations that produced their political and textual strategies. Since Asian American criticism constitutes the outermost branches of such a genealogy, its impulse to explain its own roots, to idealize its birth and hence its descent, is understandable. It is also understandable that this genealogy usually implies an evolution of racial consciousness and sophistication that culminates in the contemporary state of Asian American intellectual thought. The genealogical investigation of this chapter is conducted with a different intention than to reaffirm the need of intellectuals to find in their objects of study a reflection of their own desired self-image as being politically opposed to the dominant order. Instead, this chapter seeks to explain the structural similarity between the cultural and political locations of Asian Americans past and present. Arguing that contemporary Asian America faces similar choices to the Eaton sisters is not arguing in an ironic fashion that contemporary Asian American identity is the same in the present as in the past, because it is, no doubt, different. In other words, this chapter does not offer a return to genealogy in the conventional sense, simply exchanging a different definition of identity and origin from the one that implicitly informs the critics of the Eaton sisters. Instead, the focus of the genealogy here is on the enduring nature of what Judith Butler has called "institutions, practices, discourses with multiple and diffuse points of origin" (*Gender Trouble* ix) that construct race and the location of Asian Americans.

What we discover is that at the turns of both centuries Asian Americans are in parallel moments of racial equilibrium, the earlier one defined by violence against Asians, the later one by a consensus that includes Asians. By recognizing that Sui Sin Far and Onoto Watanna both practiced flexible strategies that are rational and calculated responses, with mixed benefits and drawbacks, we should also recognize that contemporary Asian America is faced at the present moment with *at least* the same choices, which range from accommodation with and resistance to the racial and class system of the United States. Furthermore, what we think constitutes resistance today may be no more, or not much more, radical or revolutionary than those strategies of our ancestors that we condemned as accommodationist. Consider, for example, the usual argument by outside observers of Asian America that Asian Americans must make a choice between the symbolic racial poles of black and white allegiance and identifica-

tion. These choices are construed as being about, respectively, resistance and accommodation to the racial and class order of the United States. As Gary Okihiro
(*Margins and Mainstreams*) and others have legitimately argued, however, this
dilemma is not inevitable but a construct of a dominant racial imagination that
can only see black and white options, which in the end eliminates the possibilities of an Asian American identity separate from black and white. Yet it is the
case that Okihiro and others interpret this independent Asian American identity as being oppositional to the American racial and class system, an independent identity distinct from but allied with the symbolic identity of blackness. The
actual situation of Asian America is neither this independence nor the choice offered to Asian America as a whole between accommodation and resistance.
Rather, the situation is that Asian America is divided internally between these
two poles, fractured along lines of class, ethnicity, immigration, political orientation, and language, to name only the most visible fault lines—fractures that
prevent it from achieving the resistant independence that Asian American intellectuals call for. An ethics after idealism demands that Asian American critics
and panethnic entrepreneurs recognize that the "culture" of Asian America is
neither unified nor stable in any political sense; it is ideologically impure and
contradictory.

The contemporary state of Asian America is therefore similar at this most
basic level of political options to the situation of the Eaton sisters one hundred
years prior. Such a time seems quite distant from ours, and with that distance
we might think we possess a certain clarity of vision concerning the political
choices the sisters faced. On the outside of their world, looking in, we may think
we know who did the right thing and who did the wrong thing, without reflect-
ing on how our judgments may be determined or influenced by our own moment, our own world of racial equilibrium whose outside we cannot see. We
may not be able to recognize, because of the span of years, our own resemblance
to Onoto Watanna, the panethnic entrepreneur, and we may not recognize ourselves as the ones who sometimes practice accommodation, with all the right
justifications. To the degree that a subsequent crisis in American racial relations,
brought about by the civil rights movement and its descendants, destroyed the
earlier moment of racial equilibrium and enabled Asian Americans to articulate
a different political language and envision a different world than the Eaton sisters, then we should understand that our own moment of equilibrium—our satisfaction with Asian America as a resistant political identity—needs to be
brought into crisis as well. Meanwhile, given the limits of this Asian America
that we live in, we should recognize that one aspect of the sisters' legacy from
which we need to draw a lesson is that whichever pole they tended toward—
accommodation or resistance—they both made *viable* choices that had unpredictable and not necessarily positive or negative consequences. Asian Americans
today still exist with this basic set of choices and the ability to be flexible about
bridging such choices; the fact that some choices may serve to divide Asian
America or lead it in directions that many Asian American intellectuals may

find repugnant does not eliminate their viability. It is because of this political reality that Onoto Watanna and her choices should neither be condemned nor appropriated in ways that make sense to our own assumptions, when we understand that many contemporary Asian Americans, including literary artists and intellectuals, follow in similar paths.

.

WOUNDED BODIES AND THE COLD WAR

Freedom, Materialism, and Revolution in Asian American Literature, 1946–1957

I f the Eaton sisters' lives and writing represent a basic template of ethical choice for Asian Americans, the lives and work of Carlos Bulosan and John Okada represent a midcentury update of those choices, framed in the declining moments of a racial equilibrium they shared with the Eatons. Bulosan and Okada lived and wrote in the period of the Great Depression through World War II and the Cold War, a time marked by both optimism and pessimism for Asian Americans, as new opportunities developed for people of color even as their violent suppression continued. These were conditions that ultimately gave Bulosan and Okada the ability to be moderately more confrontational with American society than the Eaton sisters. Like the Eaton sisters, Bulosan and Okada presented their concerns about racial oppression through gender and sexuality, in this case through the lives of Asian

American men who are deeply wounded by the racial violence and discrimination that often worked through emasculation. *America Is in the Heart* (1946) and *No-No Boy* (1957) are Bulosan's and Okada's attempts to recuperate the wounded bodies of Asian American men, speaking to American society in terms that it could understand: freedom and materialism. In *America Is in the Heart*, the narrator, Carlos, presents himself as someone like other Americans during the eve of World War II, concerned with being free, especially as the shadow of fascism looms. Freedom becomes a coded concept in the book, for not only the struggle against fascism, which could bind all Americans together, but also the struggle against racial discrimination and labor exploitation, which pitted Americans against each other. In *No-No Boy*, Ichiro, the "disloyal" Japanese American who refuses to swear allegiance to the United States during World War II and is subsequently sent to prison, proves that he is an American upon his return by conceding to the importance of American wealth—houses, furnishings, cars, and businesses—which has been bestowed upon the "loyal" Japanese Americans.

In both books, the authors' flexible strategies entail the use of concepts such as freedom and materialism that have deep resonance for all Americans. This resonance also entails problems for the authors, as the recuperated manhood they seek to establish is inevitably limited by the ways in which freedom and materialism are conceptually entangled with the same structure of racial discrimination and economic exploitation that targeted Asian Americans. According to David Harvey, the freedom and materialism that white Americans took for granted at midcentury is made possible to a great degree—or at least made more valuable—by the freedom and material success denied to people of color (138). Bulosan's and Okada's choices, like those of the Eaton sisters, were strategic attempts to be heard in American society as they talked about difficult issues, respectively the exploitation of Filipino Americans and the incarceration of Japanese Americans. While both were forthright about the historical events with which they were concerned and did not shy away from identifying with their ethnic descent, the rhetorical strategies they chose produced different consequences for their work. In Bulosan's case the language of freedom and antifascist struggle proved popular among American audiences, while in Okada's case the lack of such outright appeal to an America that was in the heart, an appeal that might offset the horrible events with which he was dealing, meant that *No-No Boy* would disappear almost immediately.

In both cases, however, the recuperated manhood presented at the books' conclusions is compromised or limited by the authors' flexible strategies, their decision to accommodate, even marginally and ironically, the demands of dominant society. In *America Is in the Heart*, hopeful Carlos embraces a feminized America, but he can never embrace a (white) American woman. In *No-No Boy*, Ichiro finds a lover, but his desire to reenter American society with all of its material promise comes at the cost of ignoring the significance found in the broken bodies of dead friends. Seemingly the only way out of the dilemma these authors faced as they confronted a postwar society bent on believing in itself as the bastion of world freedom, even as its own foundations were undermined by racism, was to step outside of that society altogether. This is what Bulosan does in his novel *The Cry and the Dedication*, which can be read as a companion text to *America Is in the Heart*. Set in the Philippines during the Huk rebellion, which lasted from 1946 to 1956, *The Cry and the Dedication* is the consummated romance of revolutionary struggle that *America Is in the Heart* could not be. The manhood that the United States denied to Filipino migrant laborers as an extension of its own racist colonial policies in the Philippines is reclaimed by Bulosan in *The Cry and the Dedication*, as a requirement of both political revolution and its allegory in the novel, sexual fulfillment. Bulosan is able to imagine a revolution not only of Filipino peasants against Filipino elites but also of the colonized against their Cold War neocolonial masters, the United States. Bulosan's rhetorical reliance upon the concept of freedom that is the basis of *America Is in Heart* is gone, suggesting that it is only outside of the political and cultural space of the United States—even in an imagined fashion—that Bulosan could be at his most critical of American imperialism and its related domestic racism.

These three books are signposts of an era in decline, a time of racial equilibrium marked by the racial dictatorship of whites, whose violence in the earlier part of the twentieth century is marked for Asian Americans in literary history by the work of the Eaton sisters. While the Eatons could be considered the originators of Asian American literature in English, Bulosan and Okada, by critical consensus, are the most important Asian American writers of the midcentury.[1] In these first two chapters on canonical Asian American literature, then, I consider the highs and lows of racial dictatorship for Asian Americans and their impact upon Asian Americans' literary strategies. While Bulosan and Okada are not panethnic entrepreneurs like Winnifred Eaton, their flexible strategies demonstrate that they struggled with the political and cultural regime of the United States as it transformed itself into a superpower whose rule was justified by its own sense of democratic exceptionalism. Their efforts to construct a usable manhood within the confines of this regime are testimony to the limits of a domestic Asian American literature, circumscribed not only by geographical borders but also by the ideological borders of an America that was not only in the heart but in the mind as well. The contradiction that both authors faced was the fact that while some Americans were willing to acknowledge that America was responsible for the wounded bodies of people of color, most white Americans saw America as the source of healing. Working with these expectations, Bulosan and Okada fashioned a pre–civil rights, pre–Yellow Power version of Asian American masculinity that was deeply concerned with the emasculation of men of color and emasculation's occasional subset, feminization.[2] Bulosan's and Okada's protagonists seek to reclaim what was denied to them through emasculation and feminization, the ability to be free men, which in the United States at this time means men of property or men of political power.

WORLD WAR II AND THE COLD WAR

America Is in the Heart was published in 1946, *No-No Boy* was published in 1957, and *The Cry and the Dedication* was written sometime in the early 1950s—hence one reason for the dates for this chapter, 1946–1957. These dates are also significant events in the history of the Cold War. In 1946, Winston Churchill delivered a speech in Fulton, Missouri, in which he coined the term "the iron curtain," in order to characterize the rule of the Soviet Union over eastern Europe. This speech is the rhetorical commencement of the Cold War and marks the transformation of the Soviet Union from being an uneasy ally and rival of the United States to being its outright enemy. The shifting nature of the Soviet Union's representation in the United States would also mark the changes in American society's perception of Carlos Bulosan. While Bulosan and *America Is in the Heart*, which chronicles the travails of a Filipino migrant laborer in the 1930s and his eventual reconciliation with America, were initially well received in the United States, Bulosan himself would eventually be blacklisted by the FBI and die in poverty and obscurity in 1956.[3] The transitional quality of the year 1946, in which the United States was transformed from an uneasy ally and rival of the Soviet Union to being its outright enemy, comes to signal the changing reception of Bulosan's book from its initial welcome reception to its later disappearance.

    In the year after Bulosan's death, 1957, two events of the Cold War occurred, one that we remember (the launching of *Sputnik*) and one that we forget—the death of Sen. Joseph McCarthy. The contrast in the historical significance between the two events is evidence of a drastic shift in the Cold War's domestic importance for the United States. After 1957, the Cold War was no longer characterized by the era of McCarthyism with its attendant atmosphere of hysteria and persecution. Instead, the Cold War was marked by something more insidious and dangerous than McCarthy's demagoguery, and that was the consolidation of both an internal security state and the military-industrial complex, which were cemented together by a deeply embedded American lifestyle of anticommunism.[4] Ironically, the obsession with security would lead to the creation of a "national insecurity state" (Brands 31–58). Anticommunism, as the work of Joel Kovel points out, had very little to do with real communists. Mainstream U.S. anticommunism was instead a national philosophy tantamount to a religion, and its acceptability, versus the unacceptability of McCarthy's anticommunism, was evident in the number of liberal and centrist thinkers who established it as the primary political and moral framework for intellectual thought during the 1950s.[5] The launching of *Sputnik*, which inaugurated the space race, becomes important here because of its status as a major factor in enhancing the feeling of insecurity in the American population that the internal security state and the military-industrial complex were designed to stem. Insecurity and the constant buttressing of security through military spending and domestic surveillance thus became two of the primary cultural and political forces at work within the United States during the Cold War.[6]

It was also in the year 1957 that John Okada's *No-No Boy* was published. *No-No Boy* is a book that is marked by its obsession with disloyalty, insecurity, surveillance, and confession. Like *America Is in the Heart*, one of its central characters is America itself; unlike Bulosan's book, in which America is a contradictory symbol of both democratic pluralism and international socialism, America in *No-No Boy* is an ambivalent icon primarily because of its embodiment of the limits of pluralism, limits that are defined by the dissent that bears the name of disloyalty. In *No-No Boy*, two modes of disloyalty are in operation: the original disloyalty of the no-no boy and the invisible, overarching presence of the communists and other "un-American" types who presumably infested America at the time of *No-No Boy*'s writing and publication. The promises of American pluralism and the specter of disloyalty are prominent influences in the shaping of a postwar Asian American culture. In some ways, the postwar period witnessed the growth of opportunities for Asian Americans that had been initiated during World War II, which was, as Ronald Takaki notes, a watershed moment for Asian Americans in terms of their political and economic opportunities, due to the democratic rhetoric of freedom projected by the United States during the conflict with Germany and Japan (*Strangers* 357–405). The United States found itself caught in its own contradictions, arguing that it was waging a war to protect freedom and democracy while exercising racial discrimination domestically. This recognition of contradiction compelled the United States to repeal the Chinese Exclusion Act in 1943, finally allowing legal Chinese immigration—at a quota of 105 per year. The repeal of the Chinese Exclusion Act, with its combination of political symbolism and marginal change, is emblematic of the moderate shift in conditions for Asian Americans.[7]

This pattern of progress and setback continued for Asian Americans in the 1950s. The gains in immigration made by Chinese Americans due to their status as American allies turned bittersweet when they became the objects of persecution during the McCarthy era, as all Chinese in the United States were tainted by association with Red China. In the case of Japanese Americans, incarceration in concentration camps was countered by the achievements of Japanese American soldiers that eventually would alter American perceptions of Japanese Americans and allow for the creation of a Japanese American middle class. Korean Americans finally became visible in American society, but only because the Cold War heated up in Korea in 1950. Perhaps the only Asian American group that did not suffer additional negative consequences after World War II during this time was Filipino Americans, who benefited from the American perception of them as brave allies during World War II and afterward.[8] These mixed results with marginal gains for the civil rights and domestic opportunities of Asian Americans developed in contrast with the domestic Cold War environment of surveillance and countersubversion, which saw un-Americannness in every act of nonconformity and disloyalty in any un-American act. Therefore, even as

World War II created limited political and social opportunities for people of color, the Cold War imposed greater restrictions on Americans as a whole, and American society remained a racial dictatorship. This contrast between greater freedom and greater repression demonstrates how the relationship between Asian Americans and American society during this historical period is an uneasy and tenuous one. For Asian American men in particular, there was the opportunity to pursue the economic benefits of a patriarchal society massively geared for war, while still being worried about the continuing and wounding effects of racism.

MASCULINITY AND THE MATTER OF RACE

Masculinity and heterosexuality become important dimensions of Asian American experiences because of the ways in which the American public sphere, at least by midcentury, had been defined as a masculine and heterosexual place that ruled over a feminized and maternalized private sphere.[9] While white women were relegated to the private sphere and allowed certain privileges there, people of color were excluded from participation in both spheres. The exclusion of men of color from the public sphere was based on white masculinity's claim to being the sole representative of "civilization" and "rationality," attributes deemed integral to life in the public sphere. White masculinity, particularly of the middle-class variety, has been the dominant version of masculinity in American culture since the early nineteenth century, which is not to say that it has been a stable version: as Gail Bederman notes, gender is a *"historical, ideological process"* (7) and it is not "totalizing" (10), so that the evolution of masculinity is one that is shaped by what R. W. Connell calls "configurations of practice," which he labels the hegemonic, subordinate, complicit, and marginalized (76–81), terms that will have significance for categorizing the approaches of Okada and Bulosan. Bederman argues that the period of 1880–1917 in American culture is the era of modern elite masculinity's establishment, in which mid-nineteenth-century values of restraint and self-mastery, summarized in the term "manly" as an adjective that described a specific upper-class ideal of proper male identity, was displaced by "masculine." The latter term described a broader set of traits oriented around "aggressiveness, physical force, and male sexuality," which drew their inspiration from working-class and "primitive" masculinity (18). Michael Kimmel describes the transition from manliness to masculinity for the northeastern elite as one from an "essence" to a "performance" of manhood, in which masculinity had to be proven by the acts and appearance of the body, rather than through its restraint (120).

Economic and cultural changes at the end of the century served to propel "performative" masculinity into dominance by the 1930s. Kimmel summarizes the three major post–Civil War factors that contributed to the change in masculinity as industrialization, which helped destroy the autonomy of artisans and small farmers, the increase of "others"—immigrants, women, and blacks—in economic competition and claiming political voice, and the closing of the western frontier (78–100). Hegemonic masculinity reconfigured itself into a performative series of acts that incorporated and responded to these challenges, while reasserting that the dominant group that embodied the new values of physical, sexual, economic, and political aggressiveness—represented iconically by Theodore Roosevelt—would remain middle- and upper-class white men. Roosevelt became an important icon for hegemonic masculinity because he integrated masculine identity with imperial identity, thus justifying American racial supremacy at home and abroad. Imperialism and warfare were important, in Roosevelt's perspective, for regenerating masculinity and civilization: "An effeminate race was a decadent race; and a decadent race was too weak to advance civilization. Only by embracing virile racial expansionism could a civilization achieve true manhood. This . . . was the ultimate meaning of imperialism" (Kimmel 190). The "new" masculinity of the early twentieth century was then conceived in this great imperialist's eyes as a necessary method not only for extending the sphere of American power but also for buttressing domestic American virility.

In relation to this racial discourse of masculinity and civilization expressed by Roosevelt, both Carlos and Ichiro initially occupy positions that might be defined as what Connell calls "subordinate" masculinities, which still carry the power of being a competitive threat to hegemonic masculinity. It is not surprising that Carlos and Ichiro, as men of subordinate masculinities, wrestle with the roles, privileges, and accomplishments of hegemonic masculinity, which, being denied to them, may seem both desirable and execrable at the same time. Both struggle to attain a more dominant kind of masculinity than has been granted to them. For Ichiro, the sign of dominant masculinity is the ability to own actual things, commodities, that represent the owner's access to the economic life of a wealthy American society, and the attendant ability to settle down—to buy a house and start a family. To be a patriarch, like a middle-class white man, thus entails economic privilege in *No-No Boy*. For Carlos, the important possession is not so much material things as a public identity, a life in the public sphere of politics and power that was denied to men of color, and a life that for Carlos meant being a poet and political activist. Since the public and private spheres in American society were traditionally gendered, the struggle for Carlos to be a man of the public sphere also entailed a corollary effort to define those women who might supplement him. Metaphorically, this effort is realized in the conclusion of *America Is in the Heart*, with its vision of America as a feminized, embodied land that embraces Carlos.

In both Bulosan's and Okada's visions, what becomes clear is that a masculine Asian American body politic is not only a racial subject but also always at the least a gendered and sexed subject. The history of the Asian American body politic's regulation and production through exclusionary and discriminatory legislation demonstrates this intertwined history of racial and gendered formation.[10] Domestic American orientalism was put into practice through such legislative acts as the Page Law of 1875, which forbade the immigration of Chinese prostitutes on the assumption that most Chinese women immigrants were prostitutes, and in various antimiscegenation statutes that were passed because of white fear that concerned the depraved sexuality of "Mongolian" and Filipino men.[11] These attempts to regulate the Asian American body politic were clearly designed to control the reproduction of the population and also to limit the possibilities for and potential of work and mobility. These policies about sex and family formation were designed in concert with discriminatory laws around employment and living and enforced with racial violence, to discourage workers from settling and finding permanent employment. The fact that economics determined, to a significant extent, racial and gender policies is also made evident in Hawai'i, for example, where plantation owners, in need of a rooted workforce, promoted the importation of women in order to encourage family formation and worker stability.[12]

The Asian American body politic, produced from these discourses of discrimination, is thus a material body, in the sense that Judith Butler defines materialism and beyond. Butler argues that the body's materiality is an "effect of power . . . power's most productive effect" (*Bodies That Matter* 9), meaning that any analysis of the body in terms of race, gender, or sexuality must turn not to biology or nature as the source of the body's cultural shape but to the social discourses in which the body is embedded.[13] The regulations on Asian American life demonstrate that one of the most important material dimensions of the body that Butler does not discuss adequately, however, is that of labor; from a Marxist perspective, Butler is not concerned with *historical* materialism.[14] The Asian American body politic is deeply embedded in the movement of labor and capital, and its bodily, material shape is inevitably partially determined by work. Labor, meanwhile, being racially determined in the United States, is itself distorted and shaped by the signification of race in the legal code and system that limited and limits the possibilities of Asian American life and existence in the United States.[15] For Japanese and Filipino Americans at this time, their bodies mattered because the exploitation of their labor was inseparable from the construction of their race, gender, and sexuality. Because their labor was inexpensive and their humanity was in question, Filipino Americans' lives were, according to Bulosan, "cheaper than those of dogs" (*America* 143). They could be treated like "domestic animal[s]" (142) and forced to live in surroundings "where man was indistinguishable from beast" (135). For Filipino male laborers, to be categorized by American racism as less than human is also to be denied the attributes of human gender and sexuality—to be depicted as literally less than men. It should not be surprising, therefore, that in the United States the most crucial component of the dehumanization of Filipino men, besides segregated housing and limited employment, was the criminalization of their sexuality.[16]

For Carlos, this awareness of the way Filipino sexuality is perceived in

American eyes means that his efforts to claim manhood and the prerogatives of the public sphere must be joined with a disavowal, at the same time, of the "natural" sexual desires that white men take for granted and the "criminal" sexual desires that are projected onto Filipino men. In contradistinction to the discourse of bestiality that white society used to demonize Filipino men, Carlos must enact a discourse of revolutionary morality, one that is both politically conscious and sexually chaste. This discourse finds its others in two kinds of women in the United States, those who are chaste (and who are usually white) and those who are eroticized (and usually of color). As Rachel Lee argues convincingly, eroticized women are associated with the social circumscription and economic exploitation of Filipino men (*Americas* 23–25). These women—Indians, Mexicans, or poor whites—are the only ones allowed to sexually interact with Filipino men.[17] In repeated incidents throughout *America Is in the Heart*, these women lure men into degraded behavior, maritally entrap them and destroy their futures, or turn one man against another.[18] Carlos is horrified to discover that bestiality is not simply a racist stereotype that whites have projected onto Filipinos but also actually a condition that he witnesses his fellow Filipinos—and himself—sinking into. After a scene in which one friend has sex with another friend's wife, Carlos says, "I almost died within myself. I died many deaths in these surroundings, where man was indistinguishable from beast. It was only when I had died a hundred times that I acquired a certain degree of immunity to sickening scenes such as . . . this" (*America* 135). Ultimately, Carlos's experiences with degradation and erotic women "fuel [his] desire for a less hostile and fragmented community that seems possible only by way of excluding [these women's] eroticized presence" (Rachel Lee, *Americas* 26).

Carlos turns to chaste women who represent the opposite of exclusion, exploitation, and degradation—namely, inclusion into American society, with an attendant fulfillment of America's pluralist promises. Lee lists the women in question—Eileen and Alice Odell, Miss Mary Strandon, Doris Travers, and Marian—who nurture and educate Carlos when he is at his lowest (*Americas* 31–32). Eileen is the personification of "the *America* I had wanted to find," "an America [that] was human, good, and real" (*America* 235). These chaste women who embody America are white, and their sexual unavailability is testimony to America's paradoxical qualities in *America Is in the Heart*.[19] Inasmuch as America seems to offer democracy and community to immigrants of all backgrounds, the fact that the nation is represented metaphorically through these women demonstrates what the entire text of the book makes clear: the ideal America is ultimately unreachable. The famous conclusion of the book makes the representation of America through the figure of a woman explicit:

> It came to me that no man—no one at all—could destroy my faith in America again. It was something that had grown out of my defeats and successes for a place in this vast land . . . something that grew out of our desire to know America, and to become a part of her great tradition, and to

contribute something toward her final fulfillment. I knew that no man could destroy my faith in America that had sprung from all our hopes and aspirations, *ever*. (*America* 326–327)

The feminization of the land and its representation as a body or a part of the body (the heart) in Bulosan's passage is a common trope in American literature, as Annette Kolodny has demonstrated in her book *The Lay of the Land*. Yet the metaphor of America as a female body is, for Filipino men, an irony, since this is one "lay" they cannot have, denied to them legally through antimiscegenation laws and the violent hatred of white men toward Filipino men and the sexual threat they embodied. The image of the implicitly white, feminized American body with its "huge heart unfolding warmly to receive me" can be suitably contrasted to what Carlos sees as he is being forced by other men to lose his virginity: "I trembled violently, because what I saw was a naked Mexican woman waiting to receive me" (*America* 159); the act subsequently leaves him "trembling with a nameless shame" (160) that eventually disappears with the promise of this other embrace that America offers.

For Marilyn Alquizola ("Fictive Narrator" and "Subversion or Affirmation"), the ending is ironic in another sense, namely, that it flatly contradicts the evidence of the entire book, which has been a litany of racist abuse by whites toward Filipinos. Alquizola argues that Carlos's "hopes and aspirations" are, in the end, meant to be considered as foolish ones by the astute reader, who should also understand Carlos to be an ironic narrator. E. San Juan Jr. (introduction to *On Becoming Filipino*) and Michael Denning read the ending of *America Is in the Heart* differently, arguing that it is not so much ironic as strategic. Its celebration of an America with universal potential and its seeming erasure of racist oppression should be understood as an expression of the Communist Party's Popular Front rhetoric. The Popular Front from 1935 to 1947 sought to rearticulate the language of the American Dream and American possibility in the service of anti-Nazi fascism and an alliance between the United States and the Soviet Union during World War II, temporarily submerging or muting the language of international class struggle.[20] Mainstream readership interpreted the celebration of America in Bulosan's book as an act of consent to a deeply mythological vision of the nation. Ironically or strategically, Bulosan compromises with American pluralism in the conclusion, exercising a standard rhetorical trope of a feminized America and erasing any sign of erotic desire on his part. The domestic masculinity he constructs for himself is ultimately one that disavows the erotic as a "privilege" too dangerous to claim.

CLASS, CULTURE, AND THE COLD WAR

While American readers may have initially thought of Bulosan's book as an act of consent to the nation, it was the implicit idea of consent, or consensus, as the political basis of democracy and freedom that ironically undergirded main-stream American anticommunism within only a few years of the publication of *America Is in the Heart*. According to James E. Cronin, general U.S. policy against communism did not deploy either a "crude defense of laissez-faire or . . . a Manichean anticommunism"; instead, U.S. anticommunism, excluding the efforts of Joseph McCarthy, was an "anticommunist liberalism" that stressed the need for a political consensus about American values and

> took its main themes from the effective wartime denunciation of fascism: it centered more upon communism's threat to civil liberties than to property rights, and emphasized communism's disdain for democratic rights and procedures, its intolerance of dissent, and its suppression of the institutions of civil society—the press, churches, trade unions, and opposition parties and movements. Anticommunist liberalism was a critique, in short, of totalitarianism. (9)

Despite its critique of totalitarianism, U.S. anticommunism recuperated totalitarianism's techniques. As Michael Rogin and other commentators on the Cold War have noted, the countersubversive must become like the subversive, because countersubversion sees the world divided between a defensive good and a pervasive, conspiratorial, and "demonic" evil, whose presence justifies the appropriation of the subversive's tactics.[21] This countersubversive "political demonology" is, Rogin argues, a tradition of American society that finds particular expression in the Cold War persecution of suspected communists. In the absolute, Manichean vision of Cold War political demonology, communism became associated with not only subversion but also deviance, and hence many categories of noncommunist deviance became politically suspect by association. *No-No Boy*, with its distinctions between "good" Japanese Americans and "bad" Japanese aliens, enacts the central problem for minorities and other suspected deviants during the era of the Cold War in which the novel was written, which is their default status of being political "demons." The only escape from the closed world of countersubversion was to accept as vociferously as possible its vision of good, which, to quote Robyn Wiegman, is defined by "America," "this nation's most pervasive and contested ideology . . . that rhetoric of nation, narrative of origin, and abstract locus of supposedly equal entitlements" (131).

Japanese Americans, of course, had experienced in the 1940s how abstract the idea of equal entitlements actually was. In February 1943, Japanese Americans in concentration camps were asked to prove their loyalty by the federal government through responding to a questionnaire titled "Application for Leave Clearance." Question 27 read: "Are you willing to serve in the armed forces of the United States, wherever ordered?" Question 28 read: "Will you swear unqualified allegiance to the United States of America and faithfully defend the United States from any or all attack by foreign or domestic forces, and forswear any form of allegiance or obedience to the Japanese emperor, to any other foreign government, power or organization?"[22] Ichiro and numerous others answered "no" to both questions. In the 1950s, with the memory of the internment and the loyalty questionnaire fresh in their minds, Japanese Americans witnessed the creation of a federal employee loyalty program, mandated through Truman's Executive Order 9835. By 1953 13.5 million federal workers, or a total of 1 in 5 American workers, were subject to security checks; 4,756,705 were actually checked, and the FBI conducted 26,000 field investigations. "The Loyalty Program reversed usual judicial practice by requiring the defendant to prove a negative—that is, that one is not disloyal" (Hinds and Windt 169). While the situation of federal workers and Japanese Americans is far from a perfect comparison, the loyalty program was premised upon the same logic of the internment and the loyalty questionnaire to which Japanese Americans were subjected, based upon a presumption of guilt. The difference, besides race, was that the federal loyalty program and various other state, municipal, and academic loyalty oaths and investigations subjected the entire American population to the presumption of guilt, which led to what Joel Kovel characterizes as "a time of massive conformism around a resurgent mythology of patriarchy"; society was "united around the patriarchal expulsion of the red devil as well as around a triumphant consumerism. . . . The fear of nuclear annihilation overshadowed all others . . . fear became omnipresent. It spread to all spheres of personal existence" (106). Domestic anticommunist liberalism was therefore a logical extension of two things: American anxiety over foreign threats (including the danger of nuclear war) and a long-standing American xenophobia.

In the first instance, of American anxiety over Soviet domination and manipulation, the domestic Cold War became an extension of foreign policy, represented in the Truman Doctrine, which preached the containment of communism and the support of free peoples threatened by communist insurgency or infiltration. The rhetoric of international subversion and containment in the Truman Doctrine extended easily to the issue of potential domestic subversion and its containment. A more serious policy position than the Truman Doctrine, however, was taken in NSC 68, a National Security Council document that became the blueprint for Cold War foreign policy and whose existence was to remain secret for twenty-five years. NSC 68 argued that U.S. military spending needed to be bolstered drastically, in order to allow military containment of the Soviet threat; the initial vast expenditures justified by NSC 68 were cloaked by the demands of the Korean War. Defense spending grew from $13 billion out of a GNP of $285 billion in 1950, or 4.6% of the GNP, to $50 billion of a GNP of $365 billion in 1953, or 13.8% of the GNP; the percentage of the GNP devoted to defense tripled. By 1959, defense spending had leveled off to about 10% of the GNP (Brands 39). To a large extent, domestic prosperity was accelerated because of this defense spending, so that by the mid-1950s, while "six percent of the world's population lived in the United States . . . [the United States was] producing and consuming over a third of the goods and services of the planet.

American industry used half of the world's steel and oil, and three-fourths of all the cars and appliances on earth were consumed in the United States. Real gross national product (GNP) increased from $206 billion in 1940 to more than $500 billion in 1960" (Whitfield 69–70). The reality of this Cold War prosperity filters into *No-No Boy*, where the presence and function of commodities are made explicit: commodities such as cars, televisions, houses, and furnishings are signs not only of prosperity but also of loyalty. That is, the Nisei veterans and their families live in middle-class luxury, while the disloyal Japanese Americans live in poverty. The reward for loyalty, both during World War II and then implicitly during the Cold War, is the participation in America's bounty of plenty. Communists and other "un-American," disloyal types were not allowed to share in the material wealth that was a direct product of the Cold War state and its secret emphasis on military spending.

The ownership of property and commodities, which is the most material sign of assimilation into American culture, is therefore a corollary to the willingness to sacrifice one's life and body for that American culture. Kenji, a Nisei veteran who befriends Ichiro, illustrates this most graphically. Kenji has lost a leg in the war, and the gangrene that is eating away at the stump eventually kills him. Kenji's reward for his service and his leg is a new Oldsmobile from the government. More important, the material wealth is something that his entire family of American loyalists shares in: "Hisa and Toyo are married to fine boys, Hana and Tom have splendid jobs, and Eddie is in college" (Okada 118). Their house is noticeably decorated with "new rugs and furniture and lamps and the big television set with the radio and phonograph all built into one impressive, blond console" (118). The material wealth is mirrored by the happiness of the family, a Japanese American version of the Cleavers or the Nelsons or other well-adjusted middle-class white families that filled the TV screens of the 1950s during the writing of *No-No Boy*. In contrast to Ichiro's fragmented family, where the mad mother rules over an emasculated father and Ichiro's younger brother hates him so much he organizes an assault on Ichiro, Kenji's family is depicted as loving, communicative, upwardly mobile, and fecund. Kenji's sacrifice has enabled his family to survive the community-destroying effects of relocation, which, Harry H. L. Kitano argues, is a process of internal colonization.[23]

Thus *No-No Boy* demonstrates that belonging to America means being able to claim the right to have things belong to oneself. This, like the "crimes" of draft resistance and refusal to declare loyalty, is a catch-22: Japanese immigrants could not become citizens, and in some states noncitizens could not buy property.[24] Perversely, in the eyes of Ichiro and other Americans the most tangible sign of the Issei's refusal to become American is their refusal (even when they had the chance) to buy property or, short of buying property, to buy the commodities—furniture, decorations, luxuries—that would testify to permanence. Yet when Japanese did own property or leased the farm property they worked on, other Americans perceived them as an economic threat to American small farmers. Exclusive rights to citizenship and ownership become legal methods that justified an already-existing anti-Japanese racism, and Ichiro accepts the law without seriously questioning its hypocrisies and inconsistencies. He is therefore able, without irony, to regard his brother Taro's decision to run away from home and join the army as the one he should have made: Taro will "come out [of the army] and walk the streets of America as if [he] owned them always and forever" (Okada 81).

For those suspected of disloyalty like Ichiro, the Cold War accelerated the xenophobia already present in American society. The McCarran Act, also known as the Internal Security Act of 1950, allowed for the exclusion of aliens with certain political backgrounds, required the registration of communist organizations with the attorney general, and gave the president the power to detain suspected subversives (Albert Fried 85–88). Suspected subversives were also subject to deportation. Various government agencies became actively and enthusiastically involved in policing the menace: the Justice Department, the Internal Revenue Service, the Immigration and Naturalization Service, the Post Office, and the State Department's Passport Division all regulated suspect people and materials (Albert Fried 117). New agencies were created during the 1950s that were ostensibly designed to support foreign policy in the Cold War but actually became involved in the domestic Cold War as well: these included the CIA, the National Security Agency, and the Atomic Energy Commission. While the targets of surveillance and suppression were often middle Americans, those who were already suspect due to xenophobia, racism, homophobia, and sexism were more obvious suspects. Civil rights organizations, including the NAACP, were listed with the FBI as communist front organizations. Labor unions came under suspicion. Gays and lesbians were targeted because sexual perversion was seen as one step away from political subversion, and vice versa. The Cold War created a climate of paranoia, even among the centrist and liberal factions that would eventually succeed McCarthy, and the paranoid mentality resulted in a circular logic, such that those already perceived as being aberrant in American society also became perceived as being potential communists. The civil rights movement, for example, "aroused the suspicion of those who inferred from the evidence that Communism was loathsome the conclusion that anything loathsome was communism" (Whitfield 21).

Within this climate, *No-No Boy*'s portrayal of Ichiro takes on added significance. His plight as a suspected traitor and the consequences he suffers of exclusion, isolation, imprisonment, paranoia, and stigmatization, while a direct product of and reference to the concentration camps, can also be read as an implicit commentary on the domestic Cold War. The lesson that the Japanese Americans learned foreshadows the lesson that the majority of Americans learned in the 1950s: that being American demanded a submission to a society structured around a state of permanent war, with a commensurate internal security apparatus that operated not so much by visibility as by omnipresence. Thus, while Ichiro rejected the legitimacy of detention in the concentration camps, he eventually consents to the virtual panopticon of American identity.[25] It is the all-seeing model of the panopticon that serves as the structure of countersubversive containment that *No-No Boy* as a Cold War text critiques. The panopticon limits the possibility of resistance, for Ichiro never believes that his "no" to the draft and to the loyalty oath can be construed positively, as a rejection of the contradictory demands of incarceration and patriotism. Instead, Ichiro, like a good prisoner, must learn to accept his punishment as just, his act as actually illegal, and his rehabilitation as proscribed. In short, Ichiro must learn to confess, in a manner that reflects Cold War rhetoric, which offered suspected subversives the options of annihilation or therapy (Hinds and Windt 113–118). As Foucault might have put it, the Asian American body politic is no longer punished through violent spectacles of abuse, segregation, and persecution but is instead more effectively disciplined through learning to love America (*Discipline and Punish*).

To fulfill these conditions of loyalty demanded by countersubversion, the alien must find another alien whom he can denounce and against whom he can define his necessary inclusion. Thus it is because Ichiro cannot systematically understand the American society in which he lives and its racism that he turns inward to the society with which he is most familiar in order to discover the alien. While this is generally Japanese Americans, he is most concerned with his family, demonizing in particular his mother, who stands in for both an essential Japanese racial identity and some of the forces that emasculate Japanese American men. The effects of this emasculation are represented in Ichiro's father. Ichiro compares his father to an "old woman" (Okada 6) and says that he is "a goddamned, fat, grinning, spineless nobody" (12) and someone "who was neither husband nor father nor Japanese nor American but a diluted mixture of all" (116). Indeed, the mother's domination of the father is so complete that Ichiro believes they have effectively traded gendered roles: "[Pa] should have been a woman. He should been Ma and Ma should have been Pa. Things would have worked out differently then. How, I don't know. I just know they would have" (112). The fact that Ichiro's father is a "nobody" reflects the negation of the body and the spirit that emasculation entails, as Ichiro acknowledges when he describes himself with that term (76). Ironically, the sign of being a nobody in *No-No Boy* is having a *whole* body. That is, in the context of the war, physical sacrifice for Nisei soldiers is the tangible sign of being *somebody*, of mattering in the public sphere of American life. In a slightly different but comparable way, militarism becomes a sign of masculinity in Cold War; to be "soft" on communism, a common partisan political charge, was to be reluctant to use military force (Kovel 5). In *No-No Boy*, however, war participation had to be physically evident in order to overcome that other physical stigma: racial identity. Ichiro and Kenji's relationship demonstrates this irony of masculine and racial performance. Although Kenji's wound is fatal, Ichiro envies him and remarks fervently that he would gladly trade places; Kenji, upon reflection, agrees with Ichiro's assessment (59–65, 73).

Kenji and Ichiro's homosocial relationship becomes a ground for illustrating the performance of masculinity. As Butler argues, gender is a culturally compelled, reiterative performance (*Gender Trouble*); it is the variety of social acts that men undertake, consciously and unconsciously, to prove a concept of masculine identity that is based upon the idea of an essence, a definable core of manhood that contradictorily should need no proof. Masculinity becomes a performance in the public sphere to demonstrate a private identity, as Kenji's case demonstrates (Kimmel 329–335). Kenji's missing leg and visible stump become symbols for the phallus: the missing leg is the physically disempowering price Kenji pays for the symbolic power that remains visible in the stump, so that the phallus is always absent but always present, bestowing power and extracting pain. The phallic and sexual dimensions of this missing leg are clear in Ichiro's envious appraisal of it: "Give me the stump which gives you the right to hold your head high. Give me the eleven inches. . . . [which] made it so that you can put your one good foot in the dirt of America and know that the wet coolness of it is yours beyond a single doubt" (Okada 64). It is crucial to recognize that the phallic symbolism encodes Ichiro as having power as well, which becomes clear when Kenji, referring to their respective problems, asks, "Whose is bigger?" (64). Kenji answers his own question: "Mine is bigger than yours in a way and, then again, yours is bigger than mine" (65). The narrative demonstrates that masculinity is a wound, whose degree of injury is nevertheless a testament to the amount of power that is present. The ambiguity of Kenji's answer reflects his and Ichiro's inability to assess the nature of each other's sacrifice and damage consistently. The tragedy of the situation is that either choice, Ichiro's or Kenji's, ends with an equally crippling result: the destruction of the spirit or the destruction of the body. Ichiro's fear of spiritual death resonates with the rhetoric of the Cold War that depicted communism as an internal disease or sickness; Ichiro is fearful, then, of being consumed internally by this infection of disloyalty that he must excise (Hinds and Windt 9).

These attempts at excision manifest themselves in various ways: Ichiro's rebellion against his mother, his search for sexual fulfillment with his lover Emi, the quest for worthwhile work, and the establishment of a masculine bond with Kenji. These attempts are insufficient inasmuch as they are all attempts to enact, to perform, to prove his loyalty and masculinity (an essence that should not have to be proven) against the seemingly undeniable, visible proof of his identity as Japanese—an essence that cannot be disproven. The only real resolution for Ichiro lies in renouncing the stage for that visibility: the body itself. For Ichiro, the racialized body is taken as the *cause* of racism, when it is in actuality an *effect* of racism. Okada demonstrates his ironic awareness of the difference when he writes in the preface to *No-No Boy* that Japanese Americans, as of December 7, 1941, had *become* "animals of a different breed" (vii).[26] The preface, with its extended examination of the physical features of Japanese Americans that mean one thing before Pearl Harbor and something completely different after Pearl Harbor, testifies to the contingent nature of race, that it is not inher-

ent but mutable, a product of social, political, and economic forces and negotiations that together comprise racial formation. The physical features that we
think comprise a racial appearance are not inherently noticeable in and of themselves (skin color, hair texture, eye, lip, or nose shape, etc.). They only become
visible and noticeable as markers of race through the process of racial formation. In the course of *No-No Boy*, race is naturalized for Ichiro as an inherently
visible property of the bodies of Japanese Americans.

Carlos also recognizes the problem of visibility and to some extent recognizes the production of a visible essence through racism. As he memorably
notes, "It was a crime to be a Filipino in America. . . . We were stopped each
time these vigilant patrolmen saw us driving a car. We were suspect each time
we were seen with a white woman" (*America* 121). To be a Filipino was to be
continually under surveillance, to live in a police state, with the threat of actual
imprisonment and violence always present. Carlos extends this understanding
of his virtual imprisonment metaphorically, asking: "Was everybody moving
toward a faith strong enough to blast away the walls that imprisoned our life
in America?" (280) Even more than this, he understands that the visible mark
of his criminal status—his body, rather than the uniform of the prisoner—
threatens to become not merely an imposed sign but his actual self. He says: "I
was running away from myself, because I was afraid of myself. I was afraid of
all that was despairing in that swamp of filth—that dark dungeon of inquisi-
tional terror and fear" (294). Even though Carlos is referring to the actual conditions in which he lived, the implication is that he himself could become, and
not just inhabit, that "swamp of filth," "that dark dungeon," that is his own
body—created for him, to some extent, but his nevertheless.

For Ichiro, racial criminality is also present, in both literal and figural
senses. Even though he has left prison behind him, he carries its memory with
him like any good former prisoner should, by being condemned to a "prison of
forever" (Okada 40). He wonders why "in my freedom, I feel more imprisoned
in the wrongness of myself and the thing I did than when I was in prison? Am I
really never to know again what it is to be an American?" (82) For Ichiro, to be
an American is to be free; in order to be free, he has to admit to the cryptic
crime he has committed in order be forgiven. Since this cryptic crime has its
roots not in an actual act but in the imposed stigmatization of his skin, absolution can be sought in the disavowal of his body and its significance. Although
this disavowal is not the only choice, and indeed is a choice based upon a misrecognition of race as natural rather than social, for Ichiro the narrative of his
liberation from his imprisonment is the narrative of forgetting his own body. It
is this body that he cannot forget when he is released from prison and returns
home to Seattle. Upon the return, what he fears most is being seen by other
Japanese Americans; he is constantly aware of the fact that others recognize him
for what he has done. Eventually, however, he confesses to the crime he has
committed. "I have been guilty of a serious error," he thinks. "I have paid for
my crime as prescribed by law. I have been forgiven and it is only right for me

to feel this way" (232). His internal acknowledgment of his just imprisonment, his confession to the essence of who he is perceived to be and its link to his performance of ingratitude and rebellion, is immediately rewarded. "There was room for all kinds of people," the narrative states. "Possibly even for one like him"; and indeed, this seems to be true, as he walks up to a "cluster of people . . . [who] hardly gave him a glance" (233).

In this penultimate chapter of the text, Ichiro believes that by confessing to his crime and consenting to a particular vision of America he has been liberated from his body—a liberation that is ultimately put into question by Okada's conclusion. *No-No Boy* ends with Ichiro witnessing a concluding moment of violence, as Freddie, another no-no boy, is killed in a car wreck, while his adversary, a Japanese American veteran named Bull, is reduced to an infantile state, crying "like a baby in loud, gasping, beseeching howls" (250). Throughout the novel, characters' frustration at comprehending their situations has found expression only in incoherent screams like Bull's (12, 40, 68, 176), signifying their language's inability to provide the vocabulary for articulating a positive answer to their double-bind dilemma—imprisoned at home, forced to prove their loyalty abroad. In contrast to this violence and inarticulateness, Ichiro's final, optimistic thoughts, that there is a "glimmer of hope," a "faint and elusive insinuation of promise" (250–251) that is America, are as insubstantial and uncertain as they sound. Yet the novel's depiction of Ichiro's optimism as uncertain and inarticulate is necessary, because, as Jinqi Ling argues, Okada was writing at a time in which the civil rights movement was just commencing and he was writing of a time when civil rights as a movement did not yet exist, which circumscribed Ichiro's options ("Race, Power, and Cultural Politics"). Kandice Chuh agrees, stating that in "voicing . . . uncertainty, Ichiro expresses the unintelligibility of the American nationalist narrative that at once presumed disloyalty and demanded self-sacrifice" (106). As both Ling and Chuh make clear, Ichiro's confusion about the American narrative, resulting in his concluding optimism, is partially due to his inability to recognize the injustice of the loyalty questions and to imagine anything more than an individual, alienated response.

Both Carlos and Ichiro struggle to articulate masculine, American identities at the conclusion of the books. Carlos is able to be more forceful about his conviction in American possibility, but in both cases they are constrained by the limits placed upon their imaginations by American narratives of possibility. For Carlos that narrative centers on American pluralism's promise of inclusion, while for Ichiro that narrative concerns U.S. law. It is the law that asks the questions that Ichiro cannot answer and to which he cannot demand alternatives. In a similar fashion, Carlos is trapped in the dilemma of the "American Way," as Sacvan Bercovitch has defined it. According to Bercovitch, the United States is unique among nations because it allows for dissent, but for Bercovitch dissent is ultimately limited by an ultimate form of consent to the possibilities allowed by American democratic practice. In other words, the American Way is what one must finally consent to, the common ground that allows people to agree to disagree. The American Way is an ideological space, but as Terry Eagleton argues, "Seen from within, [ideology] has no outside" (95); ideology defines the horizons of one's vision. In this limited realm of political maneuver, Carlos, as a narrator who is either ironic or strategic, must affirm the ideological basis of American society, its belief in itself as a place where true disagreement is possible. Ultimately, Carlos and Ichiro must step outside of the American Way, outside of the ideological consensus of American society, in order to be able to articulate a masculinity that is not conflicted by the contradictions of American society over race. While they do not do so in the case of these two books, Bulosan does so in a separate work, *The Cry and the Dedication*, which imagines a space outside of America, literally and ideologically.

REVOLUTION AND ROMANCE

Bulosan probably wrote *The Cry and the Dedication*, according to its editor, E. San Juan Jr., from 1952 or 1953 until 1955. The novel is set in the Philippines during the time of the Huk rebellion, which dated from 1946 until 1956.[27] San Juan argues that the novel represents Bulosan at his ideological maturity, committed to Marxist dialectics and envisioning a diasporic connection between the oppression of Filipino Americans and that of Filipino peasants in a neocolonial society still dominated by the United States after official Philippine independence in 1946. The origins and evolution of the Huk rebellion are indeed intimately tied to the role that the United States played in the Philippines throughout the 1930s and 1940s. By focusing on the Huk rebellion, Bulosan therefore alludes to a history that is parallel to the one being experienced by Filipinos in the United States. This history of U.S. involvement in the Philippines is marked by American imperial practices that are unspeakable in the ideological space defined by the American Way. The eventual suppression of the Huk rebellion is made possible by the extension of those imperial practices through U.S. intervention in the Philippines. By intervening, the United States sought to "stabilize" the country and prepare it for its eventual role in the Cold War, as the United States' key military base in the Pacific and Southeast Asia.

The Huk rebellion had its origins in peasant unrest in Central Luzon during the 1930s, as peasants began to express dissatisfaction with exploitative landowners. When the Japanese invaded the Philippines in 1941, the peasant movement formed an armed resistance, naming itself Hukbo ng Bayan Laban sa Hapon—or Hukbalahap, the "People's Army against Japan." The Hukbalahap was the only significant armed resistance offered against the Japanese, as the Philippine Constabulary (the military police) and many politicians and landowners became active or passive collaborators. Other guerrillas from the Filipino and U.S. armies who had not surrendered to the Japanese followed orders from General MacArthur to lay low; according to William J. Pomeroy, the U.S. military did not want an anti-Japanese guerrilla force to become active and popular enough to form a nationalist movement with local leaders (107–113). After the return of U.S. forces to the Philippines, the Huks found themselves being targeted by their rival guerrillas and by the local politicians and landowners, who had once again switched loyalties, to the United States. The United States, interested in reestablishing control over the Philippines as swiftly as possible, was willing to keep the collaborating landed elite in their positions of power, as a malleable class. This malleable class served the the interests of the United States, who saw the Huks as a communist movement that could threaten U.S. interests in the Philippines. While the Huks and the Partido Komunista ng Pilipinas (PKP) were separate but overlapping entities throughout the 1930s and the 1940s, the PKP did establish control of the Huks after the end of the war. The war's aftermath was marked by a rising level of military oppression directed against the Huks and their supporters, who were numerous among the civilian population. The Huks were an effective armed movement because they were also a political movement that sought to educate the peasants and organize them into a necessary economic base for the Huks. Philippine military oppression against civilians, resulting in numerous abuses and atrocities, maintained high levels of civilian support for the Huks, and in 1948 the Huks renamed themselves the Hukbong Mapagpalaya ng Bayan, or the Army of National Liberation, signaling the change in their goals from anti-Japanese resistance to people's warfare against the Philippine state. By this time, the PKP had decided to end its efforts for democratic struggle over the independent Philippine state, moving instead to a focus on the armed overthrow of that state.

The PKP disagreed with the direction that the Philippine state was taking. In the postwar years, the Philippines had become formally independent from the United States, but had also become firmly tied to the United States in a neocolonial relationship of economic, military, and political dimensions. In economic terms, the 1946 Bell Trade Act created an unequal trade relationship between the two nations, giving U.S. citizens equal rights with Filipinos in economic dealings, allowing unlimited U.S. imports into the Philippines, and tying war damage payments to the Filipino acceptance of the Act. According to Pomeroy, "The Bell Trade Act established the near total trade and investment domination of U.S. businesses in the Philippines" (161) and led to a trade deficit of $1.1 billion during 1946–1949, virtually all with the United States (184). Just as significant as the Bell Trade Act was the Military Bases Agreement, which allowed for the establishment of twenty-three U.S. bases on Philippine soil for ninety-nine years, including the rights to complete control over what occurred on the bases and to expand the bases as necessary (Pomeroy 163–164). Finally, the Military Assistance Agreement of 1947 "put the Philippine armed forces effectively under the control of the Pentagon and produced an organization, tactics and general military orientation both internally and externally that suited U.S. global strategy" (Pomeroy 164). Subsequently, Filipino troops were sent to fight in the Korean War under U.S. pay, and the United States used the Philippines as a staging ground for the Vietnam War. The Philippines were therefore a key part of U.S. Cold War strategy in Southeast Asia, rendering it nonneutral (Pomeroy 166–168).

As a result of U.S. interests in a "stable" Philippines, the United States explicitly endorsed the ruling regime, composed primarily of landlords who were interested in maintaining the economic status quo. The Huk rebellion was a protest against the agrarian conditions of inequality for peasants, enforced by the landlords. The deep class divisions and class unrest were products of much earlier colonial times, when the Spanish ruled. The United States did nothing to redress these colonial conditions of class inequality after invading the Philippines in 1898. Part 1 of *America Is in the Heart* discusses the pre–World War II economic oppression of Filipino peasants and the necessity for a revolution to overturn those conditions, but not surprisingly, little is done to connect the exploitation of Filipinos with the U.S. colonial regime. In *The Cry and the Dedication*, while there are only a few instances where Americans appear, most notably in overflying U.S. planes that are aiding the Philippine army forces and an anomalous American doctor in a village, it is clear that they are actively assisting the Philippine government. American military and material assistance was critical in the eventual suppression of the Huk rebellion, and Bulosan's novel is something of an elegy or a commemoration for a movement that was already, even as Bulosan wrote it, in decline.[28] The novel itself centers on the journey of seven guerrillas on an important mission for the revolution, heading to a rendezvous with Felix Rivas, a Filipino American who has returned with money for the revolution.[29] The mission ends with the death of the one guerrilla, Dante, who is absolutely critical to the success of the mission because only he can identify Rivas. Thus the novel depicts a rebellion that fails, although not one that dies altogether, as later in the 1960s the PKP and the Huks would reemerge as the Communist Party of the Philippines and the New People's Army, respectively (Kessler 29).

Along the way toward the final rendezvous with Rivas, the seven guerrillas each have their own individual rendezvous, at their home villages, although there is no apparent reason given for these meetings. This is an early sign that the novel is not a realistic one but is instead what San Juan calls a transnational allegory of a Third World imagination (introduction to *The Cry* xix), as Bulosan tries to go home, figuratively, in the persona of these characters and construct the critique of imperialism that he was not able to do in *America Is in the Heart*. Each of the guerrilla's arrival at home is marked by violence and education. Each village is occupied by enemies of the revolution who provoke confrontation and death. With each incident, Hassim, the leader of the revolutionaries, takes the opportunity to spell out to his followers the revolutionary program. The most significant return, however, is that of Rivas to the Philippines. Rivas is significant not only for the plot of the book, in terms of the money he bears, but also for his symbolic import. Rivas has been sexually crippled in the United States, his testicles crushed (*The Cry* 41), a clear sign of Bulosan's concerns about the sexual and racial assaults upon Filipino men that he depicts in *America Is in the Heart*. The type of damage inflicted upon Rivas is "unthinkable" for the revolutionaries and "unbearable for [Dante] to remember alone through life" (41). The revolutionaries are literally not capable of imagining such cruelty; one of the most hardened asks, "Are there such vicious men in the world?" (42). The naiveté of the revolutionaries, their utter shock at the revelation of Rivas's wound, demonstrates clearly how emasculation confirms for them the sadism and conviction of their enemies and shakes the foundations of their identities as men.

Rivas's wound also provides the opportunity for Bulosan to show how oppression, revolution, and counterrevolution are articulated through sexual identities. If Rivas's manhood has been taken away from him in the United States, there is the possibility that it might be restored in the Philippines, thanks to the revolution. Rivas's restoration is one reason that a woman, the virginal Mameng, has been assigned to the group. Dante, who is familiar with Rivas, spells out her task when he remarks that he is unsure "if [Rivas's penis] still works. That is for someone to find out" (42). Why anyone needs to know if Rivas can still have sex is unclear, from a literal perspective. What is also unclear from that same perspective is the logic behind the other ostensible reason that Mameng is brought along, which is to identify the authenticity of Rivas, for the revolutionaries are afraid that the enemy may substitute one of its own agents for Rivas, "complete with disfigurements" (26). While Dante claims he would "know Felix a kilometer away" (26), it is Mameng who must make first contact with Rivas and check his disfigurements and functionality as well (42–43). Hassim acknowledges that the task is degrading, particularly if, as he suspects, Mameng is a virgin, and also since experienced women are available. While the use of Mameng makes no literal sense, her allegorical purpose is clear and twofold: first, to mediate the homosocial relationship of the men, both among the revolutionaries and between the revolutionaries and Rivas, and second, as someone who is sexually pure, to symbolically heal the damage to Felix Rivas.

Mameng's symbolic purpose is established even more firmly when the men decide that Mameng, as a virgin, should not have to confront Rivas uninitiated (although why *any* form of sexual initiation would not be degrading is also not mentioned). Mameng's clear choice for her first lover is Hassim, but he, without any reason, chooses Dante. A stand-in for Bulosan, Dante is a writer with a poetic pseudonym who has lived in the United States for fifteen years. His writing involves "tracing our history from the revolutionary viewpoint" (5), but when it comes to thinking about America, "a land he could not forget" (25), he is torn between seeing it as a place of "bitterness" or one of "great beauty" (18).[30] Dante, who knows "everything about Hassim, all, his political and private life," understands why Hassim has passed the task of sexual initiation to him: Hassim, too, has been sexually wounded, this time by Filipino government forces (116). Hassim the revolutionary leader and Rivas the revolutionary savior are parallel figures whose sexual damage at the hands of a U.S.-sponsored government and American racism, respectively, becomes symbolic of poor Filipino men's emasculation in the U.S. empire. While this emasculation cannot be recuperated in the United States, where sex with white women is outlawed and sex with poor women and women of color is depicted by Bulosan as morally degraded, it can be recuperated in the Philippines through the instrument of revolution. The morally conscious Carlos of *America Is in the Heart*, struggling to come to dialectical consciousness, is realized in the figure of Dante, returned from America as a sexually potent warrior of the revolution capable of initiating Mameng.

The figure of Mameng and the sexual act she must engage in have another symbolic dimension as well, which is made possible through the novel's depiction of Mameng as an embodiment of the land. The significance of such an embodiment is made clear through Hassim's observation about the landscape that the revolutionaries journey through: "The land is barren" (*The Cry* 52), devastated by war and oppression. Mameng's embodiment of the land parallels the American landscape's personification as feminine in *America Is in the Heart*, but the distinct difference in *The Cry and the Dedication* is that Dante, unlike Carlos, can return the embrace that the woman offers. Bulosan writes that "because it was Dante who had seen other lands and years, it was through him that the expression of the resolution would be realized, then to be poured warmly upon Mameng, who was the denuded landscape" (*The Cry* 54–55). She, in her turn, "would inundate with all her fertility the sterility of the world they were remaking, the world of their enemies" (59). Dante and Mameng's sexual union symbolizes the power of the revolution to save the land and make it fertile once more. Even more than this, they themselves as individuals are also reborn from this union. Sexual intercourse is transformed into a fundamental act of revolution against the oppression of imperialism, capitalism, and racism that destroys an individual's humanity. Dante, who has had sex with prostitutes in the United States, tells Mameng that on those occasions he was not human but instead "like a piece of furniture, lifeless and dreamless" (62). The financial transactions of prostitution are depicted as a process of reification that makes human beings into commodities themselves, into things; unlike Ichiro, who halfheartedly latches onto the possession of commodities as a sign of Americanization, Dante recognizes that American racism, which limits his sexuality, has misshapen him into a commodity.

Intercourse between Dante and Mameng destroys these barriers between human beings that reification creates: "They knew the act would be accomplished in terror and shame if they failed to *realize* themselves. . . . and accomplishing it truly without shame, the shame would be given another name. It would become truth and beauty. . . . and they would be made human. . . . and the loneliness and fear would be vanquished forever" (54; emphasis added). The purification of this sexual act *makes real*, and therefore human, their own identities that were in some way distorted and made illusory by the conditions of oppression in which they live. Dante's act can be contrasted with Carlos's own loss of virginity in *America Is in the Heart*, with the Mexican woman, which left him "trembling with a nameless shame" (160). In contrast to the Mexican woman, Mameng is pure, having retained her virginity by scarring her face to avoid rape by Japanese troops during their occupation of the Philippines. Thus Dante's realization is with a Filipina embodiment of the revolution's potential to be a purifying and fertilizing force for a corrupt and sterile land. The consummation of their relationship is a fulfillment of the moral discourse initiated by Carlos in *America Is in the Heart*, when he recognizes that his sexual degradation is part of his economic degradation.

In the contemporary moment and in the location of the First World, the naked allegory of *The Cry and the Dedication*, with the positions that it reserves for men and women, may leave many readers uncomfortable. San Juan footnotes the problems associated with the novel in terms of gender but dismisses those problems and the critics who have noticed them when he attributes the criticism of the "alleged 'chauvinist' rendition of [Mameng]" to a refusal to "see the centrality of race and nationality . . . so that one is inclined to diagnose [such criticisms] as reaction formations, which are more symptomatic of the malaise of the critics themselves than accurate formulations of what the text is driving at" (introduction to *The Cry* xxxiv–xxxv). Of course, San Juan's attempt to recuperate Bulosan as consummate revolutionary visionary, at all costs, at once displaces the centrality of the female gender to the anticolonial, nationalist imagination, even as it makes more central the masculine gender. San Juan catalogs "the 'woman' question" with "other improbabilities" (xxviii), not noting that what we might call the man question is fundamental to Bulosan's work. In Bulosan's work, women are given importance or consciousness only to the extent that they are in heterosexual partnership or a platonic relationship with a man. In other words, men have lives outside of women, but that is not the case in reverse.[31] While this may be an issue for many readers, it is less of a concern here than the critical refusal to see that gender itself is an inextricable part of the revolutionary articulation in Bulosan's work.

Bulosan's books and the anticolonial rebellion he depicts are very much what Nina Baym calls melodramas of beset manhood, cast here in the intersecting terms of revolution and romance.[32] Filipino masculinity is beset and wounded by a wide variety of forces, practically all of which can be traced to the damage inflicted and perpetuated by U.S. colonialism and its aftermath for the Philippines in the Cold War. The extremities of U.S. oppression, cloaked in its own melodrama of liberatory democracy transcendent and embodied in the figure of an untouchable and pure white womanhood, generate equal extremities of response, represented in the moral Filipino revolutionary at the center of Bulosan's books, whose sexuality is ultimately redemptive and resistant to capitalism. The realization or consummation of sexuality is only possible, however, outside of the Unted States, outside of an ideology of pluralism and consensual dissent that could not imagine itself being incapable of healing the wounded bodies that it damaged in the first place. The flexible strategies that Bulosan and Okada practice involve an engagement with an ideology of pluralism and consensual dissent that neither author felt he could ignore and which was deeply implicated in the racial relationships and representations of their moment of racial equilibrium. As long as Bulosan and Okada stayed inside that ideological space, their criticisms were muted, distorted, or marginalized by their readership and, to some extent, by themselves, as they relied on an authorial irony about racial relations and racial identities that many readers did not understand, even though that moment of racial equilibrium was in decline and heading for crisis.

Perhaps because they could sense that decline and impending crisis and because they were never sure that America's promise of inclusion was genuine, Bulosan and Okada failed at being ethnic entrepreneurs. They created fictional personas who were not sufficiently "sold" on the American Dream and whose efforts to sell themselves as bona fide Americans were troubled by authorial suspicions about America.[33] Okada's *No-No Boy* is nevertheless the portrait of not only those Japanese Americans who refused, however ambivalently, the United States' call for patriotic duty but also of those in the ascending Japanese American middle-class and the price they were forced to pay for their success. Besides being an example of a flexible strategy, then, the novel also demonstrates a flexible strategy on the part of the members of the Nisei generation who went to war fighting for a country that had compromised its ideals and laws. It is only with *The Cry and the Dedication* that we witness what could be articulated once the author stepped outside of the ideological space of the American Way and once his characters were situated outside of the geographical borders of the United States. Bulosan is able to articulate concerns that would not be domestically heard by other Asian Americans until the late 1960s. His recuperation of a wounded manhood, healed through a virile sexuality that enables and is enabled by a violent revolution, foreshadows the work of the authors considered in the next chapter. While Bulosan avoids the ideological saturation of the American Way in *The Cry and the Dedication*, in a fashion that the next set of authors do not, he also deploys a romantic model of nationalist revolution that is common to the narratives of an emerging anticolonial Third World. In such a model, it is not only race, class, and nation that are foundational to a revolution but also masculinity and heterosexuality themselves. Like the Huk rebellion that it draws from, *The Cry and the Dedication* fails to overturn the dominance of an American neocolonialism but marks a hot spot in the Cold War whose suppression is testimony to the threat that it posed to the U.S. world order.

THE REMASCULINIZATION OF CHINESE AMERICA

Race, Violence, and the Novel

The movements for civil rights and Black Power fundamentally changed the U.S. landscape of political possibility for people of color, unsettling the equilibrium of race relations and bringing about a crisis in American culture. While Bulosan and Okada could not articulate alternatives to the political consensus demanded by the American Way as long as U.S. borders circumscribed their writings, a new generation of Asian Americans found political self-consciousness in criticizing this consensus, especially as it centered on domestic American attitudes toward race and the American denial of its own imperialism. The year 1968 signaled this change in consciousness, as many of the younger generation of Asian Americans in college became radicalized around the antiwar and anti-imperialism movements and began to connect those issues with the cause of domestic racial empowerment. In that year, Japanese, Chinese, and Filipino American student activists at San Francisco State College coined the term "Asian American." As part of their radicalization process, these young Asian American activists during and after 1968 began to see violence as a tool they could use as agents, rather than only as a weapon that targeted them as objects.[1] Without knowing it at the time, these young Asian Americans were making explicit what Carlos Bulosan had already realized in the previous decade but had been suppressed from articulating. Perhaps the most vocal of the young Asian Americans was Frank Chin, whose work, like Bulosan's and Okada's, is concerned with the recuperation of Asian American manhood. Unlike his predecessors, Chin did not have to step outside of America to make the claim that violence had been used throughout American history to emasculate Chinese American men by exploiting their labor and excluding them from American society and that young Asian Americans could use violence to *re*masculinize themselves. While Bulosan and Okada tried to speak to American society through a flexible strategy that focused on the rhetorical value of freedom and materialism in order to combat racism and emasculation, Chin's flexible strategy was more confrontational, based on turning American violence against itself in order to remasculinize Chinese American men.

Though begun in 1968, this remasculinization of Chinese America, initiated by Chin, continues in the work of contemporary authors such as Gus Lee because the gendered subordination of Chinese American masculinity persists in mainstream culture through stereotypes that have not substantially changed since their creation in the latter half of the nineteenth century.[2] Chin and Lee represent both the American and Asian American body politic as a violent one. American identity, especially of the nationalist and masculine type, certainly has a long tradition of deploying violence to define itself, and following a long line of American authors before them, Chin and Lee assert that the individual male body can be discursively transformed into a representative of the larger ethnic and national community through violence and that this male body can be regenerated through violence as well.[3] Implicitly for Lee and explicitly for Chin, this regeneration of the body personal is also a metaphorical regeneration of the ethnic and national body politic. Ironically, it is violence and its reenactment that serves as a key element of the shared experience between Asian Americans and other Americans; it is through violence that Asian Americans are first marked by others, as aliens, and then marked by themselves, as Americans. Through their familiarity with the varieties of American violence, Asian Americans are able to recognize its legitimate and illegitimate forms, embodied respectively in the regenerative violence that white mythology claims for itself and the degenerative violence that this mythology displaces onto blackness. Violence is an initiation for immigrants, Asian and otherwise, into the complexities of American inclusion and exclusion, mobility and inequality.

It is on this unequal terrain of American society that we can identify a juncture between Asian American and American studies. This inequality, defined through the contemporary practice and function of violence and the history of its deployment, has been the object of study for both fields. Scholars such as Susan Jeffords and Richard Slotkin have demonstrated the historical and contemporary functions of violence in American society, particularly the methods by which violence has served to differentiate an American Self from various racial and gendered others, but have not addressed how these others in their turn have understood the seeming necessity of practicing violence themselves. The experience of Asian Americans with violence provides evidence to supplement these earlier studies, demonstrating even further how endemic violence is to American culture and its new initiates. Asian American experience also provides material to expand upon the conclusions of these earlier studies. This is because violence, in addition to shaping the experience of Asian Americans in a national context through the struggle for assimilation, also shapes their prehistory before arrival, through immigration and its international context. The international context reminds us that while the myth of American violence as a regenerative, heroic practice legitimizes American state power to Americans themselves, this same violence functions ambiguously and precariously in the international arena. Here other states may offer a different interpretation of American violence, as being simply another, particular version of a lawless, degenerative struggle for control. For Americans, that aspect of violence is domestically displaced onto blackness and the ghetto, where it serves as the other of a state-sponsored, legitimate violence.

The legitimacy of this state-sponsored violence, realized in institutions like the military, came into question during the 1960s and 1970s, when, as a consequence of the Vietnam War, the United States suffered a "crisis of hegemony" in terms of its own national identity and its dominance of the world economy.[4] The terms of American pluralism, which held that all Americans could become one, were thrown into suspicion by racial riots and the struggle for racial equality, and the mythology of American exceptionalism, the image of America as the defender of the free world, was attacked by the antiwar movement. It was also a crisis in which Asians as foreign economic competition and Asian Americans as a model (and threatening) minority figure prominently. Jeffords argues that a process of remasculinization occurred in American culture at this time, largely through the discourse of the Vietnam War. In this discourse, the remasculinization of the (white) American male body in literature and film served to counter various cultural, political, and economic changes that exceeded the scope of the war and were thought to be eroding the social and material status of the American white male. The turmoil of the war and the economic threat of Asia, with its contribution to the real or imaginary erosion of white male privilege, exacerbated an already-present orientalist tendency in American culture to conflate Asians and Asian Americans.[5] While Asian American remasculinization is inevitably influenced by this dominant discourse, it is also antagonistic to its orientalism. Thus I situate the project of Asian American remasculinization both within and against the dominant American project to restore masculinity. Asian American remasculinization's flexible strategy partakes in American patriarchy's attempts to continue the masculine domination of political and economic public life while opposing the racialization and subordination of races that in the past characterized the male domination of nation-state and civil society.

In Chinese American literature, this remasculinization through violence, this attempt to throw the equilibrium of American race relations into crisis by foregrounding strong Asian American men, provides a vehicle for the narrative enactment of assimilation as a process of bodily change. The bodily basis of remasculinization is important because the history of U.S. legislation that concerned Asian immigration has been explicitly a "biopolitics" of bodily regulation, shaping the Asian American community through acts that target gender, sexuality, race, and class, as we have seen in the previous chapters.[6] Legislation and popular rhetoric that concerned Chinese immigrants reflected the related fears that Chinese immigrant men were, depending on circumstance, both asexual and oversexed. The asexuality of Chinese immigrants, an aspect of their inhuman dedication to work, threatened white labor, while their contradictory voracious sexuality threatened white womanhood and white patriarchy. In neither case did Americans see the Chinese immigrants as "real" men.[7] The historical legacy of such violence upon Chinese American masculinity was to render it in the eyes of dominant American society as something subordinate to a normative American masculinity; to a certain extent, this subordination affected the self-perception of Chinese Americans as well.[8]

In the era after which racial emasculation was essentially U.S. state policy, racial remasculinization through the performance of violence by the male body becomes the dominant mode of political and aesthetic consciousness for Chinese American male writers. While this chapter focuses on Chinese American writers, it uses the terms "Chinese American" and "Asian American" interchangeably, except when "Chinese American" is used to refer to specific situations or conditions that pertain only to Chinese Americans. In the case of Frank Chin, this slippage also occurs in his essays, as he makes clear that his argument about Chinese American masculinity is broadly applicable to Asian Americans as a whole.[9] In this case, the distinction between ethnic entrepreneurship and panethnic entrepreneurship is blurred, for Chin's efforts to recuperate Chinese American masculinity and literature are part of a larger effort by him and his allies during the early 1970s to carve out a literary space and eventually a market for Asian American writers. Thus while Chin is not entrepreneurial in the same sense as Onoto Watanna, aiming for a white audience, he is entrepreneurial in another sense, aiming to find and even create his own Asian American audience.[10] The collapse that Chin enacts, and that this chapter repeats to some extent, between Chinese American and Asian American is indicative of two other things besides panethnic entrepreneurship, namely, the nature of American racism and the evolution of the Asian American panethnic coalition. For the most part, American racism has not been able to distinguish between different Asian American ethnicities, tending to see all Asians as alike, even if in special circumstances certain Asian American groups can be isolated, as with Chinese exclusion and Japanese internment. The formation of an Asian American panethnic coalition therefore turns racism against itself by affirming the similarity of different Asian American ethnic groups. As this panethnic coalition has evolved, however, Chinese and Japanese American culture and issues have come to be representative of the entire Asian American experience. In some cases, Chinese and Japanese American experiences have a legacy that is defining for all Asian Americans, such as the history of emasculation and remasculinization with which this chapter is concerned. In other scenarios, the lack of ethnic symmetry—the inability of some Asian Americans to see Filipino, South Asian, or Southeast Asian experiences, for example, as Asian American—can be detrimental.

This inequity and asymmetry is a part of contemporary Asian American culture, an aspect of its contradiction in bridging the ethnic and the panethnic as it responds to the anti-Asian violence that is a fundamental part of its history. The Chinese American novel provides an important vehicle for understanding this violence and the panethnic, entrepreneurial response, because of the novel's properties, its representation of violence, its formal relation to the social contexts it depicts, and the prominence of its argument in the Asian American community. In this chapter, I am particularly concerned with the bildungsroman, or novel of formation. The bildungsroman, while narrating the public inclusion of its subjects, also enacts violent exclusion against those who do not match the profile of its ideal subjects (white, heterosexual, male, and eventually propertied). A significant strand of American literature adapts the European bildungsroman by presenting narratives that trace the successful struggle of characters who achieve this public identity and its prerogatives: the formal or informal rights to property, political participation, and patriarchal domination of women. For Chinese American authors, using the bildungsroman both proclaims a public identity for themselves and their subjects and reenacts exclusionary processes of violence found in traditional representations, this time directed at Chinese American women and African American men. Through the bildungsroman, Chinese American authors shape their own vision of an Asian American *Bildung*, or culture, in which Asian American masculinity Americanized itself in the most ironic fashion, by affirming patriarchy through the violence that had previously been directed at Asian Americans en masse.

Violence and Assimilation

Gus Lee's novel *China Boy* depicts Kai Ting, a young Chinese immigrant during the 1950s who comes to America with his father, a veteran of the Chinese army, and lives in the Panhandle, a black-dominated ghetto of San Francisco. After Kai's mother dies, the father remarries a white woman, who disciplines Kai harshly and arbitrarily, becoming the embodiment of a violent America that threatens to forestall his manhood. At the end of the novel, after Kai has been bullied by both the stepmother and the black children in the neighborhood, he assumes a fighting stance and utters this declaration of independence to his tyrannical white stepmother: "You not my Mah-mee! *I ain't fo' yo' pickin' on, no mo'!*" (322). These two sentences signify the ways in which language, violence, and duality are mutually involved in the emergence of a unique Asian American identity.[11] Kai delivers these threats of both verbal and physical violence in dual dialects, the former Chinese English, the latter Black English. Chinese American masculine identity begins to emerge in this unspoken gap between Chinese English and Black English, which respectively signify an alien exclusion *from* and a partial inclusion *in* American society. Kai's inclusion and masculine maturation is fully realized later, not in the black ghetto where he spends his immigrant youth but at a "civilized" citadel of violence, West Point, in *China Boy*'s sequel, *Honor and Duty*. The title character of Frank Chin's novel *Donald Duk* follows Kai's trajectory of assimilation from ghetto to West Point in form, if not in detail. Donald Duk sees contemporary Chinatown as a place of degradation, and he must eventually learn to reinscribe this space of exclusion from American society as a space of inclusion. His education is accomplished through a realistic dream that he experiences, in which he visits the heroic past of the Chinese railroad worker. In this dream, Donald seems to experience bodily the toil, suffering, triumph, and disappointment of the Chinese workers. Whereas Kai Ting is masculinized through the black ghetto and West Point, Donald Duk embarks on his masculine young adulthood through a journey from the Chinese ghetto to the frontier West, a space of violent character formation even more fundamental to the American imagination than West Point.

These three novels centered on the travails of young manhood are examples of the bildungsroman. The bildungsroman is centrally important to both American literature in general and Asian American literature in particular, where the genre offers a formal vehicle for representing both the outsider's desire for assimilation and upward mobility as well as the limits imposed on those possibilities by dominant society in regard to women and minorities. The bildungsroman traces a youthful individual's cultivation through various means of education that culminate in his maturity, which includes an identification with dominant national values.[12] The classical German bildungsroman and its descendant in the United States generate at their conclusions a sense of closure concerning this maturation and identification, according to Gunilla Theander Kester, who argues that "the classical genre strives to resolve the contradiction between the world and self; in a Kantian fashion, the imagination of the mature subject can overcome the restrictions of the world and thus obtain a sense of harmony" (10). Horatio Alger's rags-to-riches novels, published in the latter half of the nineteenth century, are perhaps the prototypical examples of an American bildungsroman, particularly in the conclusions that they offer their characters and audiences. In these novels, "the story of the fictional adolescent in the Republic and the narrative of the adolescent Republic were made one" (Nackenoff 271). The closures found in these novels center on the successful rise of a hardworking, self-reliant young man, who typically becomes a solid member of the middle class, rather than a capitalist. His status as an outsider in relation to dominant society is defined by class, which does not in the end erode his individuality, unlike race or gender. The narrative compromise reconciles the demands and difficulties of industrialism and unfettered capital accumulation, on the one hand, with the "traditional" values of the petty bourgeois, on the other.[13]

Another version of the American bildungsroman is the war novel, recent examples of which have been produced around the experiences of young American soldiers in Vietnam. In these novels, the disillusionment that soldier-authors often experienced with American nationalism and values complicates the issue of narrative closure. At the same time, however, the identity of the American soldier, as a representative of the youthful American and his struggles with adult identity and society in general, is secured against the representation of the Vietnamese as other.[14] In these two examples of the American bildungsroman, the role of the other is critical to the production of the dominant American Self, which, like its European version, is a white, male propertied citizen—the assumed inheritor and representative of national identity. The bildungsroman's use of the other to aid in the formation of the American Self is a formal expression of American society's exclusion of women and people of color in the development of a national identity. This tendency in the bildungsroman toward the erasure or exploitation of racial difference complicates the possibility of racialized others' adopting the form. Thus Kester coins the term "narratives of African American *bildung*" instead of using the term "African American bildungsroman" in order to indicate that the closure offered by the classical bildungsroman does not exist for African Americans in novels such as *Invisible Man*. Instead, these works exhibit a sense of perpetual double consciousness.

As with African American literature, the Asian American version of the bildungsroman is an enduring, if contradictory, subcategory of Asian American literature, because so much of the literature is concerned with the education or formation of the individual and the community as "hyphenated" Americans. Shelley Sunn Wong claims that critics often read Asian American novels as immigrant bildungsromane that "present the narrative of a 'minority' culture growing into a recognition of its place within the majority culture" (129). The central characters' achievement of an "autonomous selfhood" serves "as a prelude to the Asian American subject's achievement of political representation" (130). This "autonomous selfhood" is complicated, however, by the heterogeneities and contradictions found within Asian American texts often classified as bildungsromane. As Lisa Lowe argues, well-known Asian American texts such as Carlos Bulosan's *America Is in the Heart*, John Okada's *No-No Boy*, Monica Sone's *Nisei Daughter*, and Joy Kogawa's *Obasan* often attempt to prevent the type of narrative closure associated with the bildungsroman despite formal similarities they share with the genre. The main characters are often fragmented and divided and the narrative representations of America ambivalent. Even novels that stress realism and closure, as *China Boy, Honor and Duty*, and *Donald Duk* do, may "express a contradiction between the demand for a univocal developmental narrative and the historical specificities of racialization, ghettoization, violence, and labor exploitation" (Lowe, *Immigrant Acts* 100). All three novels exhibit this contradiction, but they are also troubled by both sexism and misogyny. The novels represent the feminine and the maternal as obstructions to both masculine development and the incorporation of the immigrant into the American national identity.[15]

In Gus Lee's *China Boy*, these contradictions of genre and national identity develop through two narratives that operate in counterpoint to each other. The foregrounded narrative features Kai Ting, the protagonist who is recording his self-formation as a man and as an American. The other, "shadow" narrative is the "antibildungsroman" of his Panhandle neighbors, who are primarily African American and primarily poor. While Kai's use of violence enables him to leave the ghetto and go to West Point, his African American neighbors' deployment of an even more threatening violence condemns them to remain in the ghetto. Thus the novel's central contradiction in relationship to the narrative of self-development is this problem of why violence functions differently for different populations. Through adopting the work of Richard Slotkin, we can lay the initial groundwork for understanding this contradiction, which involves the prevalence of violence in the ghetto, the role of violence in determining the life chances of the characters, and its importance in relation to race, masculinity, and the state. According to Slotkin, Americans hold an enduring mythological view that their national character was formed and regenerated through the violence that occurred during the confrontation between European settlers and the New World's wilderness and its inhabitants. The mythical American individual, embodied in heroic, representative figures like Daniel Boone, confronted the unknown—symbolized through the frontier—by himself and tested his individual character against danger. The American *Bildung* was one of cultivation through violence and, more important, a cultivation of violence. Through the exercise of violence, European American civilization was formed, in opposition to the dangerous violence of the American wilderness and the degenerative violence of its "savage" inhabitants. Slotkin carefully stresses the mythological dimension of this conception of *Bildung*, meaning that its power lay in its claim to a symbolic truth about European American character rather than in historical veracity. Through the political and cultural dominance of European Americans, this mythological dimension of American character that stems from the ethnocentric experience of European settlers became part of the dominant definition of American identity. Thus the power of such mythology influences even Americans of non-European descent, who must grapple with their symbolic place in such a mythology.

This white mythology is racially defined, first against Indians and then against blacks. Thus immigrants to the United States who learn this mythology are also educated into particular understandings of the place of blacks, historically the most visible objects of American violence. Asian immigrants in particular often see themselves and are seen as being caught between the white and black polarizations of the American racial order. In *Honor and Duty, China Boy*'s sequel, Kai recounts how his black peers are unsure of whether he is white or black, as if no other option exists (17). This position of being in between black and white is both contradictory and opportune for Asian Americans as they seek to assimilate, either *into* whiteness or *against* blackness.[16] In *China Boy*, Lee frames Kai Ting's choices in this regard through his relationship to the mythology of a formative violence and the degenerative violence it confronts. Kai learns this formative mode of violence through the YMCA's paramilitary boxing school, which enables him in the end to defeat the much larger neighborhood bully, who is black. Kai chooses the type of violence that allows him to fulfill the terms of the American bildungsroman, by becoming a man and an American through a disciplined violence that represses the other's dangerously unrestricted violence, manifested in lawless and murderous street fighting. He assimilates into the American *Bildung*, while his African American peers are relegated to an antibildungsroman that writes them out of the national identity. This is because, as James Baldwin puts it, "In the United States, violence and heroism have been made synonymous except when it comes to blacks" (58); their violence is unwanted because it is perceived by dominant, white society as destructive rather than formative. In white mythology, while violence is liberatory for some, it is (self) repressive for others.

Like many immigrants, Kai is prepared to believe this lesson of white mythology because of his own knowledge that concerns the importance of a masterful use of violence. Kai's understanding of Chinese history is oriented around China's decline as a national power, especially in contrast to the rise of the United States as a world power. Kai and his father are preoccupied by the significant difference between the ability of China and that of the United States to control violence. For Kai's father, the problem is twofold. On the one hand, medieval China had mastered violence to such an extent that it had created its "worst nightmare. A world at peace" (Lee, *China Boy* 19). On the other hand, the resulting Chinese culture's "immutable humanistic standards" (4) became antithetical to violence. As Walter Benjamin summarizes the problem, "When the consciousness of the latent presence of violence in a legal institution disappears, the institution falls into decay" (288). China's decay is realized in "the chaos, the irresponsibility, the waste, and the obsolescence of a culture that could not fashion an airborne corps, run a modern railway, operate a film industry, or defeat superstition" (*China Boy* 70). Through Kai's father, and in his struggles with contemporary Chinese social and moral decline, Lee creates a dualistic opposition between a vital American culture and an outmoded, feudalistic Chinese culture, as represented in their militaries. Being a pragmatic man, Colonel Ting follows the one obvious course open to him, which he sums up very aptly: "America. It has the answers" (128). Colonel Ting's proclamation reveals an implicit acceptance of the mythology that concerns American violence, which is productive for both individuals and nation-states.

As *China Boy* demonstrates, violence operates in a very similar fashion for both individuals, in relationship to each other, and nation-states, in relationship to the international context. Violence can serve regenerative and degenerative functions for both individuals and nation-states, who must master it or be dominated by the others. This similarity is masked by the fact that the state is committed to suppressing among its own citizens the enactment of violence that the state itself finds fundamental to its existence; as Benjamin puts it, the state demands a monopoly of violence. He argues that this monopoly of violence by the state masks itself through a discourse that transforms state violence into law: "One might perhaps consider the surprising possibility that the law's interest in a monopoly of violence vis-à-vis individuals is not explained by the intention of preserving legal ends, but, rather, by that of preserving the law itself; that violence, when not in the hands of the law, threatens it not by the ends that it may pursue but by its mere existence outside the law" (281). From the state's perspective, then, violence in all its forms when exercised by the state and its representatives is law, while violence exercised by unsanctioned individuals is criminality, with the critical exception being the individual, heroic violence of characters like Daniel Boone and Natty Bumppo that is enshrined safely in the past through mythology. While the state exercises a legal and civilizing monopoly of violence within its own borders, however, it cannot do so in the international arena. As Norbert Elias points out, "At this level there is no central monopoly of physical violence to restrain the participants from violent action if they believe themselves stronger and expect advantages from it" (181). The state's suppression of "illegal" violence within its own borders functions uneasily with the shadow of the "primitiveness" that is coded as international politics. Indeed, that primitiveness is displaced onto the degenerative violence of minorities through a parallel discourse of racialization and criminalization.

All immigrants exist in a critical moment of transition between the international and the national dimensions of violence, and many also exist in a critical moment of transition between being members of the majority and being members of a minority. In the United States, the relationship between the majority and the minorities has often been violent, either explicitly so for the overwhelming duration of the nation's history or implicitly so, as the case may be now for many, if not all, immigrants. Kai, as a representative immigrant, as a foreigner becoming an American and a youth becoming a man, must learn critical lessons about the culture of violence, primarily that through the variable uses of violence the American male body's masculinity becomes coded as civilized and legalized, savage and illegitimate, or decrepit and ineffective. For immigrants, appropriating violence productively becomes a sign of successful assimilation into American culture. The American bildungsroman is therefore an ideal genre for immigrant authors to use in depicting their movement from being victims of xenophobic violence to agents of violence, because the genre it-self is expressive of the dominant society's violence in both form and content. As David Lloyd argues, there is a correspondence between "the monopoly of violence claimed by the state . . . [and] the monopoly of representation claimed by the dominant culture" (*Anomalous States* 4), realized formally through such genres as the bildungsroman. Kai pursues the opportunity of vio-lent assimilation offered to him by his environment, at the cost of accepting both the American narrative about proper violence and cultural formation and the Orientalist narrative about the degeneracy of China. Frank Chin's work poses an illuminating contrast: instead of an immigrant protagonist, we have an American-born one; instead of a black ghetto, we have Chinatown; instead of a degenerate China, we have a heroic one; instead of a vision of the future, we have a vision of the past; and instead of a lawful mode of assimilation through violence, we have an *outlaw* mode.

CHINATOWN OUTLAWS AND RAILROAD WORKERS

Frank Chin's short fiction of the 1970s, collected in *The Chinaman Pacific and the Frisco R.R. Co.*, and his play *The Year of the Dragon* are set in the ghetto of Chinatown. In this setting, the Chinese American man (immigrant and Ameri-can-born) becomes conscious of his body within the embodied setting of the ghetto. American popular discourse, from explicitly racist late-nineteenth-century versions through mutedly racist versions of the late twentieth-century, depicts Chinatown as a geographic and cultural body that is separate from the civil body of the city and as a site where the individual body may degenerate physically and morally. In the same way that meanings accrue to Chinatown be-cause of its juxtaposition with the white city of San Francisco, the Chinese male body in Chin's work takes on degenerate meanings in juxtaposition with white and female bodies. The narrators of Chin's works, the workingmen of China-town, are incapable fathers, insufficient role models, and inadequate lovers, bur-dened by their bodies.[17] As Elaine H. Kim argues, Chin's work displays an "over-riding sense of the utter futility of the male protagonist's efforts to define himself" (*Asian American Literature* 186). Furthermore, according to Daniel Y. Kim, Chin's early work paints "literary self-portraits of an Asian American mas-culinity in ruins, of men who seem only to hate themselves for their inability to be men" (296).[18] Chin presents a portrait of the Chinese American man, outlaw and antihero, who is trapped within social conditions that negate his masculinity and seemingly demand an equal negation of the female body.

In his 1991 novel, *Donald Duk*, however, Chin reconsiders the image of Chinatown, especially in its relationship to masculinity, and uses the title char-acter to demonstrate his project of remasculinization. The novel shares some of the formal features of *China Boy*, being about a young boy on the brink of young adulthood, facing challenges that he has to overcome physically while not yet having to confront heterosexual sex and its gendered antagonisms. Donald, unlike the immigrant Kai, is a fifth-generation Chinese American. His Chinatown is a warmly depicted ethnic enclave, where the sights, sounds, and smells of living in close quarters are reassuring rather than alienating, so much so that "Chinatown life lay against Donald Duk's cheek like a purring cat" (Chin, *Donald Duk* 15). Unlike Chin's angst-ridden protagonists from the 1970s, who suffered for good reason in Chinatown, Donald Duk has little excuse to be what his father calls him: a "little white racist" (90). Instead, his self-hatred and resentment stem from the fact that he, according to his uncle, blames "every Chinese who ever lived, everything Chinese [he] ever heard of for the way white kids act like fools when they hear [his] name" (23). Donald's adolescent frustrations are symbolized in his yearning to be a dancer like Fred Astaire. That desire is a sign of both Donald's need for freedom and mobility and his need for control over his own body.[19] For Donald, control signals a sense of power that is lacking through all the petty humiliations of his youth, and by the end of the novel Donald learns to dance, not in the ballroom like Fred Astaire but in the Chinese lion at New Year's; he also learns what his father, King Duk, has been trying to teach him, that "Chinatown is America" (90). *Donald Duk* is thus a bildungsroman about the education of its title character into accepting the fundamentally American character of his identity, his family, and his environment. The novel accomplishes this education through a crucial double move that is also found in Lee's novels: it simultaneously remasculinizes the male body and transforms the space in which that body is situated. In Kai Ting's case, he undergoes an actual geographical move from the Panhandle to West Point; in Donald Duk's case, Chinatown becomes for him an American space after he dreams that he visits the Chinese-populated American West. Whereas Kai Ting moves outward and forward, Donald Duk ultimately moves inward and backward in his dream to the 1860s and the construction of the Central Pacific Railroad, which was built with Chinese labor.

The dream functions as a mode of time travel, so to speak, because Donald experiences it as if it were actually happening to his body. Donald becomes one of the railroad laborers, many of whom (according to the novel) were barely adolescents. In contrast to the history of passive and weak Chinese workers he is taught in school, Donald discovers a group of literate, articulate, and strong Chinese immigrants. These immigrant laborers must compete with the Irish crew of the Union Pacific Railroad, who are building the east-to-west stretch of the first transcontinental railroad (the Chinese are building the west-to-east stretch). They are competing to see how many miles of track can be laid down in one day, and the Chinese, under the direction of the backtalking, fierce foreman Kwan, win handily. Kwan physically and verbally dominates the building, including the white owners and overseers of the railroad, but even he cannot prevent the ultimate humiliation of the Chinese laborers. At the completion of the railroad, the laborers sign their names onto one final railroad tie that will mark the point of junction between the Central Pacific and Union Pacific railroads.

The white owners have the tie torn out and the Chinese shunted off under armed guard, and the famous spike-driving ceremony at Promontory Point, Utah, that is the official moment of the railroad's completion takes place without the physical or symbolic presence of the Chinese. Donald, in shock over the injustice of history and after having experienced himself the perils and hardships of railroad work with his own body, awakens to the "real" world of Chinatown determined to rediscover his heritage and integrate himself into Chinatown society. He does this by participating as one of the lion dancers in the New Year's parade, thus joining his desire for freedom through the dance with Chinese cultural expression. Donald expresses his Americanization through an acceptance of Chinatown, but only by learning how integral the Chinese were to American history. Rather than remaining as sites for exclusion, Chinatown and Chinese American history become spaces for Donald to stake a claim of inclusion for Chinese Americans.

Donald Duk therefore signals a shift in Chin's fictional strategy. Instead of confronting American racism and Chinese American self-hatred with his typical acerbity, Chin celebrates ethnic pride in the service of American pluralism. Like *China Boy*, however, the novel contains a serious discourse about the meaning of violence in its relationship to the individual, to narrative writing, and to the state that supplements the novel's pedagogical aspect as a vehicle of (counter) cultural formation. This counterculture is configured in Kwan the foreman, who is explicitly a version of Kwan Kung, the Chinese of god of war and literature and the same god that Donald Duk's father, King Duk, is famous for playing in Cantonese opera. King Duk's operatic performance of the god merges Kwan Kung as cultural icon of Chinese masculinity with King Duk's responsibility as paternal role model to Donald. Unlike the fathers in Chin's short stories of the 1970s, King Duk is a strong and virile man, a former railroad brakeman, a cook extraordinaire, and an opera performer of the best quality. His right to masculinity and paternity is enacted through performing Kwan Kung, a role so demanding that few dare take it on. To be Kwan Kung, an actor must be pure in body and soul. As Donald Duk's uncle puts it, "No sex. No meat. No talk. No company. You do everything alone. No one does anything for you. . . . Nobody wants to play Kwan Kung. Too risky" (67–68). Donald Duk is thus confronted with two father figures, one real and one mythical, and the conclusion of the book is the merger of the two when King Duk performs Kwan Kung. The performance is an ideal of discipline, a model of the male actor's body in abstinence, purity, individuality, and controlled violence that is clearly a prescription for masculinity. More important, Kwan Kung's role as god of both war and literature implies a connection between the two that is made explicit in the prime lesson that King Duk teaches Donald: the mandate of heaven.

According to King Duk, the mandate of heaven is a Confucian philosophy that explains the legitimacy of state power: "Kingdoms rise and fall. Nations come and go" (124). In this explanation, power is transitory and taken up by different kingdoms and nations in succession, legitimating their rule in the eyes of their subjects by demonstrating their monopoly of violence. The state's violence is also a discursive one, as the state deploys narratives that justify and write into history and memory its own legitimacy. As King Duk says, "History is war, not sport! . . . You gotta keep the history yourself or lose it forever, boy. That's the mandate of heaven" (123). In essence, that is the lesson Donald Duk learns when he sees the railroad tie with the Chinese names and their claim to the railroad being torn out and destroyed. Thus Kwan Kung's tasks as god of war and literature are fundamentally related, because violence and narrative jointly bring into being and legitimate the existence of the state. What Donald Duk learns in this bildungsroman is a set of lessons very similar to what Kai Ting learns, except that where Kai Ting disparages China as a model for martial power and masculine rights, Donald Duk privileges it. Whereas Kai Ting must negotiate between black and white bodies and violent modes, Donald Duk must reinhabit the Chinese male body that has lost its masculine meaning for him through racism and emasculation. Kwan Kung is the violent body politic that becomes Donald's model, versus the American soldierly ideal to which Kai Ting turns.

Ultimately, both Donald Duk and Kai Ting learn that sport and labor, two modes of disciplining the adolescent male body in order to transform it into an adult body, are themselves insufficient without violence, the most important discipline of all. Kai learns in the ghetto that the greater intent of sport is the control of violence. Boxing in the ghetto is not an apolitical mode of competition but an activity that assumes great magnitude as it incorporates all of the political and economic hopes of an isolated population. Donald discovers, in contrast, that labor for Chinese immigrants was not simply a mode of survival but ultimately a method for owning a portion of America. The fact that labor itself is not sufficient for such a claim to America is emblematized in the erasure of Chinese immigrant workers from the dominant version of history and memory that concerned the transcontinental railroad. By rewriting the history of Chinese immigrant workers, Chin metafictionally draws attention to the story of what happens when storytelling is taken away from one people through another people's greater violence. Through the figure of Kwan Kung, god of war and literature, storytelling becomes a masculine act, and the storyteller becomes the privileged enactor of that masculinity. Kwan Kung is, of course, refigured in this metafiction as Chin himself, creator of the bildungsroman that claims a space in American history and literature for Chinese Americans as both subjects and authors.

EMASCULATION AND FEMINIZATION

While racism and labor exploitation characterize the experience of Chinese American men in both the ghetto and the frontier, emasculation and feminization seem to be the deeply related threats they face in domestic and literary

spaces. In Kai Ting's formation, mothers and the female gender become important signifiers of oppression. Edna, his white stepmother, signals the beginning
of Kai's assimilatory stage, replacing the nurturing traditional Chinese mother
with her own brand of xenophobic authoritarianism that demands the removal
of all signs of Chinese culture in the household. She evicts Kai from her "protection" prematurely, into the street where no legal authority exists to regulate
the rampant violence. Kai is left no choice in the assimilation process, barred
from the house, unable to engage in reciprocal acts of violence against Edna,
threatened by the street and its inhabitants until he learns that survival is dependent upon the ability to exercise violence. Assimilation, in the lawless Panhandle, means establishing one's own law, through fighting. For Kai, the female
gender represents either this emasculating terror of white femininity that ren-
ders him inadequate in the face of the Panhandle's violent culture or the aristo-
cratic, scholarly, and ineffective Chinese culture repudiated by his father and
embodied by his mother and his Uncle Shim. Kai must find a suitable masculine
ideal, and *Honor and Duty* becomes a search for a representative patriarch, initially Kai's father and then a succession of American father figures. His search
culminates in a symbolic moment of confrontation with the statue of George
Washington, who is "a cold and unresponsive mass of melted metals forged into
the shape of an unreachable father" (Lee, *Honor and Duty* 99). Kai's personal
struggle to communicate with his own father and to replace him with substitute
father figures is emblematic of a struggle to establish manhood and citizenship
under a viable representative figure of patriarchal strength. In American society,
a young man's successful completion of this struggle culminates in the assumption of patriarchy itself, meaning the establishment of one's own authority, recognized by the state and symbolized here by George Washington.

We can follow this struggle for masculinity and patriarchy in two places,
first through examining how the inhabitants of the ghetto struggle over exactly
the same problems of authority and law as the state itself does and second
through examining the ways in which the rather straightforward path to assimilation is complicated in *Honor and Duty* through the notion of cultural hybridity. The difference between the state and the Panhandle, of course, is that
the state already has some measure of authority and law, while the Panhandle
inhabitants only have criminality. Big Willie Mack, the neighborhood bully, desires to establish and maintain his own law among the neighborhood kids, by
using force to exact tribute and subservience. As Kai's friend Toos puts it, "He
don't take 'em [Kai's clothes] ta wear. He take 'em to *take 'em*" (*China Boy*
106). The tribute and the subservience that Big Willie can extract are less important for their material value than for their symbolic value, because, as Benjamin writes, "From the point of view of violence, which alone can guarantee
law, there is no equality, but at the most, equally great violence" (296–297). At
the end of *China Boy*, Kai is able to establish his equality in both the public and
private spaces of his life through possessing a violence at least equal to and possibly superior to that of his foes, the bully and the stepmother. Kai's violent

transformation from weakling to winner is accompanied by a shift in his cultural bearing, from foreign Chinese immigrant to assimilated ghetto inhabitant, signified through his shifting dialect. In the moment of final confrontation, as we have seen earlier, Kai says to his tyrannical stepmother: "You not my Mahmee! *I ain't fo' yo' pickin'-on, no mo'!*" (322). From Chinese American dialect to Black English, Kai's triumphant line indicates the evolutionary nature of *Bildung.* Unable until this point to speak anything but his Chinese English, Kai confronts representative white authority by shifting his allegiance to blacks through the use of Black English, indicating that he has learned the violence he needs to survive, if not to assimilate. The final step, then, is a third dialect shift, to standard English, which Kai constantly employs in his role as the reminiscing narrator. Somewhere in the future, Kai has learned to assimilate into American society, an accomplishment signified by his proficient use of standard English and his writing of his own story. Presumably, the Panhandle residents would still be speaking Black English, as the irrepressible sign of their (self) exclusion, their seeming inability or unwillingness, as it is perceived by outsiders, to learn the narrative of the American bildungsroman.

But "blackness" is not only a sign of exclusion, and "whiteness" is not only a sign of inclusion. This contrast between a violence that is coded as formative (read: white) and destructive (read: black) leaves no position for a Chinese American. To survive, Kai must seemingly choose one or the other, but eventually he decides to fashion a Chinese American identity out of both choices, as becomes clear in *Honor and Duty.* This novel, which follows Kai Ting through three years at West Point before he flunks engineering, reconsiders neat binaries of inclusion and exclusion, white and black, from the very moment Kai enters the overwhelmingly white academy as someone who "had been raised as a Negro youth" (4). His early experiences at West Point are marked by these recognitions: "The cadence and emphasis of [the white cadet's] speech were almost Negro, but there was no comfort in it" (6); "'*THAT'S* WRONG, *CRAP-HEAD!*' [the white cadet] screamed in that unique, Negro-like, military meter" (10); "'Git outa mah road, damn Yankee *scum*'. . . . It was familiar and strange, as if a white man were speaking the colored dialect of Negro streets" (13–14). Thus Kai's introduction to West Point presents a strange contrast between the whiteness of the cadet population and the rhythms of black culture that arise in their voices, a return of the repressed that isn't even recognized as such by the cadets. Kai, who was "raised as a Negro youth," is thus an anomaly in the academy, a man who is able to perform his masculinity in its various versions, black and white, and able to recognize this dimension of its performative aspect. He is not able, however, to recognize an even more important dimension of masculinity's performativity, namely, the mutually necessary condition of this black and white bifurcation. West Point—at least from the perspective of dominant society—becomes the site of masculine formation, or cultural initiation, while the culture of the ghetto becomes white masculinity's necessary other, the site of masculine deformation or criminalization. Kai, not recognizing this, can do or say nothing to address the reality of such inequity.

Kai's major concern, therefore, is fulfilling the terms of dominant masculinity, becoming a "proper" man. By the end of *Honor and Duty*, Kai has met a nice Chinese girl and proven that he is neither emasculated nor feminized. The romantic closure offsets the lack of closure concerning Kai's military career, because he has left West Point having failed, ironically, engineering. He is defeated not by the physical challenge of West Point but by the very mode of intellectual work that stereotypically defines the successful Asian American. In a subtle way, Lee distances Kai from that stereotype of the scientific technician, which serves both to include Asian Americans in a technological America and also to exclude them from the public life of corporate management, public policy, military hierarchy, entertainment visibility, and so on. Kai's failure at West Point seems also to signal an ambivalence on Lee's part that concerns the possibilities of a successful assimilation via the method of state-sponsored violence, which at that time was engaged in fighting the racially defined Vietnam War. Lee is convinced about the necessary rituals and methods by which a proper masculinity is enacted, but he is uneasy about the racial dimensions that have been integral to that masculinity's definition. By introducing issues of race, Lee attempts to define masculinity as a project that every American man can participate in, through the discipline of the violent body. In this project, black men are excluded by dominant society not because of race but because of their perceived lack of discipline. Their presence in the project of remasculinization is necessary, however, because their perceived degenerative violence is the necessary other that makes regenerative violence possible.

The novels themselves exist as evidence of Lee's own claims to a public masculine identity, because the discipline of writing ultimately substitutes for the discipline of fighting in a gesture that is metaphorical. For Chin, no such substitution can occur, except metonymically. For Chin, writing is fighting, and it is an attempt to combat the "fake" with the "real," as he argues in his essay "Come All Ye Asian American Writers of the Real and the Fake," published in the same year as *Donald Duk*. In this polemical essay, Chin is explicitly concerned with the emasculation of Chinese American men and the distortion of Chinese culture in popular Chinese American literary representations. He argues that the recent popularity of Chinese American writers such as Maxine Hong Kingston, Amy Tan, and David Henry Hwang is substantially due to their exploitation of stereotypes that concern Chinese culture as patriarchal, sexist, and collectivist. Chin rejects *any* validity to the claims that there exists misogyny or collectivism in Chinese culture and divides the world into the "real and the fake" ("Come All Ye Asian American Writers" 9), proposing a literally militant stance on literature ("life is war," "writing is fighting" [35]). His virulent positions and language are all signs of a deeper crisis than simply the recuperation of Chinese masculinity against a traitorous femininity. Instead, Chin's polemics that concern masculinity and authentic Chinese culture indicate an ongoing "moral panic." As Stuart Hall and his coauthors note in *Policing the Crisis,* a moral panic is a reaction that is not commensurate to the reality it is concerned with; more important, moral panic is a sign of a social crisis, or a crisis in hegemony, that is more fundamental than the phenomena with which the panic is explicitly concerned (219–222).[20]

Chin is explicitly concerned in this essay and in much of his work in general with emasculation, which he frequently collapses into feminization: for Chin, there is little difference between being less than a man and being a woman. This collapse between emasculation and feminization signals a threefold crisis that Chin is trying to police. The first and most easily understood aspect of that crisis is the loss of patriarchal power or perhaps, to put it more accurately, the deprivation of the opportunity for Chinese American men to partake in patriarchal power. Second, as Lisa Lowe argues, there is a crisis of essentialism, a destabilization of masculinity as an essence that is refigured in literary debates between the Chin camp and the feminist camp of Asian American literature as a conflict between nationalism and assimilation (*Immigrant Acts* 71).[21]

Third, there is a crisis of the "real," a crisis of the material in addition to the essential, the historical in addition to the masculine. Chin's writings reveal a determination to assert the "reality" of history as a material, indisputable fact against the alleged distortions of writers like Kingston, and that assertion is carried through an alignment of the body personal with the body politic. Thus the conclusion to "Come All Ye Asian American Writers of the Real and the Fake" is a mantra of materialism:

> It matters that Fa Mulan was not tattooed. It matters that the Chinese and Japanese immigrants came as settlers. . . . It matters that all the Chinese and Japanese American writers in this book, no matter what they believe or what literary form they favor, make the difference between the real and the fake. It matters that the Asian American writers [in this volume] are not—with one exception—yellow engineers of the stereotype. The pleasure of these works does not depend on the reader's ignorance of the real. It matters. (92)

This passage reveals that Chin is not only, or not so much, a sexist or misogynist but also a historical fundamentalist. History is real for Chin in the sense that it is absolute. The dispute over history is a warlike dispute for Chin, as previously seen in the discussion of *Donald Duk*: the winners of war and other conflicts have the privilege of writing history. The losers must struggle to reclaim that privilege. While writing historical narrative is clearly an act of interpretation reserved for the victors, Chin, as a fundamentalist, rejects the complication of interpretation and replaces it with the charge of distortion—history cannot be interpreted, only distorted in the "fake" stories of race traitors. In Chin's perspective, the distortions implicitly help to service such fake stories as the dominant narrative that concerns the construction of the railroad.

For Chin, the disempowerment that results from being unable to write history and being subject to fake versions of it is similar. The material consequence is emasculation, the violation of the male body, the proper body for the performance of masculinity and the assertion of power in the service of the state. The "correct" legend of Fa Mulan that Chin presents in the beginning of his essay is not even an exception to the rule of proper masculine performance, because Fa Mulan has to dress as a man to act like a man. Chin is offended by Maxine Hong Kingston's version of the Fa Mulan legend not only because it is a "distortion" of Chinese legend but also because it signifies the affirmation of the materiality of the female body, as bearer of both history and vengeance.[22] In Kingston's version, Fa Mulan's body is tattooed with her parents' words; these words record what was done to their village and family and serve as a reminder of what Fa Mulan must do. Kingston's story is thus more than just a story about a woman performing as a man but also a story about a woman who *is* masculine, at least in Chin's view of violence as being the right of men: Fa Mulan is a woman whose body is marked by violence, is the vehicle of violence, and is the embodiment of violence. In response to this violation of proper gender roles, Chin engages in what Daniel Kim calls an "incessant recirculation of fury and wrath, [laying] his hands on the thing that most defines manhood in our culture: a 'promiscuous' violence" (296).

THE VIOLENT BODY POLITIC

In his obsession with the violence already inflicted upon the masculine Asian American body, a violence that emasculates and feminizes it, Chin reveals that his version of the bildungsroman is a troubled one. The closure and identification of reader with protagonist and protagonist with nation that is normally associated with the bildungsroman are not methods easily adapted by an Asian American author aware of how the biopolitics of American political economy and immigration erect obstructions to closure and identification. In a similar fashion, Lee demonstrates an awareness of racial politics and class inequality that together limit assimilation, for all. Yet both authors strive at great lengths to construct novels that do seek closure for their protagonists even as they acknowledge historical inequalities. Both turn to the military and warfare as models for masculine training, performance, and assimilation, with the critical difference being that Lee embraces American martial models while Chin turns to Chinese legend. Lee's bildungsroman deploys a distinctively American, multiculturalist model of assimilation that seeks to acknowledge historic inequality and the integral place of blackness in American culture. Chin, in contrast, uses a cultural nationalist model based upon ethnic descent and self-determination that privileges authenticity and purity, versus the cultural hybridity between black and white that Lee acknowledges. In either case, the Asian American adaptation of the bildungsroman is a flexible strategy that allows Asian American authors to claim America, which involves not only illustrating its prejudices and demanding its professed rights but also being implicated in its contradictions. Chinese Americans' appropriation of writing and the bildungsroman allow them to address exclusionary violence both formally and narratively, in terms of the subgenre and its properties in the American context and in terms of the stories of young men who become adult by transcending their status as a racial other. Ironically, in the process of transforming themselves, the characters and the authors use historically accessible tropes of blackness and femininity as the others that can be opposed to their own creation of an American Self.

While describing the Americanization of their characters, the authors also participate in their own implicit Americanization through the use of conventional literary form. Lisa Lowe's statement that "the novel as a form of print culture has constituted a privileged site for the unification of the citizen with the 'imagined community' of the nation" (*Immigrant Acts* 98) may very well apply to both the characters and creators of the novel. For the creators, the novel as a form of print culture is a commodity that can be marketed, and part of what is being marketed is a particular kind of Asian American identity: regenerated masculinity. Thus regenerating masculinity also becomes a form of panethnic entrepreneurship, as the authors' political and aesthetic maneuvers in regard to identity are inseparable from the economics of marketing that identity to a readership. This identity, this unification of an Asian American citizen with the American nation, comes with a cost, namely, the novel's suppression of inequality and contradiction and its appropriation of difference, enacted through the lives of its characters. The violence of this suppression shapes the formal dimension of the bildungsroman and finds an allegory in the violent content of the Chinese American novel. The violent body politic with which these Chinese American novels are concerned is hence threefold: the Asian American masculine body, regenerated and qualified for citizenship; the American masculine body, canonized and memorialized in the classic bildungsroman; and the body politic of the nation as a whole historically, characterized by violence of all kinds: homicidal, exploitative, racial, sexual, and gendered. Collectively, Chin and Lee demonstrate through the form of the novel the fundamental importance of violence in constituting racial and masculine identity within the conflicted territory of American identity. Reading their works as symptoms manifested by the American body politic, we can see that the violence that concerns them is neither an isolated phenomenon confined to some obscure part of the body politic nor simply a tale from our mythological past. American citizens inherit this past, while new immigrants learn from it and contribute violent legacies of their own. Reading these symptoms, we discover that violence, domestic and foreign, national and international, serves as a disturbing bond of unity among Americans new and old.

>>>→ **4** ←<<<

REPRESENTING
RECONCILIATION

Le Ly Hayslip and the Emblematic Victim

The other side of violence is the victim, and in Asian American culture the victim and her body have played an important role in shaping the relationship between America in general and particular Asian American groups. The figure of the victim is especially important in relationships where the United States has occupied a politically ambivalent role in relation to an Asian nation, usually involving war. The Vietnam War has, of course, been that most difficult of wars for the United States, and it is no surprise that the figure of the victim appears often in the American iconography of the war. One of the most important of "victims" to emerge from the war is Le Ly Hayslip, who records a remarkable story in her autobiographical books, *When Heaven and Earth Changed Places* and *Child of War, Woman of Peace*. The first volume traces her youth in a Vietnamese village torn by war and caught between the U.S. and South Vietnamese army on one side and the Vietcong on the other. Forced to leave her village after the Viet Cong suspect her of betrayal, the young Le Ly goes to the big city and works as a maid and street vendor, being impregnated along the way by a rich employer. Eventually, she meets an American civilian who marries her and takes her to the United States in 1971. Spliced into this narrative is another that follows her return to Vietnam in 1986, at a time of considerable risk for returnees, given the lack of political relations between the United States and Vietnam. The second volume follows her life chronologically in the United States from 1972 to 1986 and then in the years subsequent to her first return to Vietnam.[1]

For American readers, Hayslip has become representative of those anonymous millions of Vietnamese in whose name the Vietnam War was fought by both sides. Through her extraordinary personal story, she not only symbolically bears their collective pain but also bears the victim's burden of forgiveness.[2] Her credibility as witness, survivor, and moral truthsayer depends upon the evidence of her body—that is, her pain and her experiences and their consequent rewriting—and upon how this display is read, by both Americans and Vietnamese Americans.[3] This victimized body exists in two dimensions. The body that is imposed in American discourse is a powerless one, a silent figure whose presence is only of isolated significance in the movements of armies, nations, and capital, and one that is ultimately an object of others' politics. In contrast, the body that Hayslip uses has a voice, demonstrating her integral importance to these movements and becoming a subject of politics. In both cases, the victimized body politic draws its strength from a claim to an essential truth of experience that is resistant to discursive wrangling over meanings, interpretations, and political usefulness. The negotiation between these two dimensions of the victim constitutes Hayslip's flexible strategy, which concedes to American preoccupations in order to demand American attention.

In the dimension imposed by American discourse, Hayslip typifies the function of the Vietnamese in American debates over the war, which pivoted on the unspoken (or spoken-for) locus of the Vietnamese body. From the self-immolation of Buddhist monk Thich Quang Duc, to the My Lai massacre, to the "boat people," Vietnamese bodies have been the silent spectacle on which American discourse has been staged. Antiwar protesters, for example, used "objective" photographs of atrocities to demonstrate the inhumanity of the war. Supporters of the war fought back by attempting to discredit the stories behind the images.[4] As Trinh T. Minh-ha argues, these images, icons in the American consciousness, illustrate Vietnam's status as a spectacle for the West that served to make possible American arguments among themselves that concerned the war ("All-Owning Spectatorship"). In contrast to this exploitation, Hayslip's appropriation of the victim's body has enabled her to achieve a speech audible to the West.[5] She enters this discursive dimension by giving the victimized body voice and subjectivity. Instead of being defined only by her contact with the United States, Hayslip presents herself as a historical person, existing before the United States and located in a nostalgic fiction of Vietnam as agrarian, precapitalist, and fundamentally stable and "natural" in its social organization. American violation of this world is not unique but is instead rendered part of a sequence of wars. In this context, Hayslip's victimization speaks differently to Vietnamese audiences than to American ones. In rewriting this victimized body and making it her own, she is caught, to use her own expression, "in between"—Viet Nam and the United States, war and peace, hell and heaven, and, for my concerns, the needs of "representation" and those of "reconciliation."

In moving from silence to speech, Hayslip wavers between providing a relatively complete, representative account of her location as a Vietnamese woman in a global conflict of capital and ideology focused on Vietnam and heeding the imperative for a personal and collective reconciliation on the part of all the war's participants. An attempt at accurate representation (what Fredric Jameson in *Postmodernism, or, The Cultural Logic of Late Capitalism* would call a cognitive mapping) of her location in global capitalism is in conflict with the needs of reconciliation, which dictates the rejection of that mapping and develops in its stead a deliberately partial representation. As a result, Hayslip's flexible strategy is one that charts a dialectical and irresolvable movement between representation and reconciliation, inexorably gesturing toward the intimate connections of Cold War domino-theory politics, the global expansion of capitalism, and the creation of peripheral labor markets and exploitable migratory populations—specifically, refugee and immigrant women. This movement can be found in Hayslip's account of her journey from Vietnam to the United States. The movement is simultaneously brought to light and ultimately obscured by the concluding moments of reconciliation found in both of Hayslip's books, which are dependent upon the rewriting of her victimized body as "natural," in both the prediscursive sense and the unalienated sense.

It is this reconciliation that Hayslip sells to American audiences. She adopts the guise of and is adopted as the emblematic (female) victim. Her victimhood is intimately tied to her status as a Vietnamese, and her exploitation of her intersecting ethnicity and victimization is a form of ethnic entrepreneurship. She markets her story to an American audience more successfully than any other Vietnamese author, and she sells herself, as a figure of healing, to her readers and to donors for her charitable organization, the East Meets West Foundation, which is given prominent place in the epilogues to her autobiographies. Like Onoto Watanna, Hayslip inserts herself into perilous politics, both attempting to ameliorate certain conditions and benefiting from them herself. Some critics call Onoto Watanna a trickster author who manipulates the expectations of a dominant audience, and the same characterization can be extended to Hayslip as well, who faces an equally difficult American audience torn between its misunderstanding of the Vietnamese and its desire to understand properly. As Hayslip characterizes her own literary strategy, she has to "censor myself. And deliver my message straight to the heart without politics. Just human being feelings. Make people cry. Make people feel the pain" (Ho 111). Of course, the exploitation or provocation of emotion constitutes its own form of politics, in this case a politics of reconciliation that would be absolutely necessary in order for the United States to establish a renewed state of equilibrium after the domestic crises—political, cultural, economic, and racial—initiated by the Vietnam War.

Hayslip's attempts at reconciliation are directed not only at Americans, however, but also at other overseas Vietnamese, who are likely to perceive her as a whore and a traitor and who see her trickster strategies, her ethnic entrepreneurship, as self-promotion. To speak to them, she uses a different face of the victimized body politic that has cultural resonance for the Vietnamese. She becomes the emblematic heroine of classical Vietnamese literature—the ideal woman who retains her spiritual virtue in the face of overwhelming circumstances that deprive her of her "chastity." In either case of Hayslip's dealing with Americans or with Vietnamese, it is the totality of the damage inflicted on the victimized body, represented as prediscursive and hence truthful, that provides the power for her speech. The victimized body is a body politic because it is used by others and then by Hayslip herself for the purposes of allowing her to speak in a public context. Hayslip turns to the victimized body as a way of reconciling herself and her readers to her status as a woman caught up in the contradictory demands of globalizing capital and traditional culture. She remains as an important and controversial example of the ways by which the relatively disempowered struggle for self-representation and demonstrates that the tools available for them—the "weapons of the weak," to use James Scott's term—are oftentimes double-edged.

Studying Hayslip's strategies of self-representation through the guise or role of the victim is important for Asian American culture, given the vast history of damage that is part of Asian American experiences both within the United States and abroad. This damage and its articulation, so characteristic of American minority discourse as a result of domestic racism or foreign imperialism and intervention, has produced a substantial body of persons who might claim the mantle of victim or have it placed upon them.[6] The victim has a wounded body, just like the characters of Bulosan's and Okada's work, but the critical difference in the construction of the victim is that he or she is recognized as such by American society as a whole. While Bulosan and Okada could discuss the wounds inflicted by American society, they did not have the power of the victim to absolve American society of anything, particularly since American society at their time did not feel guilty about its crimes—or even acknowledge them, for the most part—against Filipino and Japanese Americans. In contrast to this situation, the "victim," as a subset of the wounded, is a particular mode of categorization and identification that allows its subject to enter the arena of public discourse and political representation with a degree of power, albeit only the power to forgive and exploit guilt. The Vietnam War and the subsequent attempts to cope with it on the part of the American public and intelligentsia arguably constitutes one of the most important discourses of victimization in American culture. Within this discourse, both Americans and Vietnamese (as represented by Americans) have struggled to claim the role of victims who are subject to various and contradictory modes of domination. These modes include an evil communism, a weak-willed American government, an antipatriotic media, the antiwar movement, American racism and imperialism, or domestic poverty and class exploitation. Hayslip's voice speaks to many, if not all, of these modes of victimization, within one of the most traumatic moments of American and Vietnamese history, and thus becomes a critical and representative voice for Asian American studies to examine.

THE SUBALTERN AND THE EMBLEMATIC VICTIM

Hayslip was the subaltern of whom Gayatri Chakravorty Spivak writes in "Can the Subaltern Speak?" The subaltern is that person or group that is by definition prevented from public speech, specifically in a colonial situation of imperial domination. Nevertheless, the subaltern leaves a record of "voice" in history, through nonindividual actions of protest, riot, and rebellion. In the American historical record of the war, the Vietnamese, in particular those who were actively Communist or sympathetic with the cause, were subalterns. Even the majority of the South Vietnamese, however, could be considered subaltern if the defining criterion is that Americans chose not to hear them. The creation of the Vietnamese as a subaltern in American history served the interests of the United States during the war. The facelessness of the enemy and their lack of voice—as well as the lack of voice of America's South Vietnamese allies—created a void for American discourse to dominate. In the postwar period of reconsideration and reevaluation, however, this silence has come to haunt American veterans. Numerous U.S. artists and intellectuals who fought in the war see in the recovery of Vietnam and the resurrection of Vietnamese voices the potential for their own recuperation. These artists and intellectuals have participated in a controversial postwar American debate over the meanings, motivations, and justifications of the war. As John Carlos Rowe has said, "[The Vietnam War] is the most chronicled, documented, reported, filmed, taped, and—in all likelihood—narrated war in history, and for those very reasons, it would seem, the least subject to understanding or to any American consensus" (197). Neil Jamieson expresses the importance of the Vietnamese for a resolution to this American conflict: "We must learn more about Vietnamese culture and Vietnamese paradigms in order to untangle the muddled debates about our own. . . . This is the first and most important lesson of Vietnam" (x). This perceived need to understand oneself and the character of one's nation is more than a gesture at collective therapy for a generation; it also offers the regeneration of a collective, American national will, one that has always viewed history with a selective memory. In response to a 1985 conference of writers and veterans of the Vietnam "experience," Timothy Lomperis writes: "Whether we, as individuals, liked the war or not, protested it or supported it, for this scarred generation that is now coming to power in the United States, the Vietnam War is the undeniable gateway to Asia—and to ourselves" (111).

Oliver Stone's Vietnam trilogy of *Platoon, Born on the Fourth of July*, and *Heaven and Earth* ties together the necessity many veterans experience for confronting the past in order to heal. In *Heaven and Earth*, Stone's film version of Hayslip's books, the symmetrical wholeness of Vietnam at beginning and end, separated by the trauma of the war, implies that Vietnam has healed from the wounds inflicted by the Vietnamese themselves and by Americans. Visually and narratively, Hayslip herself is identified with the landscape at beginning and end. As she has healed herself by the film's conclusion, so has the country. Hayslip's message of peace at this conclusion represents a message of peace for all the war's participants. The healing, however, is figured through one woman's story, in a strategy typical of the simplified Western representation of Vietnamese refugees. Thomas A. DuBois states that "one of the most important versions of the refugee model in popular discourse is the construct of the *emblematic victim*" (4). The "emblematic victim" is the way in which the victimized body politic manifests itself in American discourse, which makes no difference between representative and represented; that is, the fact that one of the oppressed speaks is taken to mean that the oppressed in general have spoken, hence the emblematic quality of the individual speaker.

In Spivak's argument about the subaltern, she warns her readers of the dangers and subterfuges involved in First World invocations of Third World speech. The First World, embodied in Spivak's argument through particular left-wing intellectuals, does not demand that the entire Third World speak but only particular representative voices who may or may not speak in the interests of the population at large. The speech of the liberated Third World individual allows the First World intellectual to believe that the conditions of speech for an entire population have been created. In that way, these intellectuals absolve themselves of the much more difficult business of creating conditions of speech for these populations. The mode of representation evoked by these First World intellectuals is thus only a partial one. In terms of the American debates around U.S. involvement in Vietnam, there is the danger that many American veteran-intellectuals can absolve themselves through the speech of the Vietnamese. This absolution is done by paying lip service to the "oppressed" Vietnamese, by seizing on or lifting up "representative" speakers for admiration while ignoring the uncomfortable realities of those whom these speakers ostensibly represent—realities in which the First World subject is materially implicated. Through the doubled guise of the victimized body as object and subject, Hayslip attempts both to speak about these conditions of collective oppression and victimization and to address and appease the concerns of the First World subject.

THE BODY IN BETWEEN VIETNAM
AND THE UNITED STATES

Part of the discourse of victimization centers on violation and healing, and these become important tropes in Hayslip's own writings for expressing the relationship between the emblematic victim and the American victimizer. In her writings, the technologically enhanced, masculine body of the foreign and domestic aggressors violates the natural body of the woman as representative of the nation. While this body is violated and victimized, it also has the potential to heal itself in a way that the technological body, ironically, cannot do so. Through representations of the body, Hayslip depicts the American belief that masculinity and technology could control femininity and nature. This American faith in technology's ability to persuade and control the Vietnamese is a version of the colonizer's belief in technology's ability to control nature and the colonized. As Donna Haraway notes, "[Colonialist Western discourse] structured the world as an object of knowledge in terms of the appropriation by culture of the resources of nature," with "native" bodies being merely another natural resource (134). In the situation of Vietnam, U.S. technology expended itself destructively in a useless effort to subjugate these bodies or, as articulated by the rhetoric of U.S. policy, to "win their hearts and minds." Yet, in warfare, the Vietnamese bodies were not granted the same right of humanity accorded to American bodies. As Hayslip observes, "Children and women and old people had been blown to bits and everyone [in her husband's family] just yawned, because they were *the enemy*" (*Child of War* 27–28). As Elaine Scarry argues, this apathy arises because a society's discourse of war must dehumanize the enemy, even as it exploits the dead bodies of its own soldiers. The soldier's dead body gives meaning to his nation's claims, for warfare is a conflict over which warring nation's cultural construct will prevail to become a "cultural reality" rather than a "cultural fiction" (131). In the aftermath of victory, the discourse of war uses the material reality of the soldier's dead body to substantiate the nation's cultural claims, making them "real." Thus, from the American perspective, it cannot be that Vietnamese bodies are "really" dying; they must be dehumanized, derealized, in order to allow for the humanization of the American soldier and the substantiation of his body and, through it, of American ideology and culture.[7]

The American dehumanization of the Vietnamese allows the eroticization of both their deaths and the American technology that inflicts death. Susan Jeffords discusses the literary representation of the eroticized American bodies and technology in this way:

> These machine guns, shells, and mini-guns are not described as killing . . .
> or destroying . . . they are described only as their own display, their own
> theater. . . . In an aesthetic that reproduces machinery as objects of display, technology and the body can be rejoined as "pure sex" in an erotic act

that fuses the multiplicity of the fragmented body with the unified power of
technological display. No longer pieces of body counts and machine guns, the
body is reunified through technology as aesthetic. (8–10)

In Jeffords's interpretation, the alienation of the American body from its own
functions—from sex and labor or, respectively, the reproductive and (in this
case) the destructive functions—is temporarily overcome by the eroticism of
high technology expending itself in magnificent special effects. Hayslip's autobiography counters Jeffords's concept of the body reunified through technology,
by contrasting U.S. military technology in Vietnam with its ironic opposite,
medical technology in the United States. What results is a deaestheticization
and deeroticization of technology and the body. When Hayslip visits her dying
first husband in an American hospital, she sees "poor Ed [lying] in his hospital
bed like an old car torn up at the shop. . . . Wires were stuffed everywhere;
his sunken eyes glowed dimly like headlights on a failing battery" (*Child of
War* 94). The machinery holds Ed's body together, but at the same time the me-
chanical metaphor suggests that his body is even further fragmented because it
is so dissociated from nature. Therefore, while American technology in Vietnam
unifies the American body in contrast to the Vietnamese body it destroys, it
cannot do the same for the domestic American body.

We can make sense of this contradictory aspect of American technology by
returning to Scarry's argument that the dead body in war substantiates, or realizes, a nation's cultural fiction of itself. The deaths of American bodies in Vietnam substantiated the socioeconomic system of American capitalism during the
Cold War, which found itself thrown into a state of crisis, challenged by communism abroad and the domestic unrest that ensued from the antiwar and minority rights' movements. On the one hand, this substantiation denied the reality of Vietnamese bodies and the alternative to American capitalism posed by
Vietnamese communism. On the other hand, this substantiation also denied the
domestic changes that were transforming the American working body such as
Ed's. During this emergent period of late capitalism, the working body was becoming increasingly enmeshed with technology, due to advances in automation,
microelectronics, and information and computer technology in the workplace
and in medicine, all in the service of late capitalism. As Donald M. Lowe points
out, "Biotechnical systems of all sorts are changing received meanings of birth,
life, and death" (114). In addition, "laboring bodies, already sorted out in the re-
segmented labor market, are recoded and redisciplined at the new workplaces"
(28), one result of which is the "hazards and stresses" (35) on the body as the
result of specific types of work. These changes lead to the production of the late-
capitalist American body as a kind of "cyborg," to use Haraway's term, which
aptly describes Ed's ultimate fate.

The de-eroticization and denaturalization of the American body and its
machinery that Hayslip undertakes is countered by her eroticization and naturalization of the Vietnamese body as an alternative to the American versions of

the body. This rendering of the Vietnamese body is played out most evidently in two scenes in *When Heaven and Earth Changed Places*, both set in Ky La, her home village. In one, after a battle, Hayslip has to bury a handsome young Vietcong whom she had previously noticed: "I gently covered his face and lifted—embraced—the body's head while my mother took the feet. Together, we lowered him into the dark hole my father had dug and covered him with earth" (68). As if in direct rebuttal to Jeffords's outline of the eroticized, technical spectacle, Hayslip illustrates a notion of death from the Vietnamese perspective that is simultaneously natural and erotic. The "dark hole" in "Mother Earth" suggests both the source of life and the receptacle of death. Women are the guardians at both ends of life, nurturing the products of the earth and their own wombs and guiding the return of the body to its symbolic birthplace. In a second scene, this erotic wholeness is reversed and perverted but also reinforced, by the rape of Hayslip by two Vietcong who have been ordered to execute her. She says that "the war—these men—had finally ground me down to oneness with the soil, from which I could no longer be distinguished as a person" (*Heaven and Earth* 97). A circle of identification is completed here, with Hayslip's body being joined with the earth in a metaphor that makes "woman" and "earth" become synonymous: both are trodden upon and raped by men and military technology. From Hayslip's perspective, her victimization at the hands of men, war, and ideology is complete. She finds herself caught, as she later writes, "in between" two opposing and relentless forces. On one side were the Vietcong, and on the other side were the Americans and South Vietnamese. Collectively, they "had finally found the perfect enemy: a terrified peasant girl who would endlessly and stupidly consent to be their victim as all Vietnam's peasants had consented to be victims, from creation to the end of time!" (97).

Hayslip's identification of herself as one with the earth makes her self seem that much more substantial and real, an actual body in contrast to the fluctuating character of ideology and war. The binary model that Hayslip draws from—split between genders and sexes but also split between ideology and reality—presupposes, as Judith Butler argues, the sexed body as "prediscursive," a stable platform on which the binary model is constructed (*Gender Trouble* 7). Against the "cultural" and hence seemingly ephemeral character of the war and its justifications, Hayslip posits her "natural" embodied self, the "victim." In coming to the United States, Hayslip again seeks to reinforce the nature/culture divide that situates her on the side of nature and the body. Of Americans in general, she says: "What had their cozy houses and bulging refrigerators and big, fast cars and noisy TV sets really taught them about the world: about back-breaking labor, bone-grinding poverty, and death's edge starvation?" (*Child of War* 25). Here the signs of being American are all technological, the satisfactions of wants; the signs of being Vietnamese are natural, the satisfaction of bodily needs. Americans in Hayslip's depiction are participating in what Donald Lowe calls the consumption of lifestyle, which as the "social relations of consumption has overshadowed *class* as the social relations of production [in late capitalism]"

(62). Lowe argues that this shift from production to consumption as the new center of social relations, where consumption is both destabilized and valorized, is capitalism's method of regenerating itself and its project of continual accumulation. In other words, during industrial capitalism the relationship between production and consumption was premised upon the relative stability of people's needs and wants. Production, exchange value, and the reproduction of capital constituted the problematic for an analysis of capital. Consumption, use value, and the reproduction of labor were stable and not problematic. In late capitalism, however, the commodity is no longer characterized by its fulfillment of use value in the realm of consumption but is instead characterized by its fulfillment of artificially created needs—the needs of continually evolving lifestyles that are themselves the prime objects of marketing and advertising. Thus consumption itself is the target of marketing and advertising, as people are told they "need" a certain type of car, house, TV—or, in the argument of this book, a lifestyle and racial identity—in order to "be" a particular type of person. It is the body and its needs, Lowe argues, that is the new problematic of late capitalism. Against this late-capitalist body, a body that Hayslip characterizes as distinctly American in being stimulated by its manipulated desires, Hayslip poses the "natural" needs of a body not yet valorized by late capitalism.

Through her role as wife, Hayslip highlights this relationship of contrast between the American body (one that is masculine, heterosexual, technological, violent, and consumerist) and her Vietnamese body—feminine, heterosexual, natural, peaceful, and nonconsumerist. Her second husband, Dennis, is a Korean War veteran who abuses her and kidnaps her children when she threatens him with divorce. Hayslip writes that "such atrocities as I had witnessed in both countries could only be perpetuated by men with no awareness of the sacred origins of life" (*Child of War* 174). By calling domestic violence and abuse an atrocity, Hayslip literally brings the war home. In another telling example that characterizes the homegrown nature of American violence, Hayslip writes that "'*Xin ong dung giet toi*'—'Please, sir, don't kill me!'—was our standard greeting for the American boys in uniform who came our way" (*Child of War* 25). These atrocities that are committed in Vietnam and described in *When Heaven and Earth Changed Places* could easily be distanced from contemporary American life, as past crimes and errors to feel guilty for and committed by a generation of soldiers that most Americans until recently would have liked to disavow. Through the rhetoric of atrocity dependent on the victimized body, Hayslip tries to prevent this disavowal by drawing connections between American domesticity and foreign terror. Both are inflicted by the same men or at least are inflicted by the same society capable of producing such men. Connecting foreign and domestic terror constitutes one of Hayslip's most vivid efforts in constructing a representative account of how she as an individual is caught up in the forces that bind the United States and Vietnam.

In the end, this attempt at representation is clouded by her attempt at reconciliation, which is expressed twice, once at the end of each volume. In the first volume, she proclaims herself an American, which is a fitting and traditional conclusion for an autobiographical narrative that, in one reading, traces the development of a foreign refugee into a full-fledged American. In the second volume, she renounces nationality for the sake of universality when she addresses her home village this way at the conclusion:

> I can tell you now, from firsthand experience, that America is not your enemy and never was, even during the war. Back then, America picked me up when I was scared and bloody and cared for me and educated me and helped me to raise my three wonderful sons. It made me a citizen and has let me come back with these presents which she gives you freely and without reservations. What she wants more than anything, I think, is to forgive you and be forgiven by you in return. (362)

In this conclusion, she emphasizes forgiveness rather than karma, or "soul debt," as Hayslip calls it. Soul debt is part of the cycle of action and reward or punishment, for *both* individuals and nations, which is particularly important to Hayslip's notion of redemption. In reference to nations, she says of Vietnam and the Soviet Union that "the laws of karma dictate that something good must be in store for both nations" (302). Of the United States and Iraq she says, "A bloody and tragic—but blessedly short—American-led war was fought in Iraq, paying off and creating soul debt all its own" (364). Soul debt is central to Hayslip's vision of her own life, as a justification for the suffering she has endured and seen and as part of a philosophical system that allows for the possibility of compensation. The idea of soul debt, for Hayslip, offers one systematic, or representative, way to comprehend the vast brutality of the war and its effects upon individuals; it is one "weapon of the weak" that takes a dominant spiritual philosophy and imbues it with a populist sense of justice.[8] In Hayslip's philosophy, the system of soul debt allows for the possibility of human intervention to correct what would otherwise be an unending cycle of crime and punishment.

While Hayslip's philosophy allows for individual action, her conclusion that "what [the United States] wants more than anything, I think, is to forgive you and be forgiven by you in return" implies a symmetry of power between nations that did not and does not exist. The reasons for implying such symmetry are clear. Through a symmetry of power, the individual as emblematic victim has a role to play in American consciousness. For Hayslip in particular, at the moment in her life described in the book that role is to play upon the possible guilt and genuine desire to help Vietnam on the part of U.S. veterans and concerned civilians, who provide for the financial basis of her humanitarian work in Vietnam. Engagement in a tallying of spiritual sins and debts, especially on a collective level, would be detrimental to the practical effort of healing and reconstruction; more cynically, we can argue that counting debts would damage her efforts to be an ethnic entrepreneur trading in the precious commodity of reconciliation. In erasing this system of soul debt, the resolution of her life story sounds a jarring, if not totally surprising note as it attempts to harmonize a world already shown as discordant. This harmonization is extracted from the victimized body, as used both in its deployment in American discourse and in Hayslip's appropriation of that body. In her appropriation, it is she herself, in the body of the emblematic victim, who forgives and who inserts herself not only into moral issues for Americans but also, ironically, into economic issues.

Hayslip's emphasis on forgiveness cannot be isolated from Vietnam's unique place in the history of capitalism, which is the economic subtext to the American ideological debate over the United States' actions in Vietnam. This debate has developed during a signal shift in the nature of capitalism over the past twenty-five years, since the peak of American involvement in Vietnam in 1968, the year of the Tet offensive. David Harvey argues that the late sixties saw a global crisis, as Fordism, the dominant mode of capitalist economic organization for most of the twentieth century, reached its limits.[9] Within the First World, Fordism's creation of a split-level employment environment that privileged white males and discriminated against all others combined with an increasing level of state bureaucratization and the standardization of mass culture to produce the counterculture, civil rights, and minority movements, which would collectively push the United States into a domestic crisis of national identity centered on the war abroad and race relations at home. In the Third World, whose material resources and labor proved fundamental to First World development, "discontents at a modernization process that . . . delivered destruction of local cultures, much oppression, and various forms of capitalist domination" generated "movements towards national liberation that sometimes appeared quite threatening to global Fordism" (Harvey 139). Nowhere was this move toward national liberation more threatening, Aijaz Ahmad argues, than in the Vietnam War, where the global contradictions between "revolutionary anti-colonialism; the most advanced socialist political practice in the most backward peasant economy; the direct, historic, prolonged combat between socialism and imperialism; the utterly unequal balance of forces—was condensed" (28).

The "local" conflict in Vietnam, therefore, had a number of global resonances for Americans, which included the failure of anticommunist containment policies, of American "democratizing," and of American military might. There was also the failure to comprehend the "oriental" mind, at the same moment when Asian and Arab nations were poised to enter (or to make their presence felt in) the global economy forcefully. All of these failures occurred in a world Americans perceived as Manichean, divided between good and evil, democracy and totalitarianism, capitalism and communism. In short, the American war in Vietnam was not only a political crisis for Americans but implicitly an economic crisis with global implications as well. This crisis was compounded by two related factors. The first was the overaccumulation of capital and labor that led to the need for new spaces for capitalist development; the second was "the growth of trade and direct investments, and the exploration of new possibilities for the exploitation of labour power" (Harvey 183). The situation in Vietnam was considered a threat to this search for new spaces. Today Vietnam is perceived by many Americans and entrepreneurial interests as one of those necessary "new spaces" for the expansion of capitalism. The second factor was the advent of what Harvey calls the regime of "flexible accumulation," which succeeded Fordism. Flexible accumulation promoted the downsizing of high-wage labor forces, the increasing mobility of transnational corporations, the lowering of trade barriers, the proliferation of multiple, simultaneous, and sometimes seemingly anachronistic labor systems (Fordist, artisanal, familial, domestic, patriarchal), and the continuous search for low-wage, disposable labor. This search has focused on Vietnam.

The American demand for subalterns like Hayslip to speak, and also to forgive, means that the United States can forget its past and proceed with business as usual; the moral economy of Hayslip's works, its articulation through soul debt and paternal business (as we shall see), helps to facilitate not only her own ethnic entrepreneurship but also the United States' efforts to invest in a new Vietnamese economy. For twenty years after the end of the Vietnam War, business as usual did not proceed with Vietnam because the anger and resentment that Americans experienced from their loss prevented them from engaging in diplomatic and economic relations. Reconciliation with Vietnam was critical to the larger political and economic enterprise. Hayslip is deeply invested in that need for reconciliation, recognizing the benefits that are entailed for both Vietnamese and Americans. For her desire to reconcile she has often been criticized by other Vietnamese anticommunist refugees who perceive her as willing to overlook the abuses, excesses, and mistakes of the communist regime in the name of reconciliation and personal aggrandizement. In Hayslip's autobiography, however, we will see how the underlying logic of the emblematic victim—whose power lies in the naturalization of her body—becomes extended even further in the body of the ideal Vietnamese woman who is meant to reconcile Hayslip with other Vietnamese.

VIETNAMESE WOMEN AND THE NATION

When Hayslip eventually carries out "her father's business" of learning and teaching the value of life and peace, she does so from a position that Chandra Talpade Mohanty characterizes as "writing/speaking of a multiple consciousness, one located at the juncture of contests over the meanings of racism, colonialism, sexualities and class, [which] is thus a crucial context for delineating third world women's engagement with feminism" ("Cartographies of Struggle" 36). One of her complex engagements with feminism involves recasting herself in the role of the ideal woman, who belongs to a precapitalist organization of gender and social relations in Vietnam. Casting herself as such a person involves a revision of traditional social norms born from village life and peasant society, not on Western-style feminism.[10] The ideal Vietnamese woman's role is on the private side of the public/private distinction that characterizes Vietnamese culture; as the guardians of the private sphere, women are the "ministers of the interior" who maintain family and national culture.[11] In Vietnamese society, however, a woman's social role is seen to be indistinguishable from her sexed and gendered body. This is evident immediately in her work when, after the moment of foreign intrusion that begins *When Heaven and Earth Changed Places*, the book provides a lovingly described ethnography of unspoiled village life and customs, in which labor, family, gender, and tradition are united: "Transplanting the rice stalks from their 'nursery' to the field was primarily women's work. . . . That sensual contact between hands and feet, the baby rice, and the wet, receptive earth is one of the things that preserved and heightened our connection with the land" (6–7). That women undertake the nurturing of rice, the major source of nourishment for the peasants, is a significant extension of their traditional roles in Vietnamese society as "caregivers."[12] Their roles in the literal reproduction of the means of production (their children) and in the production of food join them with the feminine figure of "Mother Earth," a Vietnamese mythical construction juxtaposed with "Mr. Sky." Thus, at the very beginning of Hayslip's autobiography, she creates a feminine wholeness— of peasant, land, rice, and seasonal cycle—as one side of a balanced heterosexual division of society and nature. This heterosexual division is premised upon the idea that men and women's bodies are distinct and serve different purposes, and it also works to reinforce that distinction, continually (re)creating the body. The type of village life that Hayslip describes is "organic" and rooted in hundreds of years of tradition. Yet its "naturalness" is also a fiction. An agrarian economy is still a mode of production that depends on a certain kind of technology: the plow, the scythe, the fishnet, and the hoe. They are not "nature," even though in a precapitalist economy they may seem natural and unalienated from the human body. It is the effect of naturalness that Hayslip exploits in order to make her own body seem a part of the nature that Americans will violate.

Both Stone's film version of *Heaven and Earth* and Hayslip's original text construct a near-mythic past "before the Americans came" on which a vision of the postwar future can be constructed. While Stone appeals to an orientalist conflation of nation and woman, Hayslip ironically turns to a conflation of nation and woman that is central to the political and literary discourse of Vietnam and made possible through the notion of chastity. For all levels of Vietnamese society, "chastity" was the prime virtue for a woman. "It was a general term for different forms of purity she was to possess in different periods of her life," that is, in her relations with her father, husband, and son (the defining men to whom a woman owed the "Three Submissions") (Nha-Trang 20). Chastity in this conventional definition is clearly a social virtue dependent upon the actions of the female body. Although it can be a "general term," it is still premised upon the idea of sexual purity and faithfulness. It can be physically tested. In contrast, the prime virtue for Vietnamese men is "honor," something much less tangible. Therefore, even though Vietnamese social roles for men and women, especially for peasants, may be rigidly tied to a binaristic heterosexual division of society based upon the differentiated body, it is only women whose social practice is defined by sexual behavior and the telltale evidence of their body.

In Vietnamese culture, the idea of female chastity becomes both a personal and symbolically national value in its re-articulation through another version of the victim's body. This is expressed most memorably and complexly in Nguyen Du's early-nineteenth-century poem *Truyen Kieu* (The tale of Kieu), which tells the story of a young woman, Kieu, who gives up her lover and agrees to a marriage of convenience to save her father. The marriage of convenience turns out to be a ploy by a brothel owner to buy Kieu into prostitution. Kieu eventually escapes but embarks on a difficult life in which she becomes the lover of three different men before she finally finds a way to return to her family and earlier lover. She is reunited with her lover in a platonic marriage that allows her to fulfill her obligations to him while paying penance for her loss of virtue. In this way, Kieu fulfills her duties to her father, lover, and society by sacrificing virtue in the name of filial duty and then sacrificing physical love for ideal love. "All marveled at her wish and lauded her— / a woman of high mind, not some coquette / who'd with her favors skip from man to man" (Nguyen, lines 3218–3220). In the end, despite all her travails, Kieu is seen as keeping the most important aspect of her chastity—the spiritual one of submissive duty. *The Tale of Kieu* became the classic of Vietnamese literature because it presented a sophisticated interpretation of chastity that took into account the contingency of circumstance and also because Kieu's plight was read as a political allegory for Vietnam itself. The poem is not only a literary classic but also a popular classic that is transmitted orally as well. It has survived in the diaspora partially because of its ability to symbolize the nation's purity through the notion of feminine chastity—that is, through the idealized woman's body. The poem's translator, Huynh Sanh Thong, writes: "To the extent that the poem implies something at the very core of Vietnamese experience, it addresses [the Vietnamese] intimately as victims, as refugees, as survivors. . . . Beyond its literal meaning, Kieu's prostitution is interpreted as a metaphor for the betrayal of principle under duress, the submission to force of circumstances. More generally, Kieu stands for Vietnam itself" (xl). Hayslip's own story, as a young girl who prostitutes herself to save her family and becomes the wife of numerous men out of necessity, eventually rejecting sex in favor of a spiritual relationship, is a partial reflection of Kieu's story. The parallels between Hayslip's story and Kieu's story are there because the same disjunction between ideal and practice for women that existed in Nguyen Du's time continues today. For Vietnamese audiences, this disjunction means that the story of Kieu becomes symbolic not only of traditional Vietnamese culture before French and U.S. intervention but also of the process of culture and the fact that national culture oftentimes consists of ideals and (contradictory) practice.[13]

The traditional woman's place in Vietnamese society is one example of ideal and contradiction, a tension between the constrictions of the Three Submissions and the marginal agency granted by the public/private, masculine/feminine power-sharing strategy that characterizes traditional Vietnam.[14] In the end, of course, it is patriarchy that determines the ultimate boundaries of a traditional woman's life. It is telling, therefore, that while Hayslip learns significant and different lessons from both mother and father, it is her father who will plant within her the seed of her future philosophy, to be nurtured by the cultural and spiritual heritage she receives from Vietnam. "Your job," he tells her, "is to . . . find a husband and have babies and tell the story of what you've seen to your children and to anyone else who'll listen. Most of all, it is to live in peace and tend the shrine of our ancestors" (*Heaven and Earth* 32–33). In retrospect, these words will provide the driving impulse behind her life, to be reconfigured later in *Child of War, Woman of Peace* as "her father's business" to which she must tend. In short, she portrays herself as the dutiful daughter, following the patriarch's instructions to fulfill her duty in the private, domestic sphere, figured as her appropriate arena of power. Yet "her father's business," as circumscribing as it may be, enables her to reject another kind of business in which she becomes involved as she tries to fulfill her duties as wife and mother: that, of course, is the business of survival in late-capitalist American society. As a wife, her relations with her husband Dennis (as later with her lovers) are strained by her entrepreneurial dealings. Dennis, for example, has no objections to her work on an electronic assembly line for National Semi-Conductor, but he does vehemently object to, and even sabotages, her independent business venture (*Child of War* 152–163). It is only after his death that Hayslip becomes successful and actually financially independent, owning three houses and a share of a restaurant. Work, however, recreates the worker as much as it creates commodities, and in Hayslip's case entrepreneurialism transforms her into "a harried 'capitalist,' [who] had lost [her] touch as a mother" (251). Likewise, her infatuations and romances with a series of men in the United States threaten both herself and her family as the men manifest their instability and even treachery in various ways. Hayslip's eventual renunciation of heterosexual relations and her return to the role of a daughter fulfilling a father's spiritual business thus constitute a rejection of the late-capitalist society she has known in the United States.[15] This rejection is also an attempt to recover the wholeness and naturalness she believes is found in the Vietnamese family, in the Vietnamese village, and in the ideal Vietnamese woman's body.

It is not, however, a rejection that grapples with the changing nature of late capitalism and its problematizing of the body through discursive, semiotic, structural, and cybernetic means. Instead, it is a rejection through a nostalgic retreat to a culture that is part of an outdated mode of production. This is not to say that resistance to capitalism necessarily has to grapple with its discursive, semiotic, structural, and cybernetic means as they are defined in the developed nations. Resistance obviously can and must be undertaken in peripheral economies as well, and their character shall be different consequent to their own specific conditions. In Hayslip's case, however, her work is written in a late-capitalist economy and addressed to an audience in that economy. She is no longer "subaltern" in any sense of the word but very much a part of the First World, and thus her textual and political strategies must be addressed in that context, where we can see that her critique of capitalism and embrace of a spiritual "business" are two ironic aspects of her ethnic entrepreneurialism. Both of those aspects are legitimized by her status as a victim, and the use of a violated, victimized body is the key flexible strategy in her texts. This strategy allows her to intervene in both American and Vietnamese discourse over the war, representing herself in both cases as an emblematic victim and a representative of the nation.

VICTIMIZATION AND VOICE

This intervention through the female body is conducted as a retreat to reconciliation, serving one function for global capitalism and for the interests of Americans after the war and serving yet another function for Hayslip's Vietnamese readers in the diaspora who articulate their dislocation and recuperation in gendered terms. This reconciliatory effort is in tension with Hayslip's need to represent accurately her location in global capitalism and Vietnamese culture. Like the young female factory workers in Aihwa Ong's account of Malaysian industrialization, *Spirits of Resistance and Capitalist Discipline*, who are caught in the irreconcilable contradiction of modernization and tradition, Hayslip must turn to the premodern past, to the "spirit of resistance" found in *The Tale of Kieu*. In Malaysia, the spirits spoke through the seemingly possessed bodies of young peasant women as a protest against the exploitation of their bodies and labor in the factories. In a similar fashion, through the figure of her own body and its travails, Hayslip addresses her American and Vietnamese audiences. She represents the connection between U.S. military violence overseas, in the name of capitalism or democracy, and domestic violence and female labor exploitation at home through an emphasis on their common gendered and sexualized nature. At the same time, she contains the damage that is inflicted on her through violence and exploitation by re-articulating it, using the traditional gender roles of a diasporic Vietnamese culture.

As a result, hers is a conflicted text. It is progressive in its attempt to understand the intimate connections between the histories of Vietnam and the United States despite the artificial boundaries of culture and nation. It is also regressive in its attempt to construct a narrative that imposes a different conclusion, with a sense of wholeness, of closure, of harmony with the past, than the story warrants. In order to make sense of this ambivalence in her autobiographical account, I found myself unwittingly following Joan W. Scott's injunction that we examine the "historical processes" and discourses that "position subjects and produce their experiences. . . . Experience in this definition then becomes not the origin of our explanation . . . but rather that which we seek to explain, that about which knowledge is produced" (401). We have never lacked the valuable stories and the recorded experiences of witnesses to conflicts and atrocities, but we should not read them naively, taking them as unproblematically authoritative or transparently truthful. We need to read these stories—Hayslip's being an exemplary one—beyond their own self-positioning and their repositioning by others: in Hayslip's case, these respective positions are found in the bodies of the ideal woman (as already violated and victimized) and the emblematic victim.

The body, especially that of the victim, is a crucial site of analysis and resistance in late capitalism, yet Donald Lowe reminds us that

> we cannot fall back on the body as an individual identity, subjectivity, private self, or any other autonomous, stable, unitary entity. Such conceptualizations might have been useful under industrial capitalism, because they presupposed the structural oppositions between public and private, work and leisure, production and social reproduction, individual and society. But the older, more stable context no longer exists in late capitalism. (175)

It is therefore in this destabilized context that Hayslip's portrayal of the victimized body needs to be examined in its function as a means of reconciliation with Vietnamese tradition and American self-absolution, becoming a body politic, something that exceeds "individual identity, subjectivity, private self." Her self-representations are a flexible strategy that attempts to speak to two very different audiences in terms deeply embedded in those respective audiences' culture and history. The strategy constitutes a struggle for speech in a situation that denies voice to the subaltern classes from which she emerged. As a peasant, she speaks to the concerns of Vietnamese as a whole, drawing on a national legacy in the figure of the violated heroine Kieu, who embodies the national plight of being a colonized country. As a Vietnamese in the United States, she speaks to American demands for a healing of their war wounds, a healing that assists the continuing movement of American capitalism and Vietnamese reconstruction (to the extent that it is dependent upon American policy), bringing to closure a deep crisis in American culture. Such a closure restores American society to a state of equilibrium, in terms of both its overall national identity and its racial relations, which were radically transformed during the time of the war. More broadly, however, we should understand that the victimized body politic in its emblematic form has played important, if varied, roles throughout the history of American involvement in Asia, either justifying intervention on the part of the U.S. government and the military or justifying protest on the part of antiwar and anti-imperialist domestic movements. Generally, these emblematic victims are silent or ventriloquized pawns in U.S. domestic politics. Hayslip's writings, while being conflicted and appropriated in various ways, speak through this guise of the emblematic victim and attain a measure of independence, constituting a crucial act of witness with which we must engage.

⫸➤ 5 ◄⫷

QUEER BODIES AND
SUBALTERN SPECTATORS

Guerrilla Theater, Hollywood Melodrama,
and the Filipino (American) Novel

While the United States has sometimes dealt with its own traumatic past through rendering it highly visible, it has also often dealt with the past through rendering it invisible. The involvement of the United States with the Philippines is one of those critical moments of invisibility where the history of the involvement has been erased from the American consciousness, because it would pose a threat to the equilibrium of an American national identity based on the idea of democratic exceptionalism. In such a situation, the task of American-based writers who seek to address the Philippines or its fraught history with the United States is a difficult one. Whereas writers like Hayslip may speak through the established role of the victim and be guaranteed an audience, writers such as Jessica Hagedorn and Ninotchka Rosca who publish in the United States must first create the awareness of the Philippines, not to mention the awareness of the history of the United States and the Philippines, for their primarily American audiences. In so doing, they become, of course, ethnic entrepreneurs; like Frank Chin's efforts in the early 1970s to bring Asian American literature to American consciousness, Rosca and Hagedorn's works are both examples of U.S.-based Filipino literature and attempts to create the consciousness of such literature in the American political environment and literary market. In order to gain a foothold in that market, both writers address one of the few times of Filipino history that American audiences may be aware of, the period of martial law under Ferdinand Marcos (1972–1986).

While their textual strategies differ greatly in addressing this period, what is common in both Hagedorn's and Rosca's works is a focus upon the anti-dictatorial revolution in the Philippines. What is also common is the central role that transvestites and homosexuals play in both authors' versions of the revolution. The queer body arises in the work of these writers because it allows them to address two related historical situations—the relationship of the Philippines to the United States and the relationship of the dominated to the dominating in the Philippines. In these situations, the queer subject's status as social outsider becomes metaphorical for the Philippines as the forgotten nation in American memory and metaphorical for the dominated within the Philippines itself. To a great extent, the relationship of class domination in the Philippines, which finds its origins in Spanish colonialism, was encouraged and perpetuated by U.S. colonialism in the first half of the twentieth century and U.S. neocolonialism after World War II. Therefore, the queer subject, in addition to representing the historical amnesia of one situation and the domination of another, links the two as well. Finally, the authors, by placing the queer body at the center of the anti-dictatorial movement, transform that movement into a sexual revolution that displaces the importance of heterosexual identity and marriage found in many constructions of nationalist revolution, such as Bulosan's. In all three of these senses—amnesia, domination, and sexual revolution—the queer body serves as an ideal postcolonial subject that demonstrates the ways by which legacies of the colonial era can be critiqued and overthrown.

Jessica Hagedorn's *Dogeaters* represents the neocolonial Philippines by being relentlessly contemporary in its structure and concerns, featuring a postmodern use of fragmented time lines, multiple narrators, and an obsession with popular culture and spectacles, especially those made in Hollywood or following in its fashion. The novel's queer subject, Joey, is a male prostitute who services Western tourists and is, in that sense, a "modern," Western-oriented version of the gay man. *Dogeaters* is therefore concerned not only with modes of desire and sexuality but also with the actual existence, visibility, and acknowledgment of the queer body through which these desires play. The novel's flexible strategy, which enables it to appeal to American audiences, is to center on the spectacle and the commodity, two things that American audiences may easily associate with the Marcos-era Philippines and the excess associated with it, such as Imelda Marcos's legendary collection of shoes. At the same time, such a strategy, which delights also in a postmodern use of form that fits the novel's exploitation of spectacle and commodity, may participate in postmodernism's tendency to avoid historical complexity and depth. Ninotchka Rosca's *State of War*, in contrast, is relentlessly historical, examining the history of two families, the Banyagas and the Villaverdes, that find their common roots in Spanish colonization dating back four centuries. The novel also features a play with queer sexuality in its use of transvestites, who move from being spectacular objects for lust and derision to being revolutionary actors in a "guerrilla theater" of their own making. It is the oppressive government's soldiers, who are in hot pursuit of the transvestites, that become their unwitting spectators.

While Joey's sexuality is "out" and visible in ways that are amenable to Western versions of queer sexuality, the transvestites are models of "native" sexuality who are comfortable with being invisible in a certain fashion, exploiting conventional expectations of their "nature." The Filipino queer subject as embodied in the transvestite is not equivalent to a modern, Western conception of a queer subject that often sees itself as the normative or universal model for gay liberation. Martin Manalansan argues that this Western conception based upon "outing" and visibility can be used to suppress the manifestation of other, non-Western types of queer practices as "unliberated" ("In the Shadows of Stonewall" 486).[1] *State of War*'s flexible strategy consists of exploiting and rejecting this Western queer discourse that features the closet-as-oppression and visibility-as-liberation. The novel's complexity, both historically and culturally (in regard to sexuality), may have made it less appealing to American audiences than the critically acclaimed and commercially successful *Dogeaters*. *Dogeaters*' treatment of queer sexuality, for example, represents it as simply another aspect of the deracinated, neocolonized present, recognizable to Western sex tourists and Western readers in the postmodern, postcolonial moment. In this moment, sexuality like everything else is a commodity, and commodities in their spectacular state are both the objects of desire for the inhabitants of Manila and the signs of their oppression. The postcolonial state in Hagedorn's novel both aestheticizes the commodity and fetishizes it, suppressing the acknowledgment of the relations of production that make the commodity both possible in its existence and impossible in its attainment for the majority of the people. The ultimate act of commodification in Hagedorn's Manila becomes the selling of one's own body in the sex trades of homosexual and heterosexual prostitution and pornography and in the more naturalized and socially acceptable versions of the sex trade found in political marriage and cinematic spectacle. It is not just Filipinos who participate in such sex trade, however; *Dogeaters* does not hesitate to demonstrate Western queer participation in a contemporary kind of imperialism, namely, sex tourism.

Even as both novels criticize the discourse of Western queer sexuality in different ways, they are also informed by that discourse. As the queer body in the West has become a political body that enables positive forms of agency for gays and lesbians, it has transformed the possibilities of using the queer body culturally. In earlier cases of Asian American literature, for example, the presence of queers, or others who did not meet heterosexual expectations, often inspired revulsion or confusion.[2] The emergence of gays and lesbians into the political and public spheres after 1968 parallels the emergence of self-identified Asian Americans, and in *Dogeaters* and *State of War* we see the convergence between these two identity formations in a new kind of queer critical practice. In these novels, the convergence leads to the argument that the queer body politic is not only about queer sexuality—its marginal status can also be used to signify something "queer" behind the facades of official narratives that concern state and nation. In the context of the Philippines, the queer body introduces a "nonheteronormative" element into the nationalist, heterosexist romance that is often used by the anticolonial struggle and which may eventually become embodied in the postcolonial state's self-representation. In the context of the United States, the queer body metaphorically "queers" the claims of the United States that it is a democratically exceptional state that has never engaged in the politics of imperialism, attempting then to destabilize the equilibrium of American national identity. In both cases, the queer body is used by the authors not simply because of an easy exchangeability between the verb "queer" and queer identity but also because the queer subject historically has occupied a position of invisibility and marginalization within both Filipino and American cultures and hence serves as a model for such invisibility and marginalization in other contexts.

COLONIALISM, THE NATION, AND SEXUALITY

Placing an emphasis upon the queer body as a way to address colonialism is appropriate, considering how, as bell hooks has phrased it, "sexuality has always provided gendered metaphors for colonization" (57). What hooks doesn't mention is that sexuality also provides gendered metaphors for decolonization. A nationalist revolution seeks to cast its language in the terms of a familial and heterosexual romance; this is the logical inversion of the colonizer's use of heterosexuality and romance to justify colonialism, summarized in Gayatri Chakravorty Spivak's phrase "white men are saving brown women from brown men" (92). In the anticolonialist articulation, the heterosexual romance of revolution might be "brown men are saving brown women from white men." Homosexuality is little better than a sickness in this heterosexual romance and must be suppressed as a sign of perversion. Feminist discourse from both the First and Third Worlds has been able to intervene in the uncritical usage of these gendered metaphors.[3] Cynthia Enloe argues effectively that although women have been significant agents in anticolonial resistance, they have existed in anticolonial discourse only as passive objects for contention and protection. This gendered discourse over colonization has, according to Enloe, accepted the terms of patriarchal politics, which delegates the public realm of state politics to men and the private realm of domestic culture—the protected object of nationalist rhetoric—to women.[4] According to Neferti Xina M. Tadiar, Filipinos have internalized those same gendered perceptions in their national self-imaging and in their desires in constructing a modern nation, so that "the excessive and fluid sexuality attributed to women as well as to colonial bodies is housed and contained in a feminized national body that hence becomes the jurisdiction of a masculine nation-state" (170). Tadiar goes on to argue that this gendered stability becomes undone at the global level because the Philippines as nation and state is regarded there as a source of feminized global labor.

Vicente Rafael has focused on this divided image of nation-as-feminine/ state-as-masculine in order to show how, in nationalist Tagalog dramas at the turn of the century, men and women did not automatically fall into this model because of the absence of patriarchal figures and the foregrounded figure of the motherland. "Gender in these plays does not come across as a series of fixed and natural categories, but as a set of negotiable positions in the articulation of nationhood" (214).[5] Of course, part of the reason for this, as Rafael notes, is the absence of a Filipino state during the period in which the plays were produced (1903–1905). Rafael also writes: "What makes these plays significant is that by imaging the nation as woman, they also project a notion of the nation as *distinct* from the state" (214). Considering that the state was cast in masculine terms, what this suggests to us is how the revolutionary Filipino state-to-be under Emilio Aguinaldo must have been "feminized" by its defeat at the hands of the United States, at least in the rhetorical configuration of colonialism. Rafael calls the gendered competition among nation-states a "homosocial affair" (211); from this we can surmise that the defeat of one's opponent in colonial war must mean that the opponent has become feminized in allowing his nation (the female body he protects) to be "penetrated." This rhetorical split allows the homosocial competition to continue without worries of anyone assuming a homoerotic position, despite the fact that the defeated state is inevitably part of the feminized body anyway. It is this vacillation of identity, this insecurity that arises from unstable gendered identities, that is the concern of both *State of War* and *Dogeaters*. Through the queer body politic, they demonstrate this instability and its implications for sexual and national identities.

THE NOVEL AS GUERRILLA THEATER

The title of *State of War* refers to the condition of war, the existence of a martial state—a state of military dictatorship during the Marcos years—and finally the Philippines under martial law through colonialism for most of its history. The novel is an allegory of the Marcos dictatorship, but it is also a historical novel that traces the impact of colonization upon Filipino identity. This identity is a product of a hybridization that takes place over 350 years of Spanish rule and an additional 50 years of U.S. rule.[6] The main characters—Eliza, Anna, and Adrian—are in a quest for their own identities, which become symbolic of the national identity. Their search for a total identity, however, will be a futile one, since the totality of the racial and cultural hybridization that comprises Filipino history and identity is beyond the grasp of any one individual. These characters will confront a dictatorship that is also interested in controlling the meaning of the historical past and the present, through language and its deployment in propaganda. The revolutionary struggle against the dictatorship is then as much a battle for the representation of history and the past as it is for the state. *State of War* not only depicts this struggle over representation but also enacts that struggle itself through its charting of the complex family histories of the main characters and their two families, the Banyagas and the Villaverdes, through the period of Spanish colonization until the present.

The state of war, as Anna describes it, is an "elusive, almost illusory war that was everywhere and yet nowhere" (Rosca 20). Both camouflage and guerrilla warfare as military practices remind the reader how important disguise and elusiveness are to both this state of war and what they signify at their metaphorical level—the contestation over the manipulation of appearances and meaning that contribute to the rule of society. It is the struggle over language and its ability to represent nothing less than "reality"—both the present and the past—that is the discursive corollary to the struggle between the state and the revolution. The elusive nature of language is analogous to the elusive nature of guerrilla war and guerrillas, whose evasiveness is signaled by their camouflage. In the novel, the most notable use of camouflage is by transvestite guerrillas, whose transvestism masks their revolutionary intentions—signaling that this is a *sexual* revolution in addition to being an antistate revolution. The queer body politic of the guerrillas is aimed at unsettling both the state and the heterosexual mores that it uses to represent itself. The transvestites and the government soldiers confront each other on the island of K— during a festival in honor of the Commander (the allegorical figure for Marcos). One might not think of associating soldiers and transvestites together, but in fact the soldiers actively pursue the transvestites (49, 144). The acceptability of this situation springs from both the local tradition of Filipino queer practices and the wider implications of the transvestite, who is, as Marjorie Garber argues, "the space of desire" (75). This local tradition of Filipino queer practices is very different from the Western homosexual tradition and provides the basis for the strategic nature of their transvestism as potentially revolutionary rather than simply escapist, which is how Eliza mistakenly perceives it when she describes the transvestites in this fashion: "In such a disguise . . . man-woman, woman-man, one could live safely in illusions and avoid all confrontations" (15).

In the Philippines, queer practices, meaning the broad range of sexual activities and behaviors that may not be considered normatively heterosexual, are rhetorically framed as an accepted part of life. The Tagalog and Cebuano terms that most closely approximate the Western terms "homosexual" and "queer," *bakla* and *bayot*, respectively, are focused more on the gendered behavior of the person specified rather than just, or only, their sexual object-choice. It is not that the *bakla*'s and *bayot*'s sexual object-choice isn't important. As we shall see in more detail later, their object-choice must be consistent with their gendered behavior; that is, a *bakla*, if he chooses a partner, should choose a masculine-gendered man. But the term *bakla* itself is not necessarily associated with sexual activity, as "gay" and "homosexual" in Western societies usually are; rather, *bakla* as a category has room for transvestism, effeminacy, and homosexual object-choice. In that sense, it is closest to the term "queer," which describes a variety of sexual practices, behaviors, and identifications. While the studies of American sex researchers such as Donn V. Hart and Frederick L. Whitam and Robin M. Mathey have concluded that *bakla* are accepted and tolerated in Philippine society, Martin Manalansan comes to a different conclusion when he argues that the acceptance is still dependent upon a rigid categorization of *bakla* identity. While *bakla* are not publicly condemned as gays are in the United States, they do face social circumscription and fulfill certain expected roles. This circumscription is due to how they are perceived, because as Manalansan argues, "[The *bakla*] possesses what is called the 'female heart' (*pusong babae*). This idiom encapsulates what is perhaps the core of the social construction of the *bakla*, that of the male body with a female heart. . . . Thus unlike his American 'counterparts,' the *bakla*'s predilections are seen to be focused on the straight male population" ("Speaking of AIDS" 199–200).[7]

Their social circumscription arises from the fact that *bakla* is not a term associated with a political identity like "gay male" but a social category with limited options for agency, which in the popular imagination are in the realms of sex, beautification, and aesthetic creation. *Bakla* are seen as being especially prominent in careers associated with the arts or beauty: the movies, dance, fashion design, hairdressing, and so on. Whitam points out how Imelda Marcos employed prominent fashion designers who were well-known *bakla*; the point to be made here is the public association of *bakla* with the creation of appearances and artificiality, even at the highest level of society and power. This association is due not to any innate or socially bred talents for the entertainment and beauty industry that *bakla* may be seen as possessing collectively, but the conception of a *bakla* as being not what he appears to be: he is a man who is a woman. The circumscription of this identity, the limits of tolerance for this "third sex," can be seen with the existence of the masculine *bakla*, "the cassowary (anomalous category) in the Philippine taxonomy of sexual behavior. . . . It is not true that the Filipino public is disinterested with the masculine *bakla*. There is no social discourse by which to discuss these kinds of 'men.' These *bakla* are met either with puzzlement or suspicion" ("Speaking of AIDS" 198). In other words, a man who looks like a man and acts like a man and also prefers men is someone who confuses the heterosexual object-choice dichotomy in Filipino popular perceptions of sexual behavior. The so-called third sex option to describe *bakla* actually is not a third sex in terms of being able to imagine a distinction between gendered behavior and sexual object-choice.

One of the other potential ways by which *bakla* undermine the social and sexual categories that they find themselves in is through mimicry. Even in the early moments of U.S. colonialism, American observers noted the Filipino capacity for mimicry. Maj. Frank S. Bourns of the U.S. colonial army declares: "They are natural imitators; it is a racial characteristic" (quoted in Rafael 198).[8] But even if this characteristic of Filipino imitation were true, imitation is not in itself a negative trait, as Fenella Cannel argues in a study of *bakla* in Bicol and their imitative performances of American culture. These performances both appropriate some of the symbolic capital associated with possessing American culture, in terms either of goods or style, and acknowledge the impossibility of owning that culture in rural Bicol. As the writings of Homi Bhabha and Sui Sin Far in chapter 1 have shown us, however, mimicry itself, even in its colonial pejorative use, can have a subversive effect upon colonial authority. What the mimic shows to the colonizer is the inevitably partial nature of identity. For colonizers, the paradox is the fact that Filipinos are perceived as essentially imitative—there is no "identity" as such there.[9] The Filipino transvestite, then, is a mimic among mimics, an imitator par excellence, which can have an unsettling effect upon notions of gender identity itself. According to Judith Butler (*Gender Trouble*), when the transvestite has the power to present appearance as identity and to show that identity is only appearance, as when a man can pass as a woman, s/he effectively destroys the boundaries between man and woman.[10] *State of War* demonstrates that the queer subject can disrupt in this and other ways as well, threatening also the heterosexual order and the state's representation of itself as a product of anticolonial heterosexual romance. When the revolutionaries start their attack upon the Commander's soldiers in the plaza at K—, the transvestites lift their skirts to reveal shotguns. The illusion of the *bakla* as being "only" a woman is ripped away with the appearance of the hidden shotgun, and a government soldier describes the scene with a combination of fear and hilarity. The soldier realizes that the *bakla* is, in effect, "really" a man because s/he has intruded him/herself into the heterosexual, homophobic discourse of state and revolutionary politics—this is a cause for fear. It is cause for hilarity because, as Mary Ann Doane says, "Male transvestism is an occasion for laughter . . . it's understandable why women would want to be men but not vice versa" (48).

There is another way to imagine this spectacle as a subversive act, however, by focusing on its nature as theatrical. The conventional theatrical presentation of *bakla* transvestism is in the form of popular cross-dressing pageants, as well as in film depictions and in everyday cross-dressing. As Manalansan notes, "The spectacle of the cross-dressed *bakla* has been woven into the social fabric" ("Speaking of AIDS" 198). The *bakla* as transvestite self-consciously performs for the sake of an audience, whether it happens to be in a theater or on the street: the spectacle accommodates homosexuality even as it makes it an object of societywide amusement. What happens on the island of K—, however, is that the transvestites are performing a political theater that operates at a level of ironic mimicry that only they recognize. Their performance approximates Augusto Boal's conception of an invisible theater, which "consists of the presentation of a scene in an environment other than the theater. . . . The people who witness the scene are those who are there by chance. During the spectacle, these people must not have the slightest idea that it is a 'spectacle,' for this would make them 'spectators'" (143–44).[11] It is precisely because transvestites are regarded as an acceptable "third sex" in Philippine society that they are able to achieve a completely different effect from the transvestites in Western society as theorized by Butler. At the festival, the transvestites appropriate their own spectacle, making the soldiers the unknowing participants in another spectacle altogether, in which the soldiers themselves are the unwitting performers in a revolutionary theater. Although guerrilla theater already has a different meaning, one might say that this is truly guerrilla theater, since in guerrilla warfare it is always the conventional soldier who is the unknowing spectator in a drama not of his own making. The transvestites thus effectively answer the problem of how to stage a spectacle when one is already a spectacle—already "out of the closet"—and they do it by exploiting the illusion that there is nothing under their skirts, that they are nothing but imitators. Here the transvestites, like any good trickster, turn their perceived limitations into literal weapons of the weak: in short, behind the spectacle and the imitation there is the potential of actual threat.[12] In the domestic queer practices of the Philippines, the transvestites find the resources to stage a sexual and political revolution that is not dependent upon Western models of queer liberation.

THE NOVEL AS HOLLYWOOD MELODRAMA

This unconventional and unique approach to antiauthoritarian resistance found in State of War may be compared with the approach in Dogeaters, which is also based on the acceptance and exploitation of the spectacular. These features of the spectacle are integral to the very nature of the commodities that rule the Philippines in Hagedorn's novel. Hagedorn's postmodern vision of the Philippines is one in which everything and everyone is either for sale or in the circuit of the production and consumption of commodities. In Dogeaters, the problematic of commodification and sexuality finds its center in the world of film and its various locations of expression: the movie theater, the film industry, the star cults, the entire "intertextual" apparatus in which the moviegoer is inserted and from which the moviegoer as spectator derives meaning from particular films and stars.[13] The world of film, with its dependency on the "ideology of the spectacle and spectacular," as Thomas Elsaesser calls it (78), is but the most explicit manifestation of an entire society that feeds upon that ideology. The ideology of the spectacle and the spectacular is designed to market the commodity, enforce its mysteriousness (i.e., fetishize it, obscure the social relations that brought it into existence), and to the greatest extent possible persuade its audience that the commodity-as-spectacle can guarantee happiness.

Hagedorn's *Dogeaters* addresses the ideology of the spectacle in both form and content, through a complex adaptation and parody of the Hollywood melodrama. The melodrama, with its emphasis on bourgeois life, romantic love, compulsory heterosexuality, emotional extremism, coincidences and contradictions, Manichean moral oppositions, forced happy endings, and commodity fetishism, is an appropriate genre in which to address the pretensions, pitfalls, and real dangers of the Filipino elite and middle class. In addition, the melodrama, with its focus on female "problems," female stars, and female audiences, was the genre that made most explicit the connection between cinematic spectacle and the marketing of commodities. In other words, the female star of the Hollywood melodrama presented a particular vision of what woman should be, in terms of appearance, dress, and behavior, all of which were aided by the use of various purchasable items: makeup, clothing, hairstyles, and so on. Melodrama therefore made explicit the relationship between film as an industry and the commodity as the basis for an entire mode of production. It did this through its use of film to market the image of the star, with all her attendant and necessary trappings, as a commodity package to an audience that was there to consume not only the film as narrative but also the film as marketing pitch.[14] *Dogeaters* alludes to Hollywood melodrama from the beginning, when we are introduced to Rio and Pucha as they watch Douglas Sirk's *All That Heaven Allows*, starring Rock Hudson and Jane Wyman, in 1956.[15] By the next chapter, the narrative has shifted gears to a time period that we understand to be in the 1980s. At the center of this contemporary narrative is Joey Sands, a homosexual prostitute and orphan who is the offspring of a Filipina prostitute and a black GI. As Mark Chiang argues, we can understand Joey's narrative to be the story told by Rio; we can even imagine Joey's story as a film, considering that Rio's primary childhood ambition was to be a filmmaker ("All That History Allows"). The fact that the novel opens with Rio as a rapt spectator of one of the greatest Hollywood melodramas then serves as a clue that we should read the events of the internal narrative that feature Joey as melodrama.[16]

Melodrama is part of the historical period and style known as classical (Hollywood) cinema and shares most of the basic narrative and stylistic features of that cinema, including a dependence upon a certain kind of spectator and a plot of heterosexual romance with (delayed) consummation.[17] *Dogeaters* demonstrates not only that melodramatic spectacle is tied to the marketing of the commodity but also that heterosexual romance is a part of this spectacle; subsequently, the novel appropriately places queer sexuality at the center of the revolution, a move that undermines the heterosexual romance that is an integral part of the cinematic spectacle to which Filipino audiences are subjected. The fact that the Filipino society of *Dogeaters* as a whole is a "society of the spectacle," to borrow Guy Debord's term, means that the novel's gesture against a certain kind of consuming spectatorship has a wider political relevance. In purely cinematic terms, *Dogeaters*'s use of melodrama to address the problems of spectacle and spectatorship is appropriate because melodrama has critically complicated the most dominant theoretical approach to spectatorship, which is one based on psychoanalytic feminism. This approach is typified by Laura Mulvey's immensely influential and controversial 1975 article, "Visual Pleasure and Narrative Cinema," which argued that the spectator's gaze was inherently masculine and directed at the feminine object of desire on the screen. As numerous critics subsequent to Mulvey have argued, the female spectator is left in an impossible position.[18] Mulvey's analysis, predicated as it is on the operations of classic cinema, is challenged by melodrama because of the fact that melodrama is marketed primarily toward female audiences and features female characters. This well-noted fact that concerns melodrama specifically is supplemented by Jackie Stacey's general claim that "historically, it has been the female spectator who has been of most interest to the cinema and other related industries" (85). It is not an accident, therefore, that most of the characters in *Dogeaters* are women, as Rachel Lee points out (81, 147).[19] Even Joey, the primary male character, is feminized, much in the same way that Rock Hudson's character of Ron Kirby in *All That Heaven Allows* is feminized through being the object of the camera and the female characters' gaze. Most important, melodrama as Hagedorn has staged it in the Philippines raises questions about how ethnicity, culture, and class, in addition to gender, problematize Mulvey's idealized and unitary model of spectatorship. Even in the first chapter, *Dogeaters* self-consciously stages the problem of defining the spectator as a unitary being, in its contrast of Rio's and Pucha's reactions to Jane Wyman and Rock Hudson. Rio identifies with Wyman; Pucha identifies with the masculine gaze that Mulvey proposes and bemoans the Hudson character's choice of Wyman, whom even Rio describes as having a "soft putty face" (Hagedorn 3). Later, outside of the theater, Pucha takes pleasure in being ogled by a group of boys; Rio is disgusted by Pucha's acquiescence to her own objectification, recognizing implicitly Pucha's "impossible position" in both being the object of the masculine gaze and identifying with that gaze.

Hagedorn's novel therefore establishes the initial premise that the spectator is always multiply situated. However, the heterogeneous spectator in the Philippines is also always in a subaltern position in her relationship to Hollywood cinema and the global capitalism that it represents. This echoes Tadiar's argument that the Philippines vis-à-vis global capital is always in a feminized position, regardless of differences internal to the Philippines itself. The subaltern spectator, by virtue of this gendered position, becomes in many ways an ideal Hollywood consumer due to material differences between metropolitan Hollywood and (neo)colonial Philippines. These material differences center on Hollywood's status as a primary factor in the export of U.S commodities and consumerist attitudes and as a primary technical site of ideological interpellation.[20] As Stacey argues,

In the same way that women are both subjects and objects of relations of looking, they can also be seen as both products and consumers of commodity exchange. . . . The work of femininity, then, requires the consumption of commodities. However, it not only involves consumption, both of images and of products, but also the negotiations of a feminine identity in a culture where women are both subjects and objects of commodity exchange. (8–9)

As a formula, this statement can apply equally well to Filipino women. Hagedorn illustrates this with the opening chapter, wherein she also makes explicit the essentially middle-class, interiorized nature of melodrama and the reliance upon heterosexual romance. In this opening chapter, Rio and Pucha watch the unlikely and socially condemned romance of lower-class Ron (Rock Hudson) and upper-class Carey (Jane Wyman) unfold. Their romance is a "miscegenation between classes" (Stern 120), which is set in two contrasting environments, Carey's life in her middle-class home and Ron's Walden-like existence in a mill that borders on a pond. Eventually, Carey succumbs to social pressure from friends and children and gives up Ron, only to find that the children for whom she has sacrificed herself have already started drifting away.[21] Yet she cannot bring herself to return to Ron. Suddenly an accident befalls Ron: he falls from a cliff, and Carey is summoned to his bedside, where she swears to take care of the now-helpless Ron. The run-down mill in which Ron lives has been transformed during the course of the film by Ron into a gorgeous, lush rural parody of Thoreau's spare hut, in anticipation of his marriage to Carey. Ron and Carey are thus reunited in another version of the middle-class house that Carey has fled, and Carey has left one patriarchal bind (her socially stratified widowhood) to enter another as wife and caretaker.

This film, remarkable as all of Sirk's major melodramas are for their combination of standard melodramatic formula with exposure of bourgeois contradictions, serves as a historical, thematic, and plot touchstone for Dogeaters.[22] On a historical level, Dogeaters' use of the film ironically exploits the figure of Rock Hudson, a male sex symbol who was secretly homosexual. The heterosexual masculinity he modeled for audiences was therefore a performance, although no less real to these audiences for being so. In the Philippine movie industry of the 1980s that Dogeaters depicts, the performance of heterosexual masculinity by gay men continues in the figures of the movie stars Nestor Norales and Tito Alvarez. They project images of both heterosexuality and cultural normality through their films, yet in their personal lives they are not only gay but also participants in the literally murderous intrigues and gossip of the political elites, who know their closeted secret. Behind the pristine and heterosexual images produced by the Filipino film industry, therefore, there is a sordid life that connects the secret sexuality of the movie stars with the corruption of those in control of the film industry in particular and the Filipino political economy in general. Dogeaters depicts the Philippines of the 1980s as a melodramatic world where a huge cast of characters, good and evil, are shown to be connected in a convoluted plot that centers on the systemic relations among money, sex, film, and the marketing of commodities. The novel in a sense "outs" this world, making clear what the fetishism of the commodity makes mysterious and what the cinematic image helps to obscure: the social relations between human beings, as they are mediated by the commodity.

Thematically, *Dogeaters* is deeply concerned with this world of the commodity and its obfuscation to consumers, and through the use of literally confining spaces the novel demonstrates the confining nature of consciousnesses obsessed by commodities. *All That Heaven Allows* becomes important again when *Dogeaters* refers to the film's use of an interior/exterior contrast, between lush middle-class interiors and the healthy outdoors, as symbolic of the bourgeois life and its bohemian counterpart. As Elsaesser has argued, the closed domestic arena of the melodrama, especially in contrast to the open space of the American western, leads to a vastly different set of choices and range of action for a film's characters. In the closed space, there is an "intensified symbolisation of everyday actions" (79) and a focus upon and fetishization of household commodities in which most of the story takes place. Likewise in *Dogeaters*, there is an intense focus on interior spaces, their sensual experience, and the claustrophobic presence of commodities: in the movie theater, in darkened bedrooms, in country clubs, in mansions, in torture chambers. The crucial revolutionary movement for key characters is chronicled as both an awakening from the induced sleep (literal or otherwise) of the movie theater and the female bedroom and the movement from confined spaces to open ones. Joey, for example, witnesses the government-sanctioned murder of opposition leader Senator Avila at the entryway to a posh hotel and must escape to the mountains with the revolutionaries he stumbles into.[23] Daisy Avila, former beauty queen who spends much of the novel weeping and sleeping in her bedroom, finally awakens and joins the same revolutionaries in the mountains. The crucial chapter of their revolutionary awareness is titled "Terrain," echoing Elsaesser's suggestion that in the open terrain of the western and in the revolutionary epic characters can find a range of exteriorized choices. They can, in short, enter into the open, public sphere and contend with the state, versus the private life of the family and the fetishized commodity.[24]

Even more crucial than this movement from interior to exterior is another theme-and-plot touchstone that *Dogeaters* finds in *All That Heaven Allows*, the heterosexual romance, which is a feature of classical cinema in general and melodrama in particular. As David Bordwell summarizes the issue, "unmotivated or inadequate plot resolutions" lead to the "importance of the plot line involving heterosexual romance," which resolves the problem that arises around the fact that the "classical ending is not all that structurally decisive, being a more or less arbitrary readjustment of that world knocked awry in the previous eighty minutes" ("Classical Hollywood Cinema" 21). In *Dogeaters*, the Ron/Carey relationship is alluded to in the relationship between Joey and Daisy Avila. Joey and Daisy are almost engaged in a "miscegenation between classes" (Stern 120), in terms both of their economic status and their racial status: Daisy is a light-skinned beauty queen, daughter of the elites, and Joey is a mestizo prostitute. Like Ron and Carey, they also fit into the divisions of younger man/older woman and social outcast/social insider. Joey and Daisy's transgression is not sexual but instead political, as two socially diametrical characters joined in the cause of revolution. While in *All That Heaven Allows* the heroine is returned to the bourgeois home made for her by the hero, in *Dogeaters* both hero and heroine break out into the open, the terrain of the jungle where the revolution is being plotted. The novel states that "they are together all the time. She teaches him how to use a gun" (233). The revolutionary romance of the man and the woman fleeing together to join the mission of overthrow and construction becomes subverted here through the presence of Joey's homosexuality and Daisy's single status. Joey's homosexuality and Daisy's single status become politically significant because of their insertion into the phallic, heterosexist romance of nationalist revolution, in which the successful revolution becomes a marriage between the liberated nation and state.

Dogeaters' vision of revolution undercuts both the heterosexual melodrama of Filipino society, which finds a reflection of itself in classical cinema, and the heterosexual themes of classic revolution, which extend into the formation of a postcolonial state. M. Jacqui Alexander suggests that in the postcolonial state homosexuality and other forms of "nonheteronormative" sexuality are considered improper:

> Heterosexuality promotes order while homosexuality, its antithesis, promotes chaos or the very dissolution of the natural. What is suggested is that some interest might intervene to establish order out of chaos. The state is one such interest, which rules by normalizing chaotic relations, and in this instance does so through a set of narrowly crafted notions of morality that informs its gestures. The significance here is that it sets the stage for . . . repressive state rule. (141)

Joey's insertion into the revolution is therefore troubling to this conception of the state in two senses, as something that "perverts" the nationalist romance and as something that might be necessary for purging upon the successful completion of the revolution. By ending Joey's narrative with his revolutionary conversion, Hagedorn endorses the first option and suspends the second option, thereby presenting the possibility of political revolution as a sexual revolution also.

QUEERING THE NATION

Both *Dogeaters* and *State of War* recognize that struggles for the state usually depend upon narratives of heterosexual romance to represent themselves. In both novels, there is a clear recognition that the antistate revolution is a necessity, but both novels also seize upon the chance to rewrite that revolution's narrative as well, staging, in effect, a sexual revolution. At the same time, both novels are troubled by the knowledge that revolutions usually depend also upon narratives that are as total as the ones used by the states to which they are opposed. As a result, both novels are undercut by varying degrees of ambivalence toward conclusive narrative of any sorts, including their own. Caroline S. Hau and Nerissa Balce-Cortes both note the metafictional quality of *Dogeaters*, the way in which the veracity of Rio's story about Joey is placed into doubt by the penultimate chapter, titled "Pucha," in which the much-maligned Pucha finally gets her say, stating that Rio's facts are greatly awry. Even Rio herself is shown ironically in her last chapter, imagining herself and her brother Raul as "nocturnal moths . . . drawn to the same silent tableau: a mysterious light. . . . We flap and beat our wings in our futile attempt to reach what surely must be heaven" (247). Obviously, Rio is not aware that "heaven" in this metaphor is also death for the moth. With its use of metafiction and other postmodern techniques *Dogeaters* creates a narrative about the spectacle and the commodity that is appealing to American audiences reared on those techniques and who may associate the Philippines with the spectacular consumption of commodities. At the same time, the novel's flexible strategy of using postmodern techniques to speak to an American audience simultaneously limits its ability to narrate with the certainty about future possibility that is fundamental to revolution.

In contrast, *State of War* integrates the ambiguity of its transvestites' identities with this necessary certainty. The transvestites are initially a symbol of illusion and passing, but this is destroyed by the revelation of the shotguns hidden under their skirts; this revelation demonstrates that the revolution, even as it exploits ambiguity, must fall back on the hard certainty of armed confrontation. This armed confrontation is necessary if the revolution is to destroy the illusions created by the government. In this regard, the revolution's most outstanding achievement before the battle at the festival takes place when the revolutionaries explode a warehouse full of dead government soldiers. The state's attempt to hide away the bodies of its own soldiers—the material testimony to an illusory war—is forced into the open by the revolutionaries, who send body parts flying all over the city. The explosion sends "limbs, heads, torsos zooming like torpedoes through the air . . . to skid along tables, demolishing the dinners of the unwary; to settle on sofas among the living who were watching television; to snuggle on the bedsheets, disturbing lovers . . ." (Rosca 113). The war between the neocolonial state and the revolutionary forces is waged around illusions, around propaganda and guerrilla warfare, but the necessity for certainty in order to stage action is embodied in these dead bodies and the phallic shotguns of the transvestites. While the representation of the transvestites forms the novel's flexible strategy, which exploits Western notions of queer visibility as political resistance, the dead bodies represent the novel's commitment to making readers confront the gruesome consequences of dictatorship.

The certainty of action that is called for by the revolutionaries' exploitation of the dead bodies is offset by the recognition that the war for meaning—the war over representation—is inherently contradictory in its attempt to assert control over that which is subject to interpretation. Characters like Adrian seek to grasp all of history, to know the totality of their own family line or even themselves. Their desire will be forever frustrated. The conclusion of the novel, then, is telling. Anna reunites the bastardized family lines of the two main families featured in the novel, the Banyagas and the Villaverdes, in the figure of her son Ismael Villaverde Banyaga. This naming of her son gestures at that hope for unity and the wholeness of a circle as the Banyagas and the Villaverdes, the two bastard lines of an unnamed Spanish friar, are reunited. This unification is undercut by the fact that Ismael is fated to become a story-teller, who "would remember, his name being a history unto itself" (Rosca 382). Storytelling and the narration of history will always be gestures of desire. The revolution must seek out the certainty of representation in order to make possible the act of revolution, even as it is aware that representation is a matter of interpretation, as the dictatorial use of propaganda on the part of the Commander and his cronies make clear. The revolution, in other words, must attempt to grasp or project totalizing meaning even as it remembers who else seeks totalizing meaning and representation.

Besides the dictatorial regime of the martial-law Philippines, another one of those totalizing agents of history is the United States itself. The United States has constructed a nationalist romance about itself, one of the components being its exceptional nature as a nonimperial, pro-democratic society. To expose U.S. involvement in the Philippines is, metaphorically, to queer this nationalist romance. This process of queering the American romance has implications for Americans, obviously, but also for Filipinos in the United States and Asian Americans as a whole. What has been forgotten in the national romance is the presence of the Filipinos within the United States itself and the fact that a colonial war was fought over the Philippines. E. San Juan Jr. laments how Filipinos, soon to become the largest component of the Asian American population, are nevertheless one of its most silent constituencies: "We are here, but somehow it's still a secret" (*Racial Formations/Critical Transformations* 117).

The foregrounding of the Filipino presence in both the United States and its history has the potential for three dramatic consequences, according to Oscar Campomanes and San Juan. The first is its impact on the self-representation of the United States as a democratically exceptional nation that is somehow removed from the era of colonialism. The historical difficulty for Americans in remembering the extent and nature of American involvement in the Philippines has everything to do with how "un-American" certain colonial policies were.[25] This also has ramifications for Asian Americans, who oftentimes participate in and agree with American nationalism and are therefore subject to the same historical amnesia. Campomanes argues that the literature of Filipinos in the United States can be understood as diametrically opposed to the assimilationist,

nationalist narrative that typically undergirds most Asian immigrant literatures and their reception by Asian American literary critics ("Filipinos in the
United States"). The assimilation narrative is fundamental to the vision of
Americanization and cultural pluralism that is at the heart of most (Asian)
American histories, literary and otherwise.[26] The alternative model Campomanes proposes is that of the exile, who occupies a place of "displacement, suspension, and perspective" in a land with which he or she has an ambivalent relationship ("Filipinos in the United States" 51).[27]

The second consequence is for Filipinos, both in the Philippines and in the
United States. While many Filipinos may remember the military and economic
imperialism of the United States, they may overlook the more long-lasting,
more damaging effects of U.S. intervention. These include the legacy of colonial
education, the U.S. support for Marcos, and the mental colonization of Filipinos
by U.S. cultural imperialism. The pervasiveness of the contemporary U.S. presence in the Philippines leads Campomanes to argue that "Americanization for
Filipinos does not so much as commence at the point of arrival in American soil
as it does from the point of departure itself" ("Afterword" 147). This continuity
of experience for Filipinos, from their time in the homeland to their immigration and settlement in the United States, signifies the arbitrary and provisional
nature of the national boundary that separates the United States and the Philippines. As San Juan puts it, Filipinos "have challenged the asymmetrical cartog-
raphy of metropolis and colony, core and periphery" ("In Search of Filipino
Writing" 214).

The third consequence of bringing Filipinos and the Philippines into
American history follows upon this recognition of an arbitrary national boundary. This boundary does not prevent the possibility of the diasporic Filipino returning home to a place from which he or she can never be completely severed.
This return is in its less important sense a physical one, although the capacity of
(certain groups of) people to traverse the globe almost at will is a fundamental
feature of the world system, what Arjun Appadurai calls the "ethnoscape" of
population flow and what James Clifford calls "traveling cultures." More crucial
to the historical representation of Filipinos is the discursive return engaged in
by writers and thinkers of all disciplines. In Hagedorn's and Rosca's novels, the
return to the homeland is not the return to paradise, utopia, or precolonial purity. Instead, it is a return to a place damaged irrevocably by the legacies of a
colonialism and anticolonialism narrated through images of heterosexual romance and conflict. These legacies endure in the postcolonial regime of dictatorship, which uses the language of an abusive love for its citizens. In these novels,
we can read the signs of that abuse in the bodies of the tortured and in the bodies of transvestites and homosexuals who defy the disciplinary rule of a dictatorial regime.

CONCLUSION

Model Minorities and Bad Subjects

The concept of a dictatorial regime and its relationship to Asian Americans can be found not only in the context of American imperialism and its support for overseas authoritarian regimes. As Michael Omi and Howard Winant argue, the United States and its domestic policies toward people of color can be conceived of as a "racial dictatorship" for a period that extends from 1790 to 1964, or the overwhelming majority of the nation's history (66). In 1790, the franchise was restricted to free white males, and the last provisions of legislated discrimination were not removed from the nation's laws until the 1964 Civil Rights Act. Frank Chin argues that for Asian Americans the result of living under racial oppression was the internalization of dominant society's perceptions of Asian Americans as generally docile and submissive, especially in comparison to the seemingly more recalcitrant African American and Latino populations. Asian Americans then became the objects of "racist love," versus "racist hate," because they had, by the 1960s and 1970s, accepted their place as a model minority subservient to whites. Unlike the stereotype of the yellow peril, which is resolutely negative and therefore easily rejected by those who are labeled with it, the sterotype of the model minority is regarded by Asian American intellectuals as insidious precisely because of its ability to be internalized by Asian Americans. Even more than the stereotype of the yellow peril, then, this specter of the model minority haunts contemporary Asian American intellectuals, who prefer to see themselves and the objects of their critical inquiry as bad subjects.

Model minorities are good subjects, those who, according to Louis Althusser, "'work by themselves' in the vast majority of cases," or adhere to the dominant ideology of their society without being aware of their adherence (181). The bad subjects reject dominant ideology (although that does not mean they are free from ideology itself) and "on occasion provoke the intervention of one of the detachments of the (repressive) State apparatus," such as the police (181). The bad subject, as the dominant form of the Asian American body politic in the imagination of Asian American intellectuals, becomes the organizing sign that Asian American intellectuals use to guide their excavation of the past and interpretation of the present. I will not argue for whether or not a bad subject truly exists; I will demonstrate instead how the bad subject as sign motivates a discourse that is fundamental to Asian American intellectuals. For Asian American intellectuals, the various forms taken by the body politic that this book has explored can in the end be interpreted as collectively reinforcing the discourse of a bad subject created by both enforced condition and voluntary choice. This retrospective collectivization of Asian American experience is at least partially a function of the fact that Asian American intellectuals inhabit what Pierre Bourdieu calls the economic world reversed, where value is determined not by financial capital but, in this case, by a symbolic capital that derives its worth from the idea of political resistance and social change.

I argue that Asian American intellectuals have created a discourse of the bad subject that not only rejects what David Palumbo-Liu calls model minority discourse but also disavows the model minority status of many Asian American intellectuals themselves (395–416). If, in Palumbo-Liu's characterization, model minority discourse's primary role is to suture the racialized individual back into dominant American culture as healed and whole consumer and producer, the discourse of the bad subject's primary role is to prevent that suture, demonstrating the fractures and ruptures of American culture in regard to racial and other inequities. If model minority discourse tends to idealize the model minority, the discourse of the bad subject responds by tending to idealize the bad subject, ignoring the contradictions and excesses that make the bad subject amenable to discipline by dominant society. Thus Asian American intellectuals often implicitly posit model minority discourse and the discourse of the bad subject as a binary, although in what follows I hope to demonstrate their mutual interdependency. Asian Americans can frequently occupy both situations simultaneously or, at the very least, alternate between them, as realized perhaps most graphically in the role of the panethnic entrepreneur. In this chapter, I turn to two different ways in which the discourse of the bad subject forms, first in Cynthia Kadohata's *In the Heart of the Valley of Love* and then in the relationship between Theresa Hak Kyung Cha's *Dictee* and the critical anthology *Writing Self, Writing Nation*. I conclude with a reading of Lois-Ann Yamanaka's trilogy of novels set in Hawai'i. The trilogy not only troubles the image of Asian Americans as a bad subject in a variety of ways, in particular complicating the distinction between the bad subject and the model minority, but also brings into question the very definition of Asian American identity. In all three cases, we continue to see the persistence of bodily representations in expressing the relationship of the Asian American body politic to the larger American body politic.

Ultimately, I wish to demonstrate how the discourse of the bad subject both enables and disables, through the process of idealization, the very type of political activity that it seeks to encourage and uncover. In other words, an idealistic construction of the Asian American body politic, even if it is ultimately inaccurate through its denial of the ideological heterogeneity of Asian America and even if it does fundamentally alter the vision of Asian American intellectuals by predisposing them to examine the past and the present for signs of resistance, does allow for political mobilization, unification, and action to take place, in the short term. In the long term, however, the inaccuracy that is inherent in the discourse of the bad subject prevents Asian American intellectuals from recognizing the ability of late capitalism to transform Asian American racial identity into a commodity and Asian America into a niche market for that commodity. Given that Asian American intellectuals are generally predisposed to be critical of capitalism because of its exploitation of racial minorities, the working class, and the poor, this inability to recognize how capitalism can transform the very basis of Asian American intellectual work—founded upon race as a resistant identity—constitutes a fundamental problem for both intellectual inquiry and political leadership. This problem of idealization and misrecognition constitutes the most important limit of Asian American intellectual work; by the end of this chapter, I will demonstrate how idealization and misrecognition result in a disavowed essentialism of racial identity and an unintentional repetition of ideological domination, where Asian American intellectuals seek to interpellate others even as we resist dominant society's attempts to interpellate us. If these are the intellectual limits of our contemporary mode of practice, which become expressed in a particular representation of Asian America, they are inextricably related with the limits of Asian America itself, our object of study and our place of work. These limits stem from the implicit pluralism found in contemporary constructions of Asian American identity, the commodification of that racial identity, the ideological heterogeneity of a diverse Asian American population, and the willingness of a considerable portion of that population to participate in and perpetuate such commodification and the social and economic practices that lead to it. Ultimately, Asian American intellectuals have to consider the possibility that we need to look beyond Asian America in order to address the goals of social and economic justice that were so important to our predecessors and, presumably, remain important to ourselves.[1]

THE MODEL MINORITY THESIS

To characterize the entire history of dominant representations of Asian Americans through the category of the model minority is, to a certain extent, ahistorical, given that the category itself did not come into existence under that name until 1966 and the publication of an article in *U.S. News & World Report*, which praised the accomplishments of Japanese and Chinese Americans, especially considering the racism that they had endured, and explicitly compared them favorably to African Americans.[2] For *U.S. News & World Report*, "the model minority" is a positive label to describe a well-adjusted minority population. While the category of the model minority has a particular historical specificity relevant to the post–civil rights era, the idea of Asian Americans functioning as a de facto model minority has deep historical roots, traceable at least to the nineteenth-century deployment of Chinese laborers as strikebreakers used against unruly white laborers in the North and recalcitrant black laborers in the South.[3] The emergence of Asian Americans as a de facto model minority in the nineteenth century constitutes a minor aspect of Asian American existence during the period of racial dictatorship; the major aspect was certainly one of being the objects of racist hate, versus racist love. Nevertheless, the historical functions of Asian Americans as a model minority in the past and present are similar and important to stress. Asian American intellectuals have generally come to a consensus regarding this historical function and its ideological import, what I will call here the *model minority thesis*, to distinguish such a position from the one held by others who simply accept the Asian American as a model minority at face value.

In the model minority thesis, the model minority works as a buffer between whites and blacks, who are separated by not only racial difference but a related class antagonism as well. Assuming that blacks are in general economically underprivileged as a whole and also economically disadvantaged as a racially differentiated segment when they are in the same class with whites, the thesis argues that the racial and class antagonism of blacks toward the structure of domination that favors whites is deflected at crucial moments toward Asian Americans through the model minority. The structure of domination that favors whites and is controlled by them positions Asian Americans as a minority that can succeed without government or social assistance, through sheer hard work and perseverance based upon a system of social values that prioritizes family, education, and sacrifice. These social values that all Asian Americans reputedly share, often referred to as Confucian, accurately or otherwise, also prioritize obedience and hierarchy, which means that Asian Americans are reluctant to blame others for any lack in their social position and are willing to accept their social position with gratitude. Asian Americans are therefore a model minority because they demonstrate to other minorities what can be achieved through self-reliance rather than government assistance, self-sacrifice rather than self-interest, and quiet restraint rather than vocal complaint in the face of perceived or actual injustice.[4]

Ideologically, the model minority becomes a scapegoat, drawing the ire of other minorities for the systemic inequities that they experience. The exploitation of Korean American small-business owners by politicians, police, and the media during the Los Angeles riots to absorb African American and Latino rage and characterize that rage as the jealousy of the have-nots is an enduring example of the ideological process that the model minority thesis critiques.[5] This ideological analysis of the function of Asian Americans in the race-class schema of American life differs, of course, from the subjective perspective of many Asian Americans who may indeed see themselves as a model minority from the perspective of the dominant class—in other words, accepting the positive attributes of the model minority while rejecting the ideological critique. These Asian Americans, who for want of a better term may be called neoconservatives, do not see themselves as existing in a state of false consciousness, as a class that is not aware of itself as a class, which is arguably the way proponents of the model minority thesis might see them. Asian American neoconservatives are, as Glenn Omatsu aptly labels them, "strange and new political animals" with whom mainstream Asian American intellectuals have difficulty reconciling themselves (42). To complicate matters further, even as Asian American neoconservatives disagree with much of mainstream Asian American intellectual leadership on political and economic issues, they do not necessarily accept the label thrust upon them as being insensitive to the racial and class dynamics of American society and the problems of economic and social inequity that hinder the attainment of a harmonious American pluralism.[6]

There is ambivalence and conflict, therefore, at the heart of the model minority's representation, disagreements over how to interpret the success Asian Americans have seemed to attain in the years since the 1964 Civil Rights Act and the 1965 Immigration and Naturalization Act. This ambivalence and conflict over the success of Asian Americans permeates the literature of Asian Americans, especially the literature that is most visible on the general landscape of American culture. While few Asian American writers demonstrate the enthusiasm for the conception of Asian Americans as a model minority that is found in its most naked terms in publications such as the U.S. News & World Report article, many writers take some of the model minority's aspects for granted as the formal foundation of their literature. "Success," for example, is one of the basic building blocks of mainstream Asian American literature, "mainstream" being defined as that which is most likely to be read by non-

Asian American readers and critics. The idea that first-generation Asian Americans sacrifice for their children and that these children are more assimilated and economically better off than their parents is almost universal in this type of literature—not necessarily as part of an argument the authors wish to explicitly advance but as a part of the cultural background and assumption against which the primary action takes place. The most notable type of primary action that is produced from this background is that of generational conflict and cultural difference, which, as Lisa Lowe argues, have become key signifiers of Asian American literature (*Immigrant Acts* 60–83). "Success" is certainly the most visible evidence of the conjuncture between the model minority and the American Dream, and just as the American Dream has generated a wide degree of ambivalence in American cultural productions, so has the model minority generated ambivalence in Asian American cultural productions. The key themes of the model minority—self-reliance versus government assistance, self-sacrifice versus self-interest, and quiet restraint versus vocal complaint in the face of perceived or actual injustice—can all be found in the mainstream literature as moments of conflict for the central characters.

David Palumbo-Liu cites *The Woman Warrior* and *The Joy Luck Club* as two texts that embody what he calls model minority discourse. This discourse is "an ideological construct not coextensive with the texts themselves, but rather a mode of apprehending, decoding, recoding, and producing Asian American narratives" (Palumbo-Liu 396).[7] Even if model minority discourse is not coextensive with the texts themselves, Palumbo-Liu goes on to show that as a matter of fact model minority discourse can be read from the texts and not simply from the popular and academic critical discourse that is wedded to the texts, given that the authors presumably are a part of "apprehending, decoding, recoding and producing" not only Asian American narratives but also the model minority narrative itself. Palumbo-Liu's conception of model minority discourse expands upon the ideological critique found in the model minority thesis. For Palumbo-Liu, this discourse is a mode of healing, and the injury in question is the damage done to minorities by the nation through racism and cultural (in)difference. These injuries are manifest in the dilemmas of racial and cultural identity that the protagonists find themselves enmeshed in, and the healing or resolution undertaken is inevitably individual and psychological: "The logic of model minority discourse argues that an inward adjustment is necessary for the suture of the ethnic subject into an optimal position within the dominant culture" (397). Therefore, "the pedagogical function of model minority discourse is its most significant aspect" (408). Pedagogically, model minority discourse serves to instruct readers that the individual is the appropriate resource to draw upon for resolving the disjuncture the individual may feel between his or her personal identity and the identity of the nation. The conception of individualism that is so important to standard narratives of the American nation is thus reaffirmed through model minority discourse, which absolves the nation of its responsibility for the individual's fate.

The fact that the discourse is a mode of interpretation on the part of both authors and readers is critical to stress, for by doing so we can see the assumptions that underlie the discourse. Possibly the most basic assumption is the one that Palumbo-Liu identifies as the reified identity crisis (413), or the assumption that all Asian Americans actually do suffer from a cultural damage that needs to be healed. This crisis ironically stems from the excess of success mentioned earlier, a success that seems to sever or damage human relations, resulting in the fetishization of material objects as compensation (this is *reification*); identity itself, however, can also become one such object, as can a crisis of identity. Many works of Asian American literature center upon this identity crisis, and within the literary market the identity crisis in one of the major features with which Asian American literature is identified and then marketed. The identity crisis is resolved and one is healed not only for an optimal cultural position but also for an optimal economic position within American society. Both of these positions are based upon the primary role of the individual over the communal or familial or at best in negotiation with the communal or familial. Thus Palumbo-Liu argues that in *The Woman Warrior* problems for the narrator that are caused by sexism and racism (inflicted upon the body) are ultimately resolved not through politics but through an "interpersonal" resolution between mother and daughter at the book's conclusion (404).[8]

The case of Asian American literature as a whole demonstrates that model minority discourse, while producing the type of docile and privatized narrative of Americanization described by Palumbo-Liu, also produces a benefit in the canonization or inclusion of Asian American literature in the American culture pantheon. Ultimately, the model minority in literature shares a similar function to the model minority in American society generally: it serves as a model of panethnic entrepreneurship, selling American society on the value of Asian Americans. I do not mean that these valued texts are not critical of American society, but they are not critical to the extent that they question the ultimate validity of American pluralism and inclusion; indeed, their very criticism of American society is taken positively by non-Asian American critics, as a necessary corrective. Hence, the combination of criticism and consensus to pluralism constitutes the flexible strategy of these particular authors. While canonization itself may be a problematic term or event, entailing, possibly, a submission on the part of artists and critics toward a dominant set of literary and cultural values, it also may entail a contestation of those literary and cultural values through the inclusion of heretofore excluded participants. The standard critique of canonization in this regard is to point to multiculturalism as an example of how the inclusion of culturally representative texts or authors does not necessarily change the social and economic conditions of those they represent or are chosen to represent by cultural arbiters.[9] Nevertheless, canonization and contestation are dialectically related forces, operating perhaps unevenly but nevertheless in tandem, as the discourse of the bad subject also demonstrates.

THE DISCOURSE OF THE BAD SUBJECT

The discourse of the bad subject, like model minority discourse, is a method of creating political meaning that concerns the place of Asian Americans in American society; the creation of such meaning is both enabling and disabling, as it is for model minority discourse. While model minority discourse allows for the inclusion of Asian Americans in American society at the cost of concessions to the legitimacy of American pluralism, the discourse of the bad subject allows for opposition to the hegemony of pluralism and capitalism at the cost of an inability to meaningfully recognize ideologically contradictory Asian Americans. The result of such a refusal is the failure of Asian American intellectuals to confront the inevitable idealization of Asian American identity in late capitalism, the gradual slide from a politically necessary strategic essentialism to a co-opted and commodified essentialism as the dominant, if not sole, form of Asian American identity, which in the end limits the degree of opposition to pluralism and capitalism that the discourse of the bad subject wishes to promote. In addition, the discourse of the bad subject has yet another ironic consequence, namely, the fact that it is also an ideological discourse that practices interpellation, not only hailing those it identifies as Asian Americans—who may think of themselves otherwise—but also hailing them to behave in particular ways as Asian Americans. Thus Asian American intellectuals who see themselves as bad subjects that resist dominant society's interpellation into a race- and class-stratified society may also seek to interpellate others.

Cynthia Kadohata's *In the Heart of the Valley of Love* offers an unambiguous example of the discourse of the bad subject. Set in Los Angeles in the year 2050, *In the Heart of the Valley of Love* presents a dystopian vision of the United States that is more of an exaggeration of contemporary affairs rather than a complete departure. In this new world, the United States is 64 percent nonwhite or poor white, a population who only make 20 percent of the legal purchases (Kadohata 33). The United States is also a police state in which being a petty criminal is almost a necessity, given that while the shortage of resources has driven most people to the black market, that market is illegal. Resources are so scarce that water is rationed, while the police state is so pervasive that extensive prisons have been built in the California desert and "disappearances" have become common. In Los Angeles, there is not only racial division between whites and nonwhites but also class division between the "richtown" of Beverly Hills/Brentwood and everyone else. Political apathy among voters is extremely high, while class riots are commonplace, and violence is endemic. The narrator, a community-college student named Francie, is Japanese, Chinese, and black, embodying the novel's conception of nonwhite identity as being a mélange of different ethnic and racial backgrounds. The fact that being nonwhite is also essentially being symbolically "black" or oppressed in terms of race and class and potentially a member of those politically opposed to the richtowns and whites is represented in the novel through the "black pearls" that have become a widespread skin disease. Francie compares the "lovely, black, shining pearls" (Kadohata 10) that grow underneath one's skin to acne, essentially harmless but "profoundly disturbing" (12). The black pearls are a marker of poverty and exclusion, of the inability to fight off the contamination of the earth and the destruction of its resources; they mark the bodies of the nonwhite as political, as different, as poor and marginalized. At the same time, the fact that there is nevertheless something lovely and valuable about the pearls demonstrates their contradictory meaning for Francie and the other outcasts, that the pearls can be reclaimed or resignified with resistant political meaning, in the same way that black skin was reclaimed and resignified during the 1960s.

Francie's recognition that being nonwhite and poor (synonymous in the text) is a political condition—that there is, in fact, a body politic composed of the excluded, who are physically marked through the black pearls—is demonstrated when she and her fellow college journalists meet with richtown journalists:

> They would tell us about what would happen if we ever made it in the real world. But what made one world real and another not? We didn't always want to be us, but we never wanted to be them. That's what they didn't understand. It was starting to become clear to us, if it was not to them, that someday it would be our children and not theirs who would be inheriting the country, if there was a country left to inherit. (Kadohata 82)

In this passage, *In the Heart of the Valley of Love*, like *The Cry and the Dedication*, couches its critique of capitalism's distortion of human relations in the language of reality. Capitalism distorts the reality of human relationships through reification, although capitalism in the guise of the richtown journalists presents itself as the "real world" to the disenfranchised, those without property. *In the Heart of the Valley of Love* also shares a common theme with other dystopian visions, such as *Blade Runner*, in which class and race warfare intersects with the depredations of capitalism on the environment and on human bodies, but it is noticeably different in its adoption of the "other" perspective, namely, of those black and blackened. Although blackness is often associated with criminality in the American imagination (see chapter 3), this novel recasts the terms of legality and illegality by arguing that the police state creates criminality through a wide-ranging net of laws. "They like to have something on you," is how one character puts it (201). The political and racial climate that is the concern of the novel is clearly sketched and particular to the United States, providing a concrete environment for the novel's political concerns, but *In the Heart of the Valley of Love* tends to idealize those politics. This is most evident in the novel's division between a white richtown and a nonwhite/poor white remainder. While poor whites can be included in the disenfranchised mix, the privileged are depicted as purely white. The ambiguities of racial and class alignment are erased. Asian Americans, for example, are not mentioned as such (the category is never used) and instead cast as nonwhite and non-rich, while contemporary experience would seem to point toward a future in which some Asian Americans will be included in categories of wealth and (possibly) whiteness.

Kadohata's novel demonstrates the basic irony found in the discourse of the bad subject, namely, that even as the discourse of the bad subject rejects the interpellative "hail" of dominant ideology that demands the subject conform to a particular identity, it also engages in a hailing or naming of its own. Kadohata's novel attempts to construct or name the Asian American as a particular kind of bad, resistant subject, allied with other people of color against a white, wealthy class that is synonymous with the state, and this gesture is clearly meant for the present, not for the future, even given the novel's fictionalized setting. The naming of the subject does not require the subject to even know that s/he is being named, as Judith Butler argues in her modification of Althusser's notion of interpellation (*Excitable Speech* 28–35).[10] According to Butler, the subject being named does not have to turn around and respond to the naming, agreeing with that name as his/her appropriate title. Indeed, "one may well imagine oneself in ways that are quite to the contrary of how one is socially constituted; one may, as it were, meet that socially constituted self by surprise, with alarm or pleasure, even with shock" (31). Asian American culture is replete with stories that detail the surprise, alarm, or shock that is experienced when we are hailed by dominant society as the Oriental or the outsider, and the discourse of the bad subject is designed to deal precisely with this type of naming. Asian American culture, however, finds it difficult to address those same emotions when it is the name of the Asian American that inspires them.[11] While those emotions can lead to an eventual acceptance of the name, they also may not, or they may result in ambivalence about such a name. More important, these emotions arise from a recognition that the one who names has a certain kind of power over the one being named. While Asian Americans may not think of themselves as possessing power, the discourse of the bad subject does enable the use of power, although not always in the direction of resistance that is intended. Butler goes on to argue that "if we concede that the one who speaks powerfully, who makes happen what she or he says, is enabled in his/her speech by first having been addressed and, hence, initiated into linguistic competence through the address, then it follows that the power of the speaking subject will always, to some degree, be derivative, that it will not have its source in the speaking subject" (32–33). The origins of the discourse of the bad subject in Asian American culture are complicated, but part of the discourse's derivation comes from its legitimation by the state. The unease one may experience upon first hearing oneself named as an Asian American does, then, have meaningful roots: that unease stems from both an implicit recognition of the history of racial formation and one's place in it and the implicit recognition that one is being subjected to another form of ideological hailing.

Theresa Cha's *Dictee* provides another example of the bad subject, at least in the case made for it by its companion volume of critical essays, *Writing Self,*

Writing Nation, edited by Elaine Kim and Norma Alarcón. The relationship between these two texts constitutes an additional instance of the discourse of the bad subject in operation, although in ways more complicated than what we witness with *In the Heart of the Valley of Love*. In *Writing Self, Writing Nation*, *Dictee* is presented as a key text that expresses many of the fundamental ideological concerns of Asian American intellectuals through complex and challenging formal experimentation with narrative, poetry, and visual bricolage. For some, perhaps many, readers, *Dictee* is a confusing text, and unlike most of the texts considered in this book, *Dictee* does not seem to exhibit either a flexible strategy or panethnic entrepreneurship but instead seems singularly willful and inflexible in its refusal to accommodate its audience; not surprisingly, *Dictee*'s adherence to principle and its refusal of the literary market attract critics and readers with similarly rigorous standards of politics and aesthetics who find in the text an embodiment of the strategies and values that might form the basis of an ideal countercanon, seemingly untainted by the demands of the literary market and the corollary commodification of racial identity. Even as *Dictee* renounces flexibility and panethnic entrepreneurship, however, it demonstrates a great reluctance, unlike *In the Heart of the Valley of Love*, to become the object of another's hail, including the hail of the critics and the hail of the discourse of the bad subject, a refusal that may ironically, in its perversity or its writerliness, further incite the act of hailing.

To the extent that *Dictee* can be said to be "about" anything, it is about the personal and historical experiences that have shaped Koreans and Korean Americans since the period of Japanese colonization that commenced in the early twentieth century and continued through colonization's aftermath in the Cold War. Japanese colonialism was of course interested in making good subjects of Koreans, through various kinds of coercion, including the forcible education of Koreans in the Japanese language and the bestowal of Japanese names; this erasure of the Korean language, and hence Korean culture and identity, went hand in hand with the violent suppression of Korean resistance to Japanese colonization. Cha summarizes the violence that can be enacted through language through the phrase "broken tongue" (75), "crystallizing, in the ambiguous meaning of 'tongue' as both organ and language, the relationship between linguistic colonialism and the material violences of which language can be only a painfully descriptive index" (Lisa Lowe, "Unfaithful to the Original" 47). While Cha in one context is referring to the domination of Koreans by Japanese, she also takes a more radical step in her critique of domination in general through her experimentation with the reader's response to her text. For Cha, the learning of language and the process of reading a narrative (textual or visual) can be a form of ideological indoctrination. In *Dictee*, therefore, Cha disrupts the way the reader may accept language as simply an instrument or tool that provides access to some type of knowledge; in actuality, the language and the way that it is used shape our understanding of knowledge as well. Thus considerable parts of the text are used to force the reader to reflect upon why language and narrative are being deployed in particular ways. In one passage, for example, the reader sees both a French paragraph and its translation into English; the translation is imperfect, however, since the grammatical directions given in French are translated literally, rather than rendered as punctuation marks (for example, "comma" versus ","). What is being criticized here is the submission a student of language makes to the process of dictation; the student is literally taking down words but is also submitting to a form of dictatorship manifested through the use of language as a tool.

The student who has taken down this dictation by writing "comma" versus "," is doing it literally, as Lisa Lowe points out, rather than figuratively (following the letter versus the spirit of translation), and in so doing is actually rebelling against the dictation, by not doing as she is supposed to, in one sense, but doing exactly as she is told to, in another sense ("Unfaithful to the Original" 38–42). Thus she is a bad subject, mimicking a good student but being subversive in actuality. *Dictee* is replete with examples of bad subjects, from the translation student, to Korean female martyrs, to Joan of Arc—bad subjects who are variously defined by dominant power but who exceed their definition. In a number of ways, then, *Dictee* foregrounds how the good subject is formed through ideology and how the bad subject rebels through a refusal to follow those types of ideological orders that are taken for granted by most. Good subjects internalize the nation, literally, as *Dictee* makes clear when it discusses the return of a Korean refugee to South Korea: "You leave you come back to the shell left empty all this time. To claim to reclaim, the space. Into the mouth the wound the entry is reverse and back each organ artery gland pace element, implanted, housed skin upon skin, membrane, vessel, waters, dams, ducts, canals, bridges" (57). The infrastructure of the nation as an allegory for the individual's body itself means that the individual and the nation are joined through a concept of the body politic, with the body-as-political, and with the political defined as a possession of the body. *Dictee* rejects this domination of the individual through national discourse and the discourses of religion, race, and patriarchy that it sees as related, and it enacts that rejection in its own relationship to the reader, challenging conventional modes of literary consumption.

Lowe argues that in resisting various forms of domination that seek to define identity in a singular fashion *Dictee* is engaged in a politics of difference, even as its commitment to exposing the history of Japanese colonization is dependent upon a politics of identity; "this dialectic between the politics of identity and the politics of difference is . . . of utmost importance, for it . . . engages with rather than suppresses heterogeneities of gender, class, sexuality, race and nation, yet [it is] also able to maintain end extend the forms of unity which make common struggle possible" ("Unfaithful to the Original" 63–64). The politics of difference, however, poses potential problems for the relationship between *Dictee* and *Writing Self, Writing Nation*, especially when it comes to the issue of difference as surplus or excess. As Shelley Wong puts it,

In the colonial calculus that identifies Korean with Japanese, the "Korean" is surplus; in the racial calculus that identifies American as white, the "Korean" is surplus; in the patriarchal calculus that identifies Korean as male, the "Korean female" is surplus; and in the formal calculus that identifies a literary work with a discrete genre, *Dictee* is surplus. In *Dictee's* economy of translation, the Korean American feminine is invariably rendered as surplus, as that which goes unaccounted for. (122)

Likewise, the fluidity of identity that Elaine Kim and L. Hyun Yi Kang note as being one of the hallmark features of the text that attracts them to it is, in the end, a surplus that the critical and political calculus of *Writing Self, Writing Nation* finds difficult to account for.[12]

We see this problem of the surplus in the concluding chapters of *Dictee*, where the text follows through on its critique of how various ideologies and discourses attempt to dominate the individual by reverting to a highly personal, highly lyrical account of subjectivity and perception, rooted in the experiences of the reader and the viewer. The account involves explicit rejection of conventional narrative, summarized in this passage that speaks of an unnamed person: "She says to herself if she were able to write she could continue to live. Says to herself if she would write without ceasing. To herself if by writing she could abolish real time. She would live. If she could display it before her and become its voyeur" (Cha 141). "Real time" finds its analogue in narrative movement, and *Dictee* seeks to abolish both that time and movement through its narrative of pastiche and juxtaposition that forestalls progress. In another passage, a moviegoer watches a movie and "follows no progression in particular of the narrative but submits only to the timelessness created in her body"—a physical sensation that, presumably, the reader of the text also may experience as s/he is immersed in *Dictee's* lack of progression (Cha 149). From these two examples, we can see that one goal of *Dictee*, besides its ideological critique, seems to be the establishment of an almost utopian space where the reader/viewer can find pleasure in escaping from the conventional demands of narrative and from the constraints of ideology and discourse. This utopian space is associated with childhood, which can be seen in *Dictee's* last two narrative fragments, both focusing on young girls, as if the book is moving backward in a person's life, toward innocence. These fragments conclude with a child's view of the world. In the second-to-last passage, the child looks "through the paper screen door" and sees that "dusk had entered and a small candle was flickering" (170). The child's view of light and shadows through a paper screen bears a resemblance to a spectator's view of a film screen, a view focused on intensely through-out *Dictee*. For a text deeply concerned with the cinematic image, *Dictee's* decision to nearly conclude with this return to the child's relationship with the basic building blocks of film—light and movement—suggests that it may only be here, in this lost time, that the viewer can have an uncomplicated relationship with sight. This lack of complication is an illusion, however, as we see in the last passage when a child asks her mother to hold her up to a window, where "there is no one inside the pane and the glass between" (179); at the same time as there is "no one" to obstruct her view of the world outside, that view is nevertheless being filtered by the glass, no matter how clear. As Kang puts it, "We perceive through layers" (95), although for the most part *Dictee* is concerned with opaque rather than transparent layers that throw one's own reflection back upon oneself, as Kim points out ("Poised on the In-between," 12).

The gesture toward a child's view of the world, whether conducted in sincerity or parody, and the general focus of the final third of *Dictee* on personal experience pose some challenges for the interpretation presented of *Dictee* in *Writing Self, Writing Nation* as a radical political text. While *Dictee* does offer a negative critique of ideology—in that sense offering a vision through the eyes of a bad subject—its own solution of a return to an innocent vision of the world does not correspond with the materialist, neo-Marxist approach favored in *Writing Self, Writing Nation*'s construction of the bad subject. The resistance to closure around issues of narrative and identity that the critics of *Writing Self, Writing Nation* note as a feature of *Dictee* also returns as a critical problem in the final, unnumbered page of *Dictee*. The page consists of two notes and acknowledgments for biographical material and calligraphy used in the text. The two notes are hardly adequate reference material for the wealth of allusions in the text and seem to be ultimately a mockery of the critical apparatus that they allude to. Providing us with marginal information that only partially explicates the text—and even then doing so only imprecisely, omitting publication dates for the citations and exact references to their relevance to *Dictee*'s own pages— the notes comically gesture at the critical desire for wholeness, for intellectual history and foundation.[13] *Dictee* in the end seems to distrust critics and their tools of exegesis, even as it obviously deploys some of those academic tools itself in order to excavate the history of Korean experiences. This distrust is symptomatic of the text's resistance to the various discourses it exposes and to ideological interpellation in general; the distrust is also a sign of how *Dictee* refuses to be part of the "textual coalition" between texts and critics that Sau-ling C. Wong argues is a feature of Asian American literature (*Reading Asian American Literature* 9). What does it mean, then, for critics to represent *Dictee* as enacting a particular political agenda that resonates with their own? Is the subversiveness of *Dictee* really a "theoretical construct," as Jinqi Ling claims (*Narrating Nationalisms* 9)? Instead of arguing for the (in)correctness of *Writing Self, Writing Nation*, I shall point instead to the resistance that *Dictee* poses to even sympathetic critics as an emblem for the relationship between Asian America and Asian American intellectuals. *Dictee* is premised upon a tension between its demonstration of a fluid subject and its own aesthetic inflexibility, its unwillingness to concede to the critic or to the market, to interpretation or consumption. This tension between fluidity and inflexibility is the emblem of the bad subject as it is constructed by Asian American intellectuals, yet it is that very same fluidity that constitutes an excess, and it is that very same inflexibility that resists interpretation and interpellation. Therefore, the relationship between *Dictee* and *Writing Self, Writing Nation* is an example of the discourse of the bad subject, built around signs of bad behavior that are at once the basis of the discourse and the limits of it. The subject who refuses to be hailed by dominant ideology can also refuse to be hailed by resistant ideology. It is that refusal that signals the limits of the discourse of the bad subject and the limits of Asian America.

THE LIMITS OF ASIAN AMERICA

I now turn to the novels of Lois-Ann Yamanaka and the controversies that surround them. The reception and location of production for Yamanaka's novels all pose challenges to Asian American cultural self-representation, and because the controversies around her work exceed the realm of literature and literary criticism, intruding into the entirety of Asian American studies and achieving national attention, an examination of her texts will be a fitting conclusion for this book and its concerns with the limits of Asian America. Yamanaka's novels, set in Hawai'i, seem to make as their implicit claim the validation of a culture that is relatively invisible to continental Americans, including Asian Americans.[14] Many Asian American intellectuals have considered Yamanaka's work to be part of Asian American literature, since the Association for Asian American Studies has recognized her work with its annual book awards, but many critics and writers of Hawaii's "local" literature insist that Hawaii's local culture, from which Yamanaka's work originates, is quite distinct form Asian American culture, due to the particular historical conditions that have shaped cultural formation.[15] It is arguable, therefore, that Yamanaka's works do not constitute Asian American literature at all. I read Yamanaka's works not so much as examples of Asian American literature but as examples of something that Asian American literary criticism has claimed as its own. Reading her work, then, helps illuminate Asian American studies' preoccupations and assumptions and the limits of a theoretical framework based on Asian America. By claiming the local literature of Hawai'i as Asian American literature, Asian American studies reveals the geographical, political, and cultural investments Asian America has made in a continental America with an imperialist history that continues to shape the present. Through these investments, Asian American studies feels safe to claim Yamanaka's novels and the culture they represent as Asian American, despite the fact that it may in doing so "operate unexpectedly in the service of American imperialism" (Fujikane, "Between Nationalisms" 24), reiterating American nationalism and the related historical amnesia that concerns imperialism and its effects. Within this context of Asian America's claim on local literature as Asian American, what we also witness is how Yamanaka's novels oppose the discourse of the bad subject in ways that are different from *Dictee*'s resistance. Yamanaka's novels willingly explore and perhaps embody the messiness of diversity and heterogeneity, represented in this case through Hawaii's local culture, where panethnicity can break down into interethnic strife.

The history of local culture in Hawai'i demonstrates some of the similarities and differences with continental Asian America, as we shall see later. The development of local culture in Hawai'i is a direct result of U.S. colonization, which first manifested itself through the arrival of U.S. businessmen and missionaries in Hawai'i in the early 1800s. U.S. businessmen who were looking for economic opportunities in building sugar plantations gradually assumed more and more power in Hawai'i throughout the course of the nineteenth century, even as the power of the Hawaiian monarchy waned. Factors in the U.S. rise and the Hawaiian decline included the devastation of the Hawaiian population due to the introduction of Western diseases and the usurpation of Hawaiian land by U.S. businessmen through the introduction of Western concepts of land tenure. The clash of interests between U.S. businessmen and the Hawaiian monarchy culminated in an 1893 coup led by U.S. businessmen and supported by the U.S. military, which successfully overthrew the Hawaiian queen. Although President Cleveland refused to annex Hawai'i, his successor, President McKinley, did so in 1898. The Hawai'i of subsequent generations bore the mark of the coup, as a white oligarchy retained economic and political power in the territory, controlling a population composed of Native Hawaiians and emigrants who primarily came from East Asia and the Philippines as contract labor for the plantations.[16]

Starting in the early nineteenth century, sugar plantations in Hawai'i depended on the labor of Hawaiians, but the planters subsequently turned to imported labor from Asia, the Pacific, and even Europe. Chinese, Japanese, Filipino, and Korean immigrants all came during the nineteenth and early twentieth centuries in successive ethnic waves. On the plantation, they found themselves facing both ethnic segregation among the labor force, whereby different Asian ethnic groups were separated from one another in order to prevent the cohesion of a potentially resistant workforce, and racial domination, whereby Americans and ethnic European immigrant laborers were able to rise to positions of influence on the plantation but not Asians (Takaki, *Pau Hana* 13–81). Eventually, however, the barriers of ethnic segregation broke down, partially through the development of panethnic labor strikes and partially through the development of common cultural connections such as Hawai'i Creole English, or pidgin, a hybrid language that incorporated both English and various other immigrant languages.[17] It is this population of people, primarily Asian, that forms a substantial portion of the population defined by residents of Hawai'i as "local," in relationship to haoles (whites) and Native Hawaiians (who may or may not also identify as local). Brenda Lee Kwon defines "local" as a label that "can be used to refer to anyone of Asian, Hawaiian, or other Pacific Islander descent, and usually designates those who have been in Hawai'i for more than one generation, although more politicized definitions call for a lineage that can be traced back to the plantation labor experience" (9). As Kwon implies, the category of the local is not without its controversies over definition, with some questions as to whether haoles can ever become locals and whether "local" simply describes a state of residence or also a state of lineage and cultural consciousness; that is, locals are sometimes seen as being direct descendants of the primarily nonwhite class of plantation workers, a heritage that also implies some type of working-class consciousness.[18]

Local culture, in any event, finds its origins in the plantation system and U.S. colonization, which led to the importation of different populations who, despite the efforts of plantation owners, developed a unique and hybrid working-class culture that Jonathan Y. Okamura claims is the result of struggle ("Aloha Kanaka"). A refusal to recognize the historical struggle over the making of culture and the allocation of resources, Okamura argues, leads to the fact that Hawai'i "while loudly and proudly embracing its ethnic/racial diversity . . . has yet to confront its perverse social inequities" (204).[19] The idea that local culture is the result of struggle is a different conception from the popular one attached to Hawai'i on the continent, namely, that local culture is a multicultural mélange that can be celebrated as a further, innocent extension of the melting pot, as evidenced by the mixing of populations, the high proportion of nonwhites among the population, and the rise to power of local Asians in the political structure.[20] This image of Hawai'i is also perpetuated by some scholars and locals, particularly those of the middle-class local Asian elite dominated by local Japanese. Other residents and scholars of Hawai'i object to such an image. These critical scholars point to the fact that the multiculturalism of Hawai'i is no less problematic than the multiculturalism of the continent, whereby cultural diversity is not necessarily a signifier of economic and social equality.[21]

Continental perceptions of Hawai'i as a multicultural paradise, with the history of U.S. colonization and the continuing U.S. military presence in Hawai'i erased, have aided in the creation of a tourist economy that is central to Hawai'i.[22] Tourism, as the economic mainstay of Hawai'i since statehood in 1959, occupies a critical place in the culture and economy. Native Hawaiians and locals regard tourism with emotions that include acceptance, ambivalence, and outright rejection. On the one hand, many residents of Hawai'i are convinced that tourism is an inextricable part of the economy; on the other hand, many residents also recognize that tourism is responsible for damaging the environment, driving real estate values to astronomical heights, creating a service-oriented economy that limits job opportunities for residents, and perpetuating an idealistic image of Hawai'i that is at odds with the complexities of Hawaii's cultures. The commodification of Native Hawaiian and local culture through tourism is also a bone of contention for residents. The touristic, multicultural image of Hawai'i also obscures the fact that there is significant tension between locals and Native Hawaiians over the question of sovereignty and the history of colonial domination, with Native Hawaiian leaders arguing that locals, despite any past history of being dominated by the plantation system, are now themselves settlers who are complicit with colonialism (Trask, "Settlers of

Color"). Rejecting the legacy of colonialism, the controversial Native Hawaiian Sovereignty Movement seeks to reclaim land ceded by the United States to Native Hawaiians but still being used by the military, corporations, and federal and state governments (Trask, *From a Native Daughter*). Meanwhile, the rise to power of local Japanese in Hawai'i does not reflect the fact that some ethnic populations, notably Filipinos, Native Hawaiians, Samoans, and other recent immigrants to Hawai'i, have not had the same economic and political benefits.[23]

Asian Americans' claiming of local literature as a part of Asian American literature can therefore be a fraught act that reiterates unacknowledged assumptions about the relationship of the continental United States to Hawai'i, which include a disavowal of the colonization of Hawai'i and its perpetuation through tourism and the military as well as an unwitting reiteration of stereotypes that concern the idealized multiculturalism of Hawai'i. The relationship between the continental United States and Hawai'i is also characterized by continental cultural domination of Hawai'i, a recognition of which by local writers led to the development of local literature, catalyzed by the 1978 "Talk Story" conference. This local literature opposed itself to the representation of Hawai'i on the continent and in the dominant, white literary establishment in Hawai'i at the time. James Michener's *Hawaii*, released in 1959, the same year as Hawaii's statehood, came to symbolize both the literary establishment and the continental representation of Hawai'i. For many local writers, a self-consciously defined local literature was an act of cultural validation in the face of continental marginalization or dismissal of local culture, imposed continental standards of cultural worthiness, and reiterated stereotypes of Hawai'i as paradise. Since Asian Americans on the continent are not immune from perpetuating these continental representations of Hawai'i and its inhabitants, local literature in its emergence not only had to contest the image of Hawai'i as tourist paradise and the image of Hawai'i as provincial and inconsequential culturally but also had to face the potential problems of being misread or appropriated by Asian Americans.[24]

There are, then, significant political, economic, and cultural tensions in Hawai'i that are tied to the historically created differences among ethnic populations, due to the legacy of U.S. colonization, the plantation system, and the development of the tourist economy; these tensions coexist with the undeniable ethnic diversity of Hawai'i. Yamanaka's work shows both the reality of this diversity and its related tensions that fueled the controversy that concerned the representation of local Filipinos as sexual monsters and deviants in *Blu's Hanging*, as Filipinos and their supporters argued that Yamanaka was drawing from a historical well of anti-Filipino prejudice. These tensions contradicted the implicit panethnic multiculturalism that is a part of Hawaii's popular image and a part of some Asian American intellectuals' image of Asian America. Asian American intellectuals, who otherwise are inclined to critique the multiculturalism of American society, generally (although with notable exceptions) accept the notion that Asian America is a multicultural alliance of different ethnic groups. This version of multiculturalism, like the national version, simultaneously recognizes and disavows the differences of power that may exist between different ethnic groups; in Asian America's case, these issues of power, manifesting themselves in discrimination and oppression between groups, are displaced onto dominant society's relationships with Asian Americans as a whole or onto Old World intranational Asian rivalries that are supposedly irrelevant to second-generation-and-beyond Asian Americans. Asian America is generally assumed by Asian American intellectuals to be oppressed *first* by dominant society, which is then a historical cause for any potential and seemingly misguided intraethnic Asian American discrimination. The local culture that Yamanaka depicts does not follow this model of oppression. Yamanaka represents the local community, in many of the most important events, as responsible for both the alienation and inclusion of its members. Thus while Yamanaka's works retain a historical memory of colonization and haole racism and recognize their consequences in such things as exploitative tourism and the destruction of self-esteem among locals, these works also demand a recognition of the community's ability to turn against itself. The community—and here I mean the local community as an allegory for the continental Asian American community—may not be amenable to the discourse of the bad subject, premised on an opposition to racism, discrimination, and exploitation, because it may practice these forms of oppression itself, contra the dictates of a political leadership that calls for unity and allegiance based on race. This is a lesson that Asian American intellectuals are still dealing with in the aftermath of the controversy around Yamanaka's work.

While the case of Uncle Paulo in *Blu's Hanging* will serve as my concluding point for investigating these claims, I will begin with more general assertions that concern Yamanaka's work as a whole. The issues of colonialism, tourism, cultural commodification, and the complexity and validity of local culture are all prominent in Yamanaka's trilogy of novels that deals with the lives of local Japanese families, in particular the lives of the young girls in these families. Viewed as a whole, the trilogy actually tells one story, given that the protagonists and their families are very similar, as are the difficulties concerning alienation and inclusion the protagonists endure. The trilogy is about narrators who do not fit into any environment easily—their families, their schools, their immediate neighborhoods, and continental American culture. By the trilogy's conclusion, these forms of alienation will be overcome; what is redeemed by the conclusion is not only the protagonist but also her local culture, which is both her home and her source of adolescent angst and perceived cultural inferiority. Thus even though the narrator of the last book, *Heads by Harry*, becomes a "good subject," that identification is defined in relationship to a unified local community, not to continental American culture. The ruptures and the fractures, the exploitation and the eventual redemption, are all ultimately centered on the bodies of children and animals, who are the most helpless members of the local community and whose fates are ultimately a commentary upon the potential of unifying the body politic of that community.

In the first novel of the trilogy, *Wild Meat and the Billy Burgers,* the pubescent narrator Lovey Nariyoshi suffers from am inferiority complex that is partly racial (she "used to wish [she] looked just like" Shirley Temple (*Wild Meat* 3)), partly cultural (she is ashamed of speaking pidgin), and partly economic (she is ashamed of her family's poverty), all of which converge to form her personal alienation from the other children her age. The fact that Lovey is a poor local Japanese is significant, because as a whole, Japanese in Hawai'i are the predominant nonwhite ethnic group, economically and politically. Lovey's sense of alienation is due to a desire not only to be like haoles but also to be like other local Japanese, who all seem wealthier, prettier, and more stylish than herself. Yet Lovey's perspective on the world around her is clearly meant to be ironic, for if she believes that all her haole and Japanese friends and acquaintances are significantly better off than she, the narrative demonstrates otherwise. Some haole girls are shown to come from poor families and to be less popular than the local Japanese girls, although for Lovey it is a flat statement of truth that it is "just better to be haole" (28). Meanwhile, one of Lovey's Japanese nemeses, who belongs to the popular Japanese girls' club at school that Lovey characterizes as being "all so rich" (186), is poignantly described as coming from a working-class background (191, 195). Lovey can notice the details of the girl's life but does not understand their significance. This girl victimizes Lovey, but the reader is able to see that this victimization is an outcome of the girl's own sense of inferiority, displaced onto Lovey, who herself has previously repeated the cycle of adolescent cruelty by picking on a Filipina in order to displace the attention of other children onto the Filipina (14–15). Lovey's world of adolescent cruelty is mirrored in the world of animals, including pets, whose experiences become lessons in the cruelty of nature for Lovey—and by extension lessons in the cruelty of human nature. In one of the more disturbing scenes in the novel, Lovey's father takes away her pet female goat and gives her to the zoo, where Lovey sees male goats forcing sex upon her goat in an act that Lovey implicitly understands to be rape (163). For Lovey, the strange act of sex is one that involves violence and domination and one that is replete with horrible consequences, which is a belief reinforced when she spies on a teenage girl she idolizes having sex; later, the girl, pregnant, commits suicide.

This threatening world of sexual violation, which finds its corollary in the abuse of animals by humans and other animals, is continued in its representation with even greater ferocity in *Blu's Hanging.* As in *Wild Meat, Blu's Hanging* features an adolescent boy, in this case Blu, the narrator Ivah's younger brother, who is struggling with his (homo)sexuality. Blu in particular becomes the object of attention for various men of different ethnicities in the neighborhood who seek to expose themselves to him and molest him. Blu is complicit in his own molestation in many cases, if "complicit" can be used to describe someone who is clearly longing for ways to compensate for his own sense of individual inadequacy that arises from his sexuality and his family's poverty; his complicity in one act of molestation is bought by an old man, for example, with money and candy—a $100,000" bar (Yamanaka, *Blu's Hanging* 20). The environment of molestation and sexual danger is embodied most graphically in the twenty-year-old Uncle Paulo, who is part Japanese and part Filipino, and his nieces, who are also half-Japanese and whom Ivah describes as "human rats" (34) because of their sadistic behavior: they torture and kill the neighborhood cats and threaten Ivah's own pet cat. Uncle Paulo has sex with at least one of the older nieces, who in turn perform oral sex on Blu; ultimately, Uncle Paulo kidnaps Blu and rapes him, but Blu himself is ambivalent about the entire event, finding at least some pleasure in the sexual act (253). Yamanaka has defended herself from charges of racism in the portrayal of Uncle Paulo by arguing that her critics cannot distinguish her perspective from her characters'. Certainly the world as seen through Ivah's eyes, as it is through Lovey's, is a horrifying and threatening one, populated by monsters in human form. Uncle Paulo is not the only sexual villain in the novel, and the novel also makes it clear that his nieces are not innately evil, as Ivah understands, but corrupted by Uncle Paulo. The two younger nieces, for example, do not participate in the same cruel activities as their elders and are terrified of Uncle Paulo and the initiations that he seems to promise (149–150).

Yamanaka's argument that her novels are told through the adolescent perspective, which readers have to understand ironically, finds support in the third novel of her trilogy, *Heads by Harry*, published in 1999 after the controversies about alleged anti-Filipino racism arose but presumably written before the controversies reached their height in 1998.[25] In *Heads by Harry*, the narrator Toni is a teenager who goes on to college and hence has a different understanding of the world and sexuality than the previous narrators, who can be seen as younger incarnations of herself. In *Heads by Harry*, the world is not as threatening as it once was, particularly in terms of sex, poverty, and ethnic difference. While Mindy Pennybacker reads this as a retreat on Yamanaka's part from confronting difficult issues, it can also be read as a maturation of an adolescent perspective that is no longer as prone to see the world in drastic terms. Again sexuality and animals are tied together in a thematic sequence of events that demonstrate the nature of Toni's perspective on the world. Unlike Lovey and Ivah, Toni does not see sex as threatening, insomuch as she sees it as something pleasurable, if still confusing. In notable contrast to *Blu's Hanging*, Toni's significant sexual encounters are with Filipino brothers. In addition, her most memorable, and secret, encounter involves both brothers simultaneously. The novel implies that sex is not an experience whose unruliness must be disciplined by bourgeois constrictions but one that should be embraced or at least accepted; what bourgeois society or small children like Ivah and Lovey may consider monstrous is at the most disruptive and kinky in the local neighborhood, once the secret is revealed. The ethnic differences and tensions between Filipinos and Japanese, magnified in *Blu's Hanging* and certainly a reality in the local society, is ameliorated by the relationship between Toni and the Filipino brothers and the deep friendship between Toni's father and the brothers' father. Meanwhile, animals, whose natural behavior and whose exploitation by human beings became symbolic of the Darwinist nature of the world for Ivah and Lovey, become symbolic of creation and art in *Heads by Harry* through the profession of Toni's father, Harry, who is a taxidermist (hence the title of the novel). As Pennybacker argues, the novel explicitly compares the taxidermist's re-creation of animal life to the artist's re-creation of life in her work. Thus the world of animals—especially hurt animals—that is so threatening in the first two novels is redeemed in the end though the artistic process in *Heads by Harry*. The last image in *Heads by Harry* is of the return of Toni to her local community, the place where she finally feels at home. While *Wild Meat and the Billy Burgers* and *Blu's Hanging* also offer closure for the narrators as they come to some sense of reconciliation with their identity and place in society, *Heads by Harry* is the only novel of the trilogy to also paint a more positive portrait of the environment, the local culture in which the narrator lives. At the same time, then, as the narrator is brought home, the novel affirms local culture.

The issue of local culture in particular, and the concept of community in general, is fundamental to Yamanaka's works, and the dynamic of inclusion and exclusion that drives the thematics of her novels is pinned upon the representation of bodies. The affirmation of a local identity is ultimately accomplished through a reconciliation of the narrator's own bodily concerns with her ability to represent the bodies of others. This nexus of bodily identification and representation is also at the heart of the controversial reception of *Blu's Hanging* and the obvious case of Uncle Paulo and Blu. In looking more closely at Uncle Paulo and his relationship to the community around him, especially Ivah's family, we can trace a chain of events *routed through the body* that implicate the community in what eventually happens to Blu. The original sin of the community, in the history of the novel, is the exile of Ivah's parents during their childhood, an act occasioned by their contraction of leprosy. Their diseased bodies are excised from the healthy bodies of their family and their community, and they are never welcomed back. Ivah's mother is so stricken by her abandonment that she swears she will never leave her own children and subsequently, fearing that her leprosy may return and again force her own removal, consumes over the course of her lifetime a dangerous amount of a drug designed to stave off leprosy. It is this drug that eventually and ironically kills her. The death of Ivah's mother leads to the emotional and physical withdrawal of Ivah's father from his children, leaving them essentially defenseless in the face of Uncle Paulo's assault. Ivah's sense of alienation from her community is thus not simply in her imagination or produced from the cruelties of adolescence but also a direct function of the community's exclusion of her parents. While Uncle Paulo's monstrousness remains inexplicable, the opportunity for him to molest and rape is provided by a breakdown in the community's body politic—the social relations that bind all members together. This breakdown commences with the exile of Ivah's parents due to their leprosy and continues in the neglect of Ivah and her siblings by their peers, their father, and their neighbors. The social relations of the body politic are ruptured by the fear of otherness and contamination symbolized in the disease of leprosy and reenacted continuously through various cruelties, major and minor, that the local children commit upon one another.

Yamanaka's work and its reception demonstrate the complex and contradictory ways that power works, blurring the lines between "good" and "bad," the insider and the outsider, the model minority and the bad subject. Even as Yamanaka's novels affirms local culture, for example, they repeat the colonization of Native Hawaiians by erasing their presence, as Pennybacker points out:

> Though Hawaiian myths, artifacts, place names and ghosts fill the threatened landscape, there aren't any living Native Hawaiians among Yamanaka's main characters. But the Big Island and Molokai, where her novels are set, have relatively large populations of Kanaka Maoli. Instead, their culture is appropriated as a sentimental, beautiful backdrop, like the forest itself, indigenous but nearly extinct.

Pennybacker's comment points to an ongoing dilemma for local residents of Hawai'i, constituted by the history of colonization, the theft of land from Native Hawaiians, and the accusations by Native Hawaiian leaders that locals, even if they are not white and have a history of being oppressed themselves, are nevertheless settlers (Trask, *From a Native Daughter* 79). Thus locals, who may imagine themselves as participating in some kind of "oppositional regionalism," as Rob Wilson calls it, or at least may imagine themselves as being descendants of and proponents for the disenfranchised and the marginalized, find that they are being targeted as participants in oppression (129).[26] Addressing the same problem, Jeff Chang argues that "local knowledges are split, sometimes mimicking and other times resisting colonial narratives" (3), a phenomenon clearly visible in Yamanaka's work.

The ruptures and fractures in the local community and the greater society of Hawai'i and the methods of resolving those ruptures and fractures serve as analogous examples for continental Asian Americans as they consider their own practice of community. The fact that Hawaii's local community derives largely from Asian populations helps to advance this analogy, although there are clear and significant historical differences in the formation and practices of the local and the Asian American communities. The most useful analogy to be drawn from Yamanaka's work, detailing the limits of Asian America, would concern the panethnic possibilities and limits of an Asian American community, especially as it has arisen to a position of demographic prominence and all that this possibly entails in terms of economic, cultural, and political power. Yamanaka's novels send a mixed message about the possibilities of a pan-Asian population, because even as they suggest that individuals and communities can "grow up" or evolve beyond prejudices, the world of terror is nevertheless reproduced anew for every generation.[27] It is this adolescent world of children misbehaving and terrorizing one another, of people who do not subscribe to the doctrines of ethnic equality and respect, that presents critical problems for Asian America and its hopes of panethnic unity. Asian American intellectuals, who have prided themselves on their alignment with America's bad subjects, must contend with those who are not "hailed" by the discourse of Asian America as the bad subject, who do not respond to the call that they are Asian American, or at least do not respond in the way desired. As Asian America grows larger and more complex in every way imaginable, as they become a significant minority in a society of minorities in the twenty-first century, it will become increasingly more difficult for a "mature" Asian American political and cultural leadership to maintain a cohesive ideology about what constitutes Asian American subjectivity.

It may, indeed, be impossible to even entertain the idea of an Asian American subject that has any significant political meaning in a postmulticultural society, that is to say, a society in which the importance of multiculturalism is no longer a political issue but simply a fact of American life. To the extent that an Asian American political subject exists today, it is premised upon the idea of Asian Americans as a "race" who must struggle against oppression, which is clearly a contemporary social construction born out of a posture of political self-defense on the part of people of Asian descent in the United States. If multiculturalism eliminates the power of racial identity as a political bond in this sense, given that multiculturalism ostensibly creates a racially equal society, then an Asian American racial identity itself will have no clear ideological orientation, since the struggle for racial and cultural *validation*—versus a more complicated notion of socioeconomic equality—will no longer exist. Certainly race will continue to matter, since it is embedded in relations of class and economic difference, privilege, and exploitation that will remain into a multicultural future, but it will be increasingly difficult to convince Asian Americans *as a whole* that their common political interests involve anything more than their own immediate racial self-interest. The specter of Pres. George W. Bush nominating the ideologically conservative Elaine Chao for a cabinet position and having that nomination endorsed by progressive groups such as the Organization of Chinese Americans is indicative of the future of Asian America where for many race itself, rather than certain kinds of goals or practices, becomes politics. In that scenario, the picture that Yamanaka paints of intra-Asian rivalries—rivalries that are resolutely domestic and not a function of the Old World—may very well characterize a contradictory set of Asian American intrarelations. Once Asian Americans take their common racial identity for granted and evacuate it of any substantive political meaning, that is to say, any ideological orientation except the orientation toward race as identity, Asian American populations will be free to fracture around more concrete political and economic interests.

BEYOND ASIAN AMERICA

Given that Asian America has claimed Hawaii's literary products for itself through the rhetoric of racial formation that extends continental assumptions to Hawai'i because it is a part of the nation, I have taken the opportunity to read Yamanaka's works because of their significance within Asian American culture. At the same time, I read her works not as Asian American literature but as a counterexample, an analogy, and a parallel, in order to demonstrate how Asian America is divided, often against itself. The lesson we can draw from Yamanaka's work about local culture is that the practice of Asian American communities and their politics can run counter to idealized visions of Asian American consensus, which demands a recognition that an Asian American political identity may be most clearly articulated in defensive postures against racism, where being an Asian American has its most concrete meaning. Anti-Asian violence and discrimination creates Asian American consensus as nothing else will. This is illustrated vividly in Steven Okazaki's pseudo-documentary film *American Sons*, which has four Asian American actors reenacting interviews done with Asian American men about their experiences with racism. The film concludes with the actors reading from newspaper articles that document anti-Asian hate crimes. Preceding the litany of hate crimes, which in itself constitutes a particularly important trope of Asian American cultural production, the actor Kelvin Han Yee, in the voice of his character, states:

> [Some] Asian Americans have forgotten about being Asian American. They've forgotten the sacrifices that their parents and grandparents made. They don't give back to the communities they came from. They've got their cars and their houses and their good jobs and they think they can create a comfort zone where racism doesn't affect them. They're living in denial! They read these newspaper stories and they think, well, that doesn't affect us. They read about some Southeast Asian kid who gets his head bashed in with a baseball bat, and they think, well, we're not Vietnamese. . . . You see, these Asian Americans who think they're safe, who think that all this Asian bashing and hatred and violence has nothing to do with them, they're not Asian Americans. They're something else. You see, to me, saying that you're an Asian American, that means something to me. It means you carry a sense of pride and solidarity when you say it. Don't give that up.

In this monologue, which echoes Mari Matsuda's argument that being Asian American is a conditional, political identity from which certain people can be excluded (177), many of the foundational elements of Asian American intellectual work and the discourse about Asian American identity are evident, including the call to historical memory, community commitment, coalitional alliances, political resistance, and ideological homogeneity. The call, or the interpellation, is dependent upon the specter of anti-Asian violence, the seemingly inarguable mark that is used to distinguish the Asian American body politic from the rest of the American body politic. This reminder of violence works in more subtle ways as well, circulating through the everyday ways that I, for example, and possibly many others structure a course syllabus on Asian American studies: punctuated by the history of anti-Asian violence and discrimination and shaped by a "sense of pride and solidarity" in the formation of Asian American communities and identities, the syllabus and the teaching is implicitly, if not always explicitly, an exercise in interpellation, in the education and making of future Asian Americans.

If classrooms and universities are some of the spaces where the underlying theories of Asian American intellectuals are exercised in practice, they are also spaces where we may see these theories falter as they run up against those types of recalcitrant Asian Americans—or non-Asian Americans, as the case may be—of whom Kelvin Han Yee's character and Mari Matsuda speak. Yen Le Espiritu argues that even though Asian America was born from a protective reaction against racism, as ethnic groups cohered for political survival, Asian America "may outlive the circumstances and interests that produced it, creating conditions that sustain and revivify it" (*Asian American Panethnicity* 164). Perhaps it is these recalcitrant Asian Americans who do not take Asian American studies classes, for example, who will constitute the new other and the mirror to our contemporary Asian American self and who will help to create different conditions for demographically defined, rather than self-identified, Asian American communities to grow and change in unpredictable ways. It has been my argument that these new conditions of sustenance and what they produce may very well run counter to the ideological beliefs of many Asian American intellectuals, who are deeply invested in the analysis of the original circumstances and interests of their own production, which are essentially the dialectic between the racist, capitalist exploitation of Asian Americans and the resistance they have posed against such exploitation. In these new conditions, many Asian Americans may see themselves as equal participants and beneficiaries in a global capitalism that many Asian American intellectuals view with despair. What may be worse for Asian American intellectuals than fractures within Asian America, however, is the ironic prospect that there can still be a relatively unified Asian America that will operate under a different set of signs from antiracism and anticapitalism. Thus when Espiritu warns in 1992 that "without shared worldviews, collective modes of interpretation, and common class interests, the prospects of a viable pan-Asian ethnicity appear bleak" (*Asian American Panethnicity* 173), she may not be taking into account that global capitalism may very well provide that shared worldview, collective mode of interpretation, and common class interest for many—perhaps a majority of—Asian Americans. Whether this group constitutes a viable pan-Asian ethnicity or is the only voice for Asian Americans, they may nevertheless contest the leadership of

Asian America and the definition of Asian Americans as a political, cultural, and economic interest group in the eyes of other Americans.

Asian American intellectuals are beginning to worry about these future directions of Asian America. Patricia Chu, for example, asks: "When will Asian Americans write as assimilated subjects, and when we do, what will it mean to write as Asian Americans?" (189). My speculation is that once (some) Asian Americans write as assimilated subjects, their literature and their subjectivity will enter the realm of ethnicity rather than race; in this scenario, (some) Asian Americans may become white or become aligned with whiteness, in effect assuming a position as the "new Jews" who are "ethnic" rather than "racial," as Eric Liu argues in *The Accidental Asian* (145–174). These two options of becoming white or becoming aligned with whiteness are not exactly identical. In both options, Asian Americans become ethnic rather than racial, but in the first option whiteness is not redefined; it retains its identity as the powerful, dominant ethnic/racial identification and category in the United States into which other groups must assimilate. In the second option, whiteness is forced to change, losing some of its dominance and allying itself with other, competing ethnic groups with whom it must share power. The possibility that, in either option, (some) Asian Americans may become an ethnic group that either assimilates into whiteness or transforms whiteness by becoming its ally is objectionable to mainstream Asian American intellectuals, whose discourse of the bad subject is predicated upon the insistence of a fundamental racial difference from whites. While this racial difference is (of course) articulated by Asian American intellectuals as a social and historical construction, it is also nevertheless quite often construed, implicitly, as an essential—and not a strategically essential—difference.

One example that illustrates my claim about an implied reliance upon essentialism is Ronald Takaki's argument with the neoconservative intellectual Nathan Glazer that concerned the possibilities of minority assimilation. Glazer, in an article originally published in 1975, compares the situation of blacks, Chinese, and Irish from the nineteenth century until the present and argues that if the Irish, once characterized by American society as "white negroes," can overcome hurdles of discrimination and become a part of the white mainstream and if the Chinese by the 1970s have almost done the same, then so can blacks, if they learn to rely on themselves rather than on government assistance, which was never proffered to the Irish or the Chinese (1994). Takaki claims that Glazer's argument blurs the line between race and ethnicity, implicitly positing that Chinese, Irish, and blacks are equivalent ethnic groups ("Reflections on Racial Patterns"). In reality, Takaki argues, an overarching racial difference separates the Irish, as white, from the Chinese and blacks, as nonwhite; the eventual success of the Irish is partially predicated upon their whiteness and the opportunities this affords. Takaki's argument about the subordinate nature of ethnicity under race is fundamental for Asian American intellectuals, but it is based upon a tautology: the Irish can become white because they look white, and the Chinese cannot become white because they do not look white. Yet historical evidence demonstrates that in the nineteenth century the Irish *did not look white*, at least to other European Americans who had already claimed the mantle of whiteness.[28] If the Irish can become white, when they were seen by others as black, or at least nonwhite, then what is to prevent any other nonwhite group from doing the same? The situation of the Irish demonstrates that race is not inherently visible through physical characteristics such as skin color, hair texture, and eye and nose shape, but that race is instead something that we learn to see. Robyn Wiegman's question about the visibility of race is worth quoting here: does the "fact of blackness" (or any other color) "lie in the body and its epidermis or in the cultural training that quite literally teaches the eye not only how but what to see?" (22).

Against Wiegman's question, the discourse of the bad subject implicitly assumes that Asian Americans simply do not look white, cannot look white, and therefore can never be white, a set of assumptions produced from a history of cultural training in regard to how we see race. My point in demonstrating this assumed (and denied) essentialism on the part of many Asian American intellectuals is not, in the end, to argue that my speculations about (some) Asian Americans becoming white or becoming aligned with whiteness will come true. Rather, it is to argue that the meanings and perceptions of race are dynamic and unpredictable and that the discourse of the bad subject is, in many ways, not prepared to address the possibility of changes in racial identity and perception that are antithetical to its own assumptions. Of course, one of the basic assumptions of the discourse of the bad subject is that the establishment and maintenance of an Asian American subjectivity as a resistant identity is a good thing, yet as David Li argues, there is a paradox in such efforts: a "definitive Asian American culture would be premature at this point. If there were, there would also have been a complete resolution of the American democratic contradiction, and accordingly, the expiration of 'Asian America(n)'s categorical and historical functions" (16). Li suggests that a *definitive* Asian American culture can exist only—and ironically—when the *need* for such a culture has expired. Hence, a definitive Asian American culture implies the transformation of Asian Americans from a racial group predicated upon the need for political defensiveness to an ethnic group predicated upon a successfully completed assimilation into American pluralism—a complete transformation, in other words, of the very nature of the Asian American body politic.

At the present moment, such a formulation of Asian Americans—as an ethnic group—would be inaccurate and is indeed anathema to most Asian American intellectuals who are convinced that Asian Americans are racially different from whites (and rightfully so, in the contemporary context). The work of Asian American intellectuals is dependent, to some extent, upon the continuing validity of such a characterization and the endurance of the conditions that mark Asian Americans as being racially different. Practitioners of Asian American culture and politics, as they strive to create a space for Asian Americans in the American nation, must then ask themselves to what end that space—Asian America—is created. Disagreements over the meaning of that space among academics, artists, activists, and panethnic entrepreneurs, split over the priority of multiculturalism as the definition for that space or conflicting notions of social and economic justice, will serve to dilute the usefulness of Asian America in the future. Ironically, this dilution comes about even as it seems inevitable that Asian Americans will become more influential in the nation's economy and, we hope, in its culture and politics as well. In these circumstances, when prosperity and inclusiveness for *some* Asian Americans blunt the power of Asian American leadership to maintain a political cohesiveness, Asian America itself as a category will be thrown into crisis, if it is not already in one. We can only hope that crisis will force Asian American intellectuals to determine new strategies that are not completely or finally dependent upon racial identity as a vehicle of long-term social change. As Deepika Bahri argues, the "performance of categorical identity for strategic political purposes may indeed be unavoidable but cannot be the goal for the long term. Even as we use these categories to combat the problems of the moment, we cannot ignore the reification that is inherent in their deployment" (41).[29] The space of racial identity itself will no longer serve as a place for consensus, which has significant ramifications for Asian American intellectuals who have proceeded on the tacit assumption that, regardless of ethnic and other diversities, Asian America at least had ideological common ground. While Asian America will undoubtedly have political uses in the future, it will have to serve an ideologically diverse constituency, and Asian America as a result will continue to see a polarization between those Asian Americans who perceive themselves and are perceived as the model minority, the inheritors of the American Dream, and those who perceive themselves and are perceived as bad subjects. It is doubtful that Asian America as a category, a space, or an identity will be adequate in addressing the needs and desires of those "bad subjects" in a future after multiculturalism.

NOTES

Introduction

1. Tomo Hattori in his article "Model Minority Discourse and Asian American Jouis-Sense" also notes the use of race as capital in ethnic studies and the negative connotations attached to such a valuation. He argues that "what is unnecessary is the shame and fear of selling out that rules the discipline of Asian American Studies" (244); in this introduction, I argue that it is not only Asian American studies that is subject to such a fear but also Asian American intellectuals generally.

2. The articles in the annual volumes published by the Association for Asian American Studies are some examples of the academic field's self-representation as an intellectual community that is oppositional to American racial and class domination. See Hune and Okihiro (introduction to *Reflections on Shattered Windows*). In general, however, almost any influential book-length work in Asian American studies professes a similar ideological perspective. The fiction writers treated in this book often exhibit similar tendencies toward opposition, although they often are more amenable to moderation or compromise than their academic counterparts.

3. Yamanaka's supporters argued that her critics blatantly disregarded the aesthetic complexity of Yamanaka's depictions of Filipinos, which was done from the perspective of the local Japanese narrator. Various articles published in the *Association for Asian American Studies Newsletter* address the controversy. See Association for Asian American Studies ("Letter from the AAAS Board"), Espiritu ("From the AAAS President"), Okamura ("When Will It End?"), Revilla, and Simpson, Eng, and Ho.

4. An account of the politics of the protest can be found in Zia (109–135).

5. See Marx for a discussion of commodity fetishism, the basis of his theory of reification (163–178). Lukács provides a detailed account of reification, which is helpfully summarized by Carolyn Porter and applied to a study of American literature.

6. Donald M. Lowe examines the treatment of lifestyles as commodities in his work *The Body in Late-Capitalist USA*. Both Glenn Omatsu and Vijay Prashad (*Karma of Brown Folk*) argue that Asian American culture can resist capitalism by drawing upon the cultural traditions of particular Asian countries. China and India, in their respective arguments, offer legacies of revolution and radicalism that have been forgotten or obscured through the pressures of assimilation or exclusion on Chinese and Indian immigrants and their decendents. While their arguments are persuasive that these traditions exist and can be used productively by ethnic-specific Asian groups, it is not clear that a hybrid, panethnic Asian American culture will be able to draw as effectively upon such traditions in the face of a multiculturally oriented capitalism.

7. The range of works that embrace the contestatory position is vast. In sociology and urban planning, the work of Paul Ong, Edna Bonacich, and Lucie Cheng; in history, Ronald Takaki and Sucheng Chan; in literary and cultural criticism, Elaine Kim, Robert G. Lee, David Li, Jinqi Ling, Lisa Lowe, David Palumbo-Liu, and Sau-ling C. Wong; and this is only a brief selection. One of the few contestatory works to draw attention to the phenomenon of conservatism and accommodation among Asian Americans is Prashad's *The Karma of Brown Folk*, but it does so in order to demonstrate the dire necessity for a radical South Asian American politics.

8. This argument about the need for a self-critique is inspired by Rey Chow's claims in *Ethics after Idealism* that concern the conflict between "theory" and "cultural studies." In her book, Chow argues that the power of theory has come from the negative stance it has maintained as Western culture's other, a position that cultural studies has threatened to usurp. In so doing, however, cultural studies has tended to overlook its own idealization of culture. Chow defines "theory" narrowly as that which stems from the European philosophical tradition, while "cultural studies" is a broad-based term that includes postcolonial and minority discourse studies. She argues that "whether the claim to otherness is through the route of theory or through the route of culture . . . the fundamental fact of the accruing of privilege, capital, and class superiority through otherness has not been adequately challenged" (xix). Chow qualifies her call for otherness with this caveat: "This would be an arduous task, implying as it does the need to work negatively on those who are already bearers of various types of negation—of poverty, deprivation, abuse, distortion, discrimination, extermination. But this is also the reason their encounter with the *well-established* negativity of Western thought would prove poignant and provocative, providing as they will instructive antidotes to facile idealist and idealistic projections" (xxi).

9. These Filipino and South Asian scholars include Deepika Bahri, Oscar Campomanes, Nazli Kibria, Susan Koshy, Vijay Prashad, E. San Juan, Jr., Lavina Dhingra Shankar, Rajini Srikanth, and Urvashi Vaid. They are not alone, however. Early reconsiderations of the limits of Asian American studies came from founders of the field like Elaine Kim ("Beyond Railroads and Internment") and Michael Omi ("It Just Ain't the Sixties No More"). A growing number of Chinese and Japanese American scholars are also moving toward this reassessment of Asian American studies and its basis in panethnicity. These include Bill Ong Hing, Peter Kwong, Li, Shirley Geok-lin Lim, Colleen Lye, Aihwa Ong (*Flexible Citizenship*), and Palumbo-Liu. Tomo Hattori in his article "*China Man* Autoeroticism and the Remains of Asian America" also raises the topic of "the limits of Asian American studies" (216), which he identifies as the re-

liance upon authenticity and essentialism in the critical definition of Asian American literature.

10. Dana Takagi, in her book *The Retreat from Race*, examines the politics of racial discourse in the admissions controversies that concerned Asian American students and American universities in the 1980s. She argues that the result of the controversies was a retreat from race in the discourse around admissions specifically and the place of people of color in American culture in general. The retreat from race did not signal a decline in the importance of race to various modes of differentiation but instead signaled a discursive retreat that masked ideological agendas that were frequently race-based. The retreat from race was often partnered with a return to class as a mode of preference in college admissions, but addressing class in and of itself could not compensate for the entrenched social differences found between races as a legacy of American racism. Ironically, the turn to class was pioneered by conservatives and adopted by liberals. Takagi's work warns ultimately that a dependency on class solutions cannot address the complexity of social inequality in the United States, because it dismisses the embeddedness of racial difference. It may also actually enhance a conservative reliance on class difference as an ongoing aspect of American society that can be addressed by traditional American values of hard work and self-reliance.

11. I thank Tina Chen for pointing out to me the possibility of Asian American neoconservatives' assuming the status of organic intellectuals (personal communication, March 11, 2001).

12. Edna Bonacich argues that the university is able to discipline and absorb oppositional practices because of its reproductive and stabilizing function. According to Bonacich, the university in general serves to advance the interests of the state by creating the conditions for reproduction of a new middle class.

13. This claim may be most suitable in the context of literary criticism and the institution of the English department, where it seems that the study of Asian American literature has reached a significant degree of acceptance. This may not be the case for other disciplines, and it is critical to note that in some circumstances where Asian American studies is relatively autonomous in the university it must engage in constant struggles for its existence. I thank Abdul R. JanMohamed for pointing out to me the distinction between disciplines for Asian American intellectuals.

14. Their influence can be seen in almost any subsequent work of Asian American studies; a broad-ranging selection includes Espiritu, Robert G. Lee, Tuan, Palumbo-Liu, and San Juan (*Racial Formations/Critical Transformations*).

15. One of the most important ways Asian Americans became aware of their racial identity was in regard to the advantage such an identity posed in a state partially defined around the distribution of resources along racial lines. South Asian Americans, who have a troubled history in regard to the ways that they have been defined by the American state racially, petitioned in 1974 to be included in the census as Asian Americans. See Shankar ("The Limits of [South Asian] Names and Labels") for an account of the fluctuations in state definitions of South Asians.

16. Pierre Macherey argues that "the act of knowing is not like listening to a discourse already constituted, a mere fiction which we have simply to translate. It is rather the elaboration of a new discourse, the articulation of silence" (6); following upon this, King-Kok Cheung uses the term "articulate silences" to describe the use of meaningful silence in Asian American literature. I adopt their use of the term—and the method of listening to silence—to demonstrate how the disavowal of hegemonic reproduction by the majority of Asian American intellectuals proceeds by a refusal to speak its existence rather than an active disclaimer.

17. While Espiritu does not mention academics in this panethnic group of middle-class leaders, David Li does characterize Asian American academics as a "professional-managerial class" (200). In his important article on the evolution of Asian American identity politics in relationship to political activism, Glenn Omatsu also notes the phenomenon of the rising middle class assuming the mantle of leadership, at the expense of class- and community-based Asian American leadership.

18. The most forceful proponents of such a position are Campomanes, San Juan, and Koshy.

19. Southeast Asian refugees and Pacific Islanders are usually the groups referred to when Asian Americans wish to point to ethnic groups that are economically disadvantaged in relation to other Asian American groups. Higher rates of poverty, lower rates of college attendance, etc., are related to both the histories of immigration and reception and the immigrant groups' original socioeconomic status in the nation of origin. In contrast, groups like Japanese Americans and legal emigrants from Hong Kong and Taiwan are associated with economic and educational success. The correlation between ethnicity and class often leads to an analytical blurring between the two, so that interethnic conflict and prejudice is attributed solely to ethnic difference, rather than the equally, if not more, important class difference.

20. As many critics have noted, multiculturalism is a deceptively egalitarian program for cultural inclusion that masks serious inequalities and unevenness across economic and political representation and inclusion. See Lowe (*Immigrant Acts*) and Chow for two particularly incisive critiques. See Goldberg for a defense of multiculturalism in a "critical" stance. Asian America in its multicultural deployment serves to include Asian Americans in American pluralism even as internal differences of ethnicity and class in the Asian American coalition are elided. In the contemporary context of pluralism and its associated idea of equal possibilities for national assimilation for all ethnicities and races, Asian Americans serve as a model minority who demonstrate the potential for American inclusiveness, disciplining other, less successful minorities. For critical analyses of the ideological uses of the model minority in dominant American discourse, see Gotanda, Osajima, Omatsu, Palumbo-Liu, and San Juan (*Racial Formations/Critical Transformations*). While Asian American studies has maintained a relatively uniform theoretical front in critiquing multiculturalism, it has implicitly affirmed a practical multiculturalism within the academy.

21. Asian Americans, for example, constitute a potential and actual workforce in the expansion of U.S. interests in Asia, while the existence of a substantial portion of the Asian American community in the United States is a direct consequence of labor needs in post-1965 American technological and medical industries (on Asian American immigration, see Hing, Chan [*Asian Americans*], and Takaki [*Strangers from a Different Shore*]). The United States as a powerful presence in that global capitalism is one aspect of the nation-state to which Asian America consents.

22. Kwong is one of a body of scholars who are united around the argument that Asian American studies as a whole has drifted away from its original base in class analysis and community activism into an emphasis upon panethnicity. See Bonacich, Kiang, Kwong, and Mar.

23. David Harvey, in his book *The Condition of Postmodernity*, traces the bourgeois commodification and appropriation of a modernist art that was intent on rejecting bourgeois values of art as a consumable object. The revolutionary aesthetic advances made in modernist art are precisely what make it unique and hence valuable in a bourgeois economy. Thomas Frank develops an argument that concerns the contem-

porary capitalist exploitation of rebellion as a marketable lifestyle, peddled to consumers and capitalists alike.

24. Using Bourdieu does have its limits. From Asian American studies the primary objection may stem from the fact that Bourdieu's theory works best in the context of a homogenized conception of French society in which class is the primary mode of social distinction, while other characteristics such as race and gender are treated as "secondary." See Bourdieu's *Distinction* in regard to the treatment of race and gender as secondary characteristics.

25. The body politic is not simply an easy metaphor I use to bridge the representation of the body in literature with a conception of the state as being analogous to the human body itself. Certainly the idea of the state as being a body politic has deep roots. These roots date to Plato, as many scholars of the history of the body have charted. See Grosz, Schatzki and Natter, Synnott, and Turner.

26. Here I appropriate from Elizabeth Grosz, who speaks of the body in general, not only the Asian American body. The work of Grosz and Judith Butler on the cultural dimensions of the body makes its presence felt throughout this book.

27. Elaine Kim and Lisa Lowe also present this periodization in their editorial introduction to a special issue of *positions: east asia cultures critique* on Asian America ("New Formations, New Questions"). The relationship of Asian Americans to the nation, as either alien object or abject subject, is rendered metaphorically in the American political and cultural imagination as a bodily relation, according to Robert G. Lee. Asian Americans during the period of formal exclusion (1882–1952) were portrayed in literature, film, and political cartoons with great attention to their bodily images as well as their relationship to American bodies. A useful collection of the visual representations of the Chinese in American periodicals can be found in *The Coming Man: 19th Century American Perceptions of the Chinese*, edited by Choy, Dong, and Hom. Histories of the "yellow peril" in American culture can be found in Robert G. Lee, Okihiro (*Margins and Mainstreams*), Thompson, and Wu.

28. Edward Said provides the larger cultural and historical justification for this argument about the West's construction of the Orient as a servile and threatening other. In *Orientalism*, he argues that a worldview divided Europe and the Orient into distinct categories through which values, capabilities, and epistemologies could be filtered. In the European imagination, the Orient became associated with various weaknesses and degeneracies seen to stem from the body, leading the Orient into decline and feminization, vis-à-vis the masculine and rational Occident. While Said was addressing French and British versions of orientalism, American orientalism existed since at least the eighteenth century (Schueller) and manifested itself in visible and memorable ways in the legal, political, and popular treatment of Chinese immigrants in the nineteenth century.

29. Numerous scholars have put forth the argument, in different disciplinary contexts, that concerns the Asian as a perpetual foreigner in dominant American discourse. Angelo N. Ancheta studies the legal representations, Robert G. Lee discusses the popular culture representations, David Li and Lisa Lowe (*Immigrant Acts*) analyze the usage of such representations in culture and political economy, and Mia Tuan uses the idea in a sociological study of contemporary Asian Americans. The fact that Asian Americans are depicted as a cancer emphasizes their utterly bodily dimension, a critical component of racist discourse, which posited that Europeans and European Americans possessed rationality while all others were trapped by their body and its desires. The division between the West and rationality, on the one hand, and the rest and bestiality, on the other, justified European domination. This argument can be found in

numerous works concerned with the role of the body in both European and American society. See Cameron, Falk, Grosz, Sánchez-Eppler, Schatzki and Natter, Synnott, and Turner.

30. The legal scholar Alan Hyde claims that U.S. law separates "bodies" from "persons" in a repetition of Cartesian dualism (258), so that the human body is described in "cold metaphors" of "machine, property, privacy" (104). This abstraction of the human subject serves "the chief function of law in advanced societies [, which] is to provide a totalizing vocabulary under which people will become incapable of articulating any modalities of human interaction except as the relations between buyers and sellers in markets, and between bearers of abstract rights" (48).

31. The much-maligned category of identity politics is about the commodification of ethnicity, in which human relations of difference become objects of exchange and supplementation. Rey Chow argues that ethnicity in this commodification is "idealized" because it becomes an object removed from its material history as a social construct and instead becomes an ahistorical, essential property. Lisa Lowe supplements this argument, however, when she argues that cultural identities "are always in the process of, on the one hand, being appropriated and commodified by commercial culture and, on the other, of being rearticulated for the creation of oppositional 'resistance cultures'" (*Immigrant Acts* 82). If we consider identity politics as being premised on the body, there is also the possibility that, as Bryan S. Turner argues, "the pleasures of the body are never wholly incorporated by consumerism; they may become features of individualistic protest and opposition," leading to what Dorinne Kondo calls a politics of pleasure (227) that may be profitably theorized for Asian American culture.

32. According to Chris Schilling, "The body has become a project for many persons [, which] entails recognizing that its appearance, size, shape and even its contents are potentially open to reconstruction in line with the designs of its owner. . . . This involves a practical recognition of the signification of bodies" (5).

33. Turner claims that the "body is a site of enormous symbolic work and symbolic production. . . . The body is both an environment we practice on and also practice with. We labour on, in and with bodies. . . . Our body maintenance creates social bonds, expresses social relations and reaffirms or denies them" (191).

34. See note 28.

35. The 2000 census's allowing people to check off multiple racial identifications, instead of a singular one, is an example of a change in the cultural and political definition of both racial identification and the body.

36. Frank Chin argues that Asian Americans can be divided into the "real" and the "fake," into those who reject racism and those who are complicit with it. This position has been roundly rejected by Asian American critics as divisive. Yet while his rhetoric is more confrontational than Matsuda's, their positions on this one issue are essentially the same, and I would venture that many Asian American intellectuals may at least tacitly agree with Matsuda's stance.

37. While the term "false consciousness" has fallen into disrepute from a Marxist perspective, it seems applicable to the debates within Asian America given Matsuda's position that some Asian Americans are not real Asian Americans given certain conditions. Bill Hing addresses the issue of false consciousness and Asian American ideological unity directly: "Asian American activists themselves seem not to appreciate how a diversity of Asian experiences and interests might impede political unity. . . . Rarely do they acknowledge that the absence of a unified Asian front does not reflect

false consciousness so much as carefully considered responses to a host of socioeconomic and political circumstances that discourage groups from forming alliances or involving themselves in political institutions" (13).

38. Koshy's argument climaxes with a harsh, and rather unfair, critique of Sauling C. Wong's "Denationalization Reconsidered." Koshy gives short shrift to a critical element of Wong's argument, which is the cautionary note that Wong strikes in regard to the celebratory romanticization and the depoliticized quality of many arguments that concern diaspora, transnationalism, etc.

39. According to Louis Althusser, the "bad subjects" resist the interpellative power of dominant ideology; bad subjects "on occasion provoke the intervention of one of the detachments of the (repressive) State apparatus. But the vast majority of (good) subjects work all right 'all by themselves,' i.e., by ideology" ("Ideology and Ideological State Apparatuses" 181). I take up the implications of a discourse of the bad subject for Asian Americans in the conclusion.

40. Rachel Lee also diagnoses Asian America's resistance to a certain Asian-Pacific (or Pacific Rim) discourse as a function of the latter's heralding of the Asian transnational capitalist as the new "model minority" ("Asian American Cultural Production").

41. See note 20 for sources on this critique of multiculturalism.

42. In purely literary critical terms, Asian American critics, according to Jinqi Ling, equate textual "complexity" with a greater sophistication about racial and political matters that finds its analogue in contemporary critics' predisposition toward postmodern and poststructural theories. In this theoretical bias, resistance is viewed as complex and accommodation as simple (and vice versa in both cases). This, in the end, also means that critics favor contemporary texts over earlier texts, through a reluctance or refusal to historicize earlier texts' strategies. As I will argue in the next chapter, the exception to this tendency is an ironic one, when critics look to earlier texts not necessarily to historicize them and to understand their unique strategies but to project their own critical values onto the past and to discover that these texts share *contemporary* values.

43. The years 1943 through 1965 mark the transition from alienation to abjection, according to Li. In 1943, the U.S. Congress lifted immigration restrictions against the Chinese, allowing a symbolic quota of 105 per year. The changes in U.S. attitudes toward race and immigration climaxed with the passage of the immigration law of 1965, which opened the door for massive emigration from Asia. In an article on the landmark 1965 Immigration and Naturalization Act that transformed Asian immigration, however, Eithne Luibhed criticizes the tendency to see it as affirming a neutral and fair immigration policy. As she points out, the Act was only passed because, ironically, U.S. senators believed that it would not substantially change the nature of American immigration. In addition, the act is dependent upon and perpetuates a number of inequities and biased attitudes that concern race, class, and sexuality.

44. Hing, for example, warns explicitly about the dangers of speculating on the future of Asian America when he states that "no one can claim to know what Asian American ethnicity is or what it will become. No one can claim that a uniform identity exists. And certainly no one can claim to speak for Asian America" (183).

45. Prashad offers a detailed explanation for how and why an "antiblack racism" is created among South Asian Americans, who tend to refuse an identification with symbolic blackness, given the pejorative meaning of such blackness in the United States (157–184).

Chapter One

1. Throughout this chapter, I will be using the actual names and the pen names of the sisters interchangeably, although usually I will use the name that is appropriate to the context of my argument. Focusing on the Eatons as the originators of Asian American literature is to some extent arbitrary, but as the rest of this chapter will make clear, "origins," rather than existing absolutely, are often determined by the descendants of a genealogy. In the case of Asian American literature, a number of other moments, texts, and writers, anonymous and otherwise, might be chosen as an originary point for Asian American literature, depending on how one defines this literature, with language, genre, medium, and distribution all being variable factors that might be considered. Asian American literature in languages other than English constitutes the most significant other source of origins, as Chinese immigrants wrote about their experiences in their own language starting in the latter half of the nineteenth century.

2. All of the Eaton children looked white, and the combination of their surname and their appearance meant that they could pass as white. All of them except Edith and her sister Winnifred did so.

3. The primary sources for Sui Sin Far's life are White-Parks (*Sui Sin Far/Edith Maude Eaton*) and Amy Ling ("Edith Eaton" and *Between Worlds*).

4. While this is generally true for most Asian American literary critics, perhaps the ones who put the search in these terms most nakedly were Chin and the other editors of the groundbreaking *Aiiieeeee!: An Anthology of Asian-American Writers*, in their introduction to that work.

5. David Palumbo-Liu presents a lengthy and detailed argument that concerns the various ways by which Asian American culture has been formed out of the interaction between Asia and America. He uses the term "Asian/American" to signify the overlap and slippage between Asia and America that creates an ambivalent space where Asian American culture exists.

6. Angelo N. Ancheta coins the term "differential racialization" but uses it in the context of intraethnic differences between the Asian American communities. I take Ancheta's original concept and adapt it to my own purposes here. The critical exception to this trend of distinguishing Asian Americans as the yellow peril or the model minority is embodied in those capitalist and allied nations, such as Japan during the 1980s, whose economic success becomes too threatening to the United States. Japan is then cast again as the yellow peril. In these circumstances, the latent ideological content of the model minority concept reveals itself, demonstrating that the model minority stereotype is simply the reverse image of the yellow peril.

7. Larry Shinagawa and Gin Pang, in their article on Asian Americans and intermarriage, note that Asian Americans have their own ethnic hierarchies of preference when it comes to intraethnic dating and marriage.

8. In addition to Annette White-Parks's literary biography of Sui Sin Far, see White-Parks's article "'We Wear the Mask'" for additional arguments about trickster-ism in Sui Sin Far's writing, and Matsukawa for tricksterism in Onoto Watanna's work.

9. Even if one argues that the situation of the Chinese in nineteenth-century America is not a "colonial" situation, their treatment still bears many resemblances to colonial methods of cultural representation and domination. In our increasing awareness of the world as being dependent upon a transnational economic system that has been in development ever since the age of colonialism, we can see how American "minority discourse" exists on a global imperialist continuum that has on its other end an-

other set of local phenomena, which are colonial discourses. As Amy Kaplan summarizes this continuum so aptly, "Imperialism as a political or economic process abroad is inseparable from the social relations and cultural discourses of race, gender, ethnicity, and class at home" ("'Left Alone with America'" 16). China itself exists at the end point of American imperial policy at the turn of the century; as Takaki (*Iron Cages*) and Schirmer and Shalom have shown, the American wars in Cuba and the Philippines were conceived as strategically necessary steps to secure the Pacific as an "American lake" and route to China's markets.

10. For an early source on internal colonialism, see Blauner; for a critique of Blauner's model, see Omi and Winant.

11. Johannes Fabian makes this argument that concerns the suspension of time in regard to anthropology's representation of "natives" in general.

12. The 1882 Exclusion Act and the 1875 Page Law effectively excluded women from entry and therefore prevented the formation of families and the propagation of subsequent generations.

13. On the history of Chinese women, including the American perception of them as prostitutes, see Yung, especially pages 1–105.

14. Robert G. Lee and David Li both provide detailed accounts of the alien status of the Asian American subject in American culture and history from the nineteenth through the twentieth century.

15. Previous to Annette White-Parks, Xiao-Huang Yin was the only critic of Sui Sin Far to consider her work "authentic," and this reading is largely due to the ethnographic depictions of Chinatown life that one can find in some of Sui Sin Far's stories.

16. For feminist critiques of Gusdorf's limited definitions, see Benstock and Heilbrun.

17. In their respective introductions, David Lloyd (*Nationalism and Minor Literature*) and Lisa Lowe (*Immigrant Acts*) have argued in separate contexts for genre's ability to determine, to some extent, the ideological possibilities of works written within the genre. Barbara Foley (*Radical Representations*) qualifies these arguments by proposing that the generic politics of form should be countered by the doctrinal politics of content.

18. The critical audience (editors and reviewers) for autobiographies was certainly male. Whether the large female reading audience for popular literature also extended to women autobiographers is not clear in Smith's work.

19. This racial identity is Chinese, which would seem to presuppose a commitment to national identity. Yet if we think of her as a proto–Chinese American, this presupposition would not be true, to the extent that Chinese Americans make no claim to China. The racial identity of a Chinese American, born out of a reaction against racism, is supposed to lead through political efforts to dominant society's recognition of that person's individuality and humanity *despite* his or her race. The fact that this is all very contradictory is a function of racial formation's contradictions in the first place.

20. Werner Sollors offers a very well known paradigm for explaining assimilation and cultural self-effacement, using the model of "descent" and "consent" to explain how ethnic immigrants shed their ties of blood descent and agree to consent to an American identity.

21. One finds this type of narrative often in autobiographical and historical accounts of Asian American activists and writers. Most of these accounts are taped or are published in periodicals, but several book-length accounts are notable "classics" of Asian American literature, namely Bulosan (*America Is in the Heart*), Chin et al. ("Introduction"), and Mura (*Turning Japanese*).

22. Oppositional politics of identity generally freeze at this moment of cultural "rediscovery" and skirt the questions of self-knowledge and self-representation. In Frank Chin's work, for example, one can trace a paradoxical retreat to Chinese culture as the source of authentic Chinese American culture. One can find this most prominently in "Come All Ye Asian American Writers," in which he advocates a Chinese legend of heroic outlaws as an appropriate model for Asian American behavior. This can be contrasted with his position in earlier essays like "Backtalk" (1972), where he recounts how Chinese American college students were forced to list, in two separate columns, their "Chinese" qualities and their "American" qualities. This division refused the recognition of a third identity, the Chinese American, which was a uniquely American-bound product. The dominant hero for Chin at the time was the Chinese American railroad worker. See chapter 3 for a more detailed account of Chin.

23. *Me* was published anonymously but became the subject of notoriety as critics and readers tried to guess who the author was. She was eventually revealed as Winnifred Eaton, the "real" author behind both the anonymous authorial identity and the pseudonymous authorial identity of Onoto Watanna. The self that is being constructed here is not, then, Onoto Watanna, half-Japanese author and literary celebrity, but Winnifred Eaton, whose "basic" whiteness is being affirmed.

24. Eve Oishi provides the most detailed argument for reading the figure of the "new woman" into the works of Onoto Watanna.

25. The closest Nora comes to acknowledging her ancestry is to mention that she herself was "dark and foreign-looking" (Eaton 41), with a mother from a foreign land (125).

26. Hattori also examines this critical scene that involves Burbank. He argues that Burbank's Jewishness is produced retrospectively by Nora as an explanation for Burbank's wealth (which, in her eyes, is surprising for a black man to possess): "Burbank's Jewishness, and his large hooked nose, are revisions of his body that help Nora to naturalize his color with his capital" ("Model Minority Discourse" 237).

27. Samina Najmi notes that Eaton was also friends with James Weldon Johnson (xxiii).

28. These are: boy and girl meet and face an initial obstruction to their romance that they overcome, only to face a second obstruction that leads to a prolonged separation, after which they are finally reunified. Ling cites Janice Radway's study of the romance novel to help account for the formulaic qualities of Onoto Watanna's novels.

29. Amy Ling's critical work on Onoto Watanna represents an interesting shift from dismissal to qualified reappraisal. Najmi, Oishi, and Yuko Matsukawa are among the critics who attempt to find more transgressive elements in Onoto Watanna's novels. Najmi presents an interesting argument that one reason for the critical neglect of Onoto Watanna is her refusal to discuss race in terms that fit "contemporary multicultural agendas," an argument that touches upon my concerns here (xxxiii).

30. Passing is distinct from racial "drag," which has its limits as a transgressive form. Traise Yamamoto notes in discussing the differences between gender drag and racial drag that "the subversion, 'resignification and recontextualization' of drag do not, in fact, tend to manifest themselves when transferred from gender to race largely because the success of racial drag performances, like yellowface, relies on its ability to simultaneously transgress and reify categories of racial difference through mirroring, reconfirming race as an originary site of essential alterity" (31). For a provocative examination of the transvestite in Sui Sin Far's work, see Song.

31. Onoto Watanna's use of the Irish is probably intentional. Noel Ignatiev and

David Roediger argue that the Irish "became white" in their assimilation into American society, shedding their colonial status as "white negroes."

32. *Sunny-San* is also published much later than Onoto Watanna's other Japanese fictions, at a time when American anger at Japanese immigration had culminated in the passage of various alien land laws that forbade the ownership of property by Japanese immigrants and the 1917 immigration law that closed all further emigration from Japan. The Cable Act, which stripped American citizenship from citizens who married aliens ineligible for citizenship, was passed in 1921. Interestingly, Najmi notes that Onoto Watanna retracted her claim to Japanese ancestry in the 1940s when such ancestry became unfashionable, to say the least (xviii).

33. Najmi, in her introduction to the reprint of Onoto Watanna's 1903 novel *The Heart of Hyacinth*, also argues that that novel "questions the very concept of biological race" (xxxvi); this concern about the fiction of race as biological is one that crosses many of Onoto Watanna's works.

34. The gaze in the works of Onoto Watanna is an ambivalent one, seemingly coded from a Western perspective through an assumed audience and the value system expressed in her writing, which favors the status quo of race, class, and gender. The gaze is occasionally returned, however, sometimes by characters and sometimes by the implied perspective of the novel, as we shall see in *Miss Numè of Japan*. These reversals of the Western gaze create moments of ambivalence as the contradictions of the status quo are revealed in the figures of marginal women engaged in boundary-crossing romances that hint at class and cultural miscegenation.

35. This is an example of Numè's speech as she expresses her affection for Sinclair: "'Me? I lig' you,' she said, shyly. 'You are *big*—and thad you nod lig' poor liddle Japanese womans—still I lig' you jus' same'" (*Miss Numè* 87).

36. In the frontispiece to *The Wooing of Wistaria*, Onoto Watanna has signed her name in Japanese, reinforcing the authenticity of her adopted identity. Matsukawa presents an interesting reading of the meaning of Onoto Watanna's name. The photographs in *Miss Numè of Japan* are found in the original edition, not the reprint.

37. One sign of this parody on the part of Sui Sin Far is her naming of the Spring Fragrances, the only characters in the collection with their Chinese names translated into English. The very naming of the characters suggests their function as translators and mediators.

38. Yin has already pointed out how even here Sui Sin Far plays with notions of ethnic difference by making the Carmans, an Irish family, ascendant and accepted in the social order over Alice Winthrop, bearer of that prestigious colonial name (63).

39. Other critics besides Lorraine Dong and Marlon K. Hom who have seen Sui Sin Far in this fashion include S. E. Solberg, who argues that "she was not a great writer . . . but her attempts deserve recognition" (27); and Amy Ling, who was to later repudiate her own claim that Sui Sin Far was not "a writer for all ages, [although] she was certainly an extraordinary person in her own time" ("Edith Eaton" 297).

40. Racial awareness as a sign of political consciousness obviously does not imply any distinct ideological orientation, aside from the acknowledgment of identity itself. While it could be argued that racial awareness/political consciousness may constitute the "content" of the literature Asian American literary critics choose to read, more than "value," it is difficult to distinguish the two in this particular context. Critics of Asian American literature place "value" upon literature that exhibits racial awareness, because it is this type of literature that is a clear object of identification and categorization for the critics. Also, as the introduction argues, this type of racially aware literature produces "value" by being a distinct commodity in the business of literary study.

Chapter Two

1. For critical views of Bulosan in book-length surveys of Asian American litera-ture, see Elaine Kim (*Asian American Literature* 43–57) and Wong (*Reading Asian American Literature* 133–136), and for Okada, see Kim (*Asian American Literature* 148–156). The critic E. San Juan Jr. has made it his lifework to expound on the impor-tance of Bulosan to Asian American and radical literatures. For a recent selection of San Juan's critical work on Bulosan, see *Racial Formations/Critical Transformations*, "In Search of Filipino Writing," and his introductions to *On Becoming Filipino* and *The Cry and the Dedication*. Finally, in Frank Chin's afterword to *No-No Boy*, he de-scribes the historical importance of John Okada's work, at least to Chin and his col-leagues. For an account of the literary history of this time period for Asian Americans, and the impact of politics and publishing on *No-No Boy* in particular, see Jinqi Ling ("Race, Power, and Cultural Politics" 360–362).

2. Jinqi Ling argues that the two terms, "emasculation" and "feminization," are often and inaccurately collapsed in the case of Asian American criticism: "'Emascula-tion' more fully suggests the overall social consequence of the displacement of Asian men's subject position, whereas 'feminization' constitutes but one specific form of Asian men's racial gendering in America, as differing from (but not opposed to) an-other form to which they are sometimes subject—the perception of them as sex fiends" ("Identity Crisis and Gender Politics" 314).

3. For autobiographical information on Bulosan's life, see Evangelista and Mor-rante. According to E. San Juan Jr., Bulosan was the most visible of all Filipino Ameri-can writers during the 1940s. His decline and downfall are illustrated in his death in 1956. He died on the steps of Seattle City Hall, after a bout of drinking and pneumonia (San Juan, introduction to *On Becoming Filipino* 37). By then, the FBI had already blacklisted Bulosan as a subversive. The University of Washington Press would not reprint *America Is in the Heart* until 1973.

4. For general histories on this time period and the impact of the Cold War do-mestically, see Leffler (56–126), Gillon and Kutz (2–41), and Mason (8–22).

5. For an account of intellectual thought during the 1950s and the turn to liberal centrism, partially as a reaction against the perceived excesses of the American Left of the 1930s and its debts to Stalinism, see Schaub.

6. For accounts of the impact of McCarthyist anticommunism, see Richard M. Fried and Albert Fried. For accounts of the more entrenched and structural version of anticommunism, see Whitfield and Kovel.

7. Other immigration openings followed upon the repeal of the Chinese Exclu-sion Act. Subsequent to the war, the War Brides Act allowed U.S. servicemen to bring home wives of Asian nationalities. In 1946, Asian Indians were allowed naturalization rights and a small immigration quota. The McCarran-Walter Act of 1952 eliminated the racial restrictions of the 1790 naturalization law and allowed emigration from the "Asian-Pacific Triangle," but with only 100 emigrants from each nation of the triangle allowed. For a fuller account of these changes, see Takaki (*Strangers* 357–418).

8. The Philippines, even after becoming independent from the United States in 1946, remained a critical part of the U.S. strategy in the Pacific in the Cold War years. For detailed information on the changing situations of various Asian American groups in the immediate post–World War II era, see Takaki (*Strangers* 357–405) and Chan (*Asian Americans* 121–142).

9. For a history of American manhood and its relationship to the construction of public and private spaces, see Rotundo, Kimmel, and Bederman. Rotundo is primarily

concerned with pre-twentieth-century middle-class New England manhood, Kimmel with middle-class American manhood from the same period through the twentieth century, and Bederman with late-nineteenth- and early-twentieth-century American manhood in the imperial context.

10. Asian American studies, however, sometimes treats the Asian American subject as genderless, such that gender only appears in the infamous "women's chapter." Elaine Kim, for example, has criticized Takaki for organizing his history in this way, treating women's appearances as contributions or exceptions to the normative, masculine narrative of Asian American history ("Critique"). See also Okihiro for an argument on "recentering women" and gender in historiographical narratives (*Margins and Mainstreams* 64–92).

11. On the history of the Page Law, see Chan (*Asian Americans* 54) and Takaki (*Strangers* 40). On antimiscegenation laws and their eventual repeal, see Takaki (*Strangers* 101–102, 330–331, 342, 406, 473) and Chan (*Asian Americans* 59–61, 116).

12. On Asian immigrants in the Hawaiian economy, see Takaki (*Pau Hana*).

13. I use Butler here because of her language of materialism, but numerous feminist theorists have preceded Butler in proposing similar arguments, including Gloria Anzaldúa, Chandra Talpade Mohanty, and Trinh T. Minh-ha. In addition to them, many critics have specifically addressed the intersection of at least gender and race in relationship to Asian Americans. In regard to literature, see Cheung (*Articulate Silences*), Eng ("In the Shadows of a Diva"), Kim and Alarcón (*Writing Self, Writing Nation*), Amy Ling (*Between Worlds*), Jinqi Ling ("Identity Crisis"), and Sau-ling C. Wong ("Ethnicizing Gender"). In relation to Asian American studies, culture, and politics in general, see Leong (*Asian American Sexualities*), Lisa Lowe (*Immigrant Acts*), Matsuda, and Shah.

14. For Kathi Weeks, one of the problems with Butler's otherwise useful concept of performativity is that "Butler fails to situate these compulsory discursive practices within a socioeconomic matrix: language is attributed a determinative power that isolates and exaggerates its constitutive force" (95). In this vein, the Asian American body politic assumes shape and substance not only through language but also through acts of labor, and this materiality of the working body impinges upon the performative acts of gender. Rosemary Hennessy focuses on this aspect of labor's impact on the subject when she accuses Butler of restricting her analysis of the "social to the domains of culture and the law" (225), while historical materialism would consider labor as an equally important site for the formation of the social and the subject.

15. On the partiality of law in relation to race in general and Asian Americans in particular, see Matsuda (21–27, 51–59). On the usefulness and limitations of Butler in relationship to the representation of the body in law, see Hyde (147).

16. Hysteria over the heterosexual desires of Filipino males was crystallized in various antimiscegenation acts. See Takaki (*Strangers* 327–331, 341–343).

17. See Parreñas for an account of white women's status in the dance halls frequented by Filipino laborers during the 1930s. Ironically, these dancers were mostly poor or working-class women who also, Parreñas argues, found some upward social mobility through the pay they received.

18. A list of these characters in *America* follows: an Indian woman who entraps Carlos's friend into marriage (103), a blond woman who works in a taxi dance hall (105–110), a girl who is raped (113–115), anonymous women at an orgy (131–132), and a wanton Mexican wife (149–151). When their sexuality is unchecked white women of the wealthier classes or from more educated backgrounds also pose threats to Carlos and other Filipino men: the wealthy woman who displays her naked self to

Carlos (141–142); Helen, the agent provocateur and labor organizer who seduces Carlos's brother (202–203); and another labor organizer, Lucia Simpson, who is motivated by sex (290–293).

19. Sheng-Mei Ma argues that Carlos's desire for or admiration of white women stems from the legacies of Spanish and U.S. colonialism and the construction within them of the "white" or "fair" woman as an idealized object of desire whose capture, for a Filipino man, is a sign of assimilation. Carlos and other Filipino men engage in "eroticizing America" (79) in order to "validate their own masculinity" (80). Bulosan's precedent for doing so, Ma argues, is found in the nationalist Filipino classic *Noli Me Tangere*, by the national hero José Rizal, which also features a fair-skinned mestiza heroine named Maria Clara. It is this eroticization, in contradiction with the revolutionary class politics in Bulosan's work, that produces the ambivalence toward America that Ma finds troubling.

20. See Denning, Rideout (241–254), and Foley (243) for accounts of Popular Front strategy and its impact on the development and history of the proletarian novel in the United States. Bulosan's Marxist sympathies become extremely clear—that is, shorn of the language of American pluralism and celebration—in his journalism, as Susan Evangelista also notes (213). See Bulosan ("Labor and Capital").

21. Other commentators on the Cold War with perspectives similar to Rogin's include Whitfield and Kovel.

22. Question 28 was eventually rewritten for the Issei, the immigrant generation, who faced an impossible dilemma with the original phrasing because they were ineligible for U.S. citizenship; answering yes would render them effectively stateless. The revised question read: "Will you swear to abide by the laws of the United States and to take no action which would in any way interfere with the war effort of the United States?" The information in this note comes from Daniels ("Concentration Camps").

23. For other sources on the social and economic effect of relocation on the Japanese American community, see Daniels; Daniels, Taylor, and Kitano; and Weglyn.

24. On various alien land law acts that prevented Asians from owning property in states that included Arizona, Arkansas, California, Idaho, Kansas, Louisiana, Montana, New Mexico, Oregon, Utah, Washington, and Wyoming, see Chan (*Asian Americans* 47) and Takaki (*Strangers* 203–208, 411–413). For legal restrictions on Japanese that prevented them from becoming citizens, see Chan (*Asian Americans* 47) and Takaki (*Strangers* 207–209).

25. A panopticon is a penal structure built around a central watchtower. The prisoners' cells surround the watchtower and are all visible from the watchtower. Surveillance is thus always a possibility. For an explanation and theoretical account of the panopticon, see Foucault (*Discipline and Punish* 170–228).

26. It could be argued that Japanese Americans were already of "a different breed" due to a number of legislative acts like the 1790 naturalization law, the 1924 Gentleman's Agreement, and others that prevented Japanese Americans from attaining citizenship or that barred them from immigration. War, internment, and the deprivation of civil rights, however, are completely different matters, transforming Japanese Americans from undesirable aliens to incarcerated subversives.

27. The subsequent information on the Huk rebellion comes from Kerkvliet, Kessler, and Pomeroy. While their assessments of the Huk rebellion are fairly similar, William J. Pomeroy, as a member of the rebellion himself, is the most sympathetic to their cause and the most critical of U.S. motivations. The date for the end of the rebellion, 1956, comes from Kerkvliet; there seems to be some disagreement among schol-

ars over the exact end of the rebellion, however, as different dates in the second half of the 1950s have been offered.

28. Money and certain material—weapons, ammunition, and communications equipment—were absolutely critical to the rebellion, and the lack of them ultimately contributed significantly to the rebellion's failure (Kerkvliet 210).

29. How much money, in this case, is unclear. At one moment Bulosan writes that it is 1 million pesos (*The Cry* 25), and at another that it is $5 million (101).

30. According to San Juan, Bulosan, like Dante, was interested in tracing Filipino history from the revolutionary viewpoint, with a four-novel series that depicted a hundred years of Philippine history. The only one of those novels that he completed was *The Cry and the Dedication* (ix).

31. This is a more critical issue than the possibility that women exist in Bulosan's imagination as either whores or heroines, which is certainly the case; Bulosan's imagination is allegorical, however, and the men are cast in the same terms of relative good and evil.

32. Baym's argument, which concerns American men authors during the nineteenth century, posits that they feel beset specifically by women, both women authors and readers. In this appropriation of Baym, I borrow her language to indicate that what besets men in Bulosan's work is not so much women as racial discrimination and economic oppression.

33. I use the term "ethnic entrepreneur" rather than "panethnic entrepreneur" because neither Bulosan nor Okada demonstrated much penchant for building an Asian American identity or using cross-Asian relationships or confusions as Onoto Watanna did. The one exception is Bulosan's mention in *America Is in the Heart* of the inspiration he drew from discovering Asian American authors (265–266).

Chapter Three

1. For a history of Asian American student and community movements, including accounts of the rising consciousness of violence and its role in revolution, see Wei and Omatsu. The period of 1943–1965, when a series of legislative actions started to lay the groundwork for a change in the legal, economic, and political status of Chinese Americans, formed a preliminary history to Asian American formation. In 1943, Congress repealed the bans on Chinese immigration that had endured since 1882 and instituted symbolic quotas for Chinese immigration. In 1952 the McCarran-Walter Immigration Act eliminated all further Asian immigration bans, and the 1965 Immigration and Naturalization Act eliminated discriminatory racial quotas for immigration, opening the way for a tremendous flow of immigration from Asian nations. For more information on the details and ramifications of the Immigration and Naturalization Act, see Takaki (*Strangers* 406–471) and Chan (*Asian Americans* 145–165).

2. On the relative permanence of anti-Asian stereotypes and the culturally and politically fraught position of contemporary Asian Americans as an "abject" population despite their seeming success, see Li. For the endurance of Asian stereotypes in popular film through the contemporary period, see Marchetti.

3. In her essay "Of Men and Men: Reconstructing Chinese American Masculinity," King-Kok Cheung also focuses upon Chin and Lee as authors who try to "measure up to American notions of manliness by valorizing physical aggression" (190). Cheung's project of reconstructing masculinity involves finding alternative models of masculinity not dependent upon violence, and even within the works of

Chin and Lee, Cheung is able to detect an "ethic of caring" in the behavior of violent men that can be redeemed and emphasized (192–194).

4. The term "crisis of hegemony" is developed more fully through the context of Great Britain in Hall et al.

5. The representation of Asians as a military and economic threat has a long history within the United States, through the image of the "yellow peril"; see Okihiro (*Margins and Mainstreams* 118–147) and Wu.

6. For the concept of biopolitics and biopower, see Foucault (*The History of Sexuality* 139–143).

7. For a visual history of these racial depictions, culled from American newspapers and magazines, see Choy, Dong, and Hom.

8. The exemplary case of this impact can be found in Frank Chin's body of work. While this chapter is concerned primarily with his work in the 1990s, the most revealing texts that concern his simultaneous antiracism and possible self-hatred are found in his writings of the 1970s. See Daniel Y. Kim for an analysis of this period of Chin's writing and psychology. It is important to note in the context of Chinese subordination that Chinese immigrants vigorously resisted, through legal means at the very least, the discrimination directed against them. See McClain for a history of the legal cases that involved anti-Chinese discrimination and their contestation by Chinese immigrants.

9. See, for example, the introductions to *Aiiieeeee!* and its sequel, *The Big Aiiieeeee!*

10. The introduction to *Aiiieeeee!* makes this clear.

11. There is also, of course, a comic dimension to his speech. For the comic properties of the novel, see So.

12. *Bildung* literally means "culture" or "cultivation." My information on the bildungsroman, and especially its literary history as a German cultural form, comes from Martini and Sammons.

13. Carol Nackenoff provides a rereading of Alger's work and legacy, arguing that he has been falsely maligned as an apologist for capitalism. In actuality, according to Nackenoff, Alger, while advocating so-called American values of self-reliance, thrift, industriousness, etc., was highly ambivalent about the social upheavals created by late nineteenth-century industrialism.

14. For an account of American novels that concern the Vietnam War and their representation of the Vietnamese, see Christopher. While there are many other critical accounts of this literature, most of them repeat the basic prejudice of perspective found in the novels they study, namely, the ethnocentric one of their young characters.

15. For more on Asian American literature and the adaptation of the bildungsroman, especially in relationship to gender and assimilation, see Chu (12–17).

16. For accounts of Asian Americans as being caught between the racial polarizations of black and white, see Tuan and Okihiro (*Margins and Mainstreams* 31–63).

17. Chin is able to engage in this literature of emasculation—he must engage in this literature—because the key works of John Okada and Carlos Bulosan on this topic had only recently been republished or rediscovered, by Chin and his fellow editors of *Aiiieeeee!* Thus the argument about Asian American emasculation, even though it had already been produced, had not yet entered the public consciousness of Asian Americans or, to put it more accurately, had been suppressed or forgotten.

18. Elaine Kim's assessment of Chin's writing in the 1970s generally sounded the tone for subsequent critical assessments of his work by academic critics until recently (*Asian American Literature*). Jinqi Ling, while acknowledging the problematic dimen-

sions of Chin's writing, especially in regard to women and polemics, argues that Chin's theatrical work "remains vital and productive" if seen in its historical context (*Narrating Nationalisms* 109).

19. On the importance of mobility as a motif in Asian American literature, see Sau-ling C. Wong (*Reading Asian American Literature* 118–165).

20. Eriche Goode and Nachman Ben-Yehuda discuss the history and terminology of moral panic in great detail, including definitions of "moral entrepreneurs" and "folk devils" that are helpful in discussing Chin's moral crusading against the threat of feminization.

21. These debates have been focused on the status of Maxine Hong Kingston's writing, in particular *The Woman Warrior*. Kingston's critics, led most vocally by Chin, accuse her of distorting Chinese culture in order to curry favor with American readers, who are generally predisposed, in Chin's opinion, to have orientalist tastes for the exotic. King-Kok Cheung states the position most clearly between a feminist critical approach and Chin's cultural nationalism ("The Woman Warrior"). Li provides an account of the criticisms directed against Kingston (49–55).

22. Sau-ling C. Wong traces the different Chinese legends that are amalgamated in Kingston's work ("Kingston's Handling").

Chapter Four

1. While the first volume is focused on war, dislocation, and family life, the second one is focused on immigrant travails and cultural conflicts. Sex and romance also serve as major themes through both books. This difference in thematic focus, in addition to differences in writing styles, led to the first volume being substantially more popular among critics than the second. See note 3.

2. Oliver Stone's film version of Hayslip's books, as we will see later, uses the victim as an absolver of guilt. As one prescient reviewer wrote after the publication of Hayslip's first book, "Ms. Hayslip never slides into bitterness, although she has good cause. She never chooses sides or places blame. . . . She manages so gracefully to transcend politics, keeping her humaneness as the focus. . . . If Hollywood has the courage to turn this book into a movie, then we Americans might finally have a chance to come to terms with the tragedy in Vietnam" (Shipler). I will continue to refer to Stone's work, which is exemplary of the American reception of Hayslip's books.

3. The audience is classified here ethnically, because the major distinctions in reaction toward Hayslip's work can be divided along Vietnamese American and American lines. Since these reviews have also generally been written by men, a distinct gender bias is also displayed, with American reviews generally favoring *When Heaven and Earth Changed Places* for its dramatic wartime setting and dismissing *Child of War, Woman of Peace* for its domestic melodramatic qualities (see Berger).

4. The classic example of this is the My Lai massacre; despite photographic evidence and eyewitness accounts, much of the American population refused to believe that the massacre actually occurred. For an account of My Lai, see Hersh.

5. Regarding the possibilities of speech and its filters, both of Hayslip's books are co-written, with some controversy over the extent of the co-writer's control over language and content. In this way, Hayslip shares a problem that all American minority collaborative autobiographers have faced: as Paul John Eakins has put it, "The balance of power is distinctly lopsided" between the "informant" and the white co-writer (8). It is the work of future scholars to determine what effect co-writing has had on the

final shape of Hayslip's books; it would hardly be surprising if that work traces ideo-logically crucial contributions to her coauthors, considering the history of co-written narratives. On complications with Vietnamese American co-written narratives, see Truong.

6. See Abdul R. JanMohamed and David Lloyd's introduction to *The Nature and Context of Minority Discourse* for a discussion of minority discourse as a product of damage.

7. It is only in antiwar discourse that the Vietnamese body becomes substantial, as victim rather than enemy; but this seeming substantiation does service in yet an-other conflict over cultural constructs, one in which the Vietnamese have no direct in-terest: the internal conflict over the definition of American society. Although it can now substantiate discursive claims, the victim's body here is objectified as the enemy body, because it has no part in the debate between the American political left and right, being instead evidence.

8. In *Weapons of the Weak*, James C. Scott argues that "the process by which any system of political or religious beliefs emanating from above is reinterpreted, blended with pre-existing beliefs, penetrated, and transformed is characteristic of any stratified society" (319).

9. I use Harvey's work and later Fredric Jameson's with the knowledge that both participate in the typical Marxist maneuver of rendering race, gender, and anticolonial-ism as secondary factors in the development of global capitalism and cultural forms such as modernism and postmodernism. I hope this chapter demonstrates the extent to which race and gender are constitutive factors in capitalism and that imperialism and colonialism and the revolutions against them shaped the First World as much as the Third World.

10. The evolution of nationalist feminism in colonized countries has followed a different mode of development from that of dominant (white, middle-class) feminism in the West. The development of feminism in Vietnam goes hand in hand with the an-ticolonial struggles against the French. The pressures on Vietnamese nationalism—from the Chinese, the French, the Americans, and Cold War isolationism—meant that feminism was often articulated within the needs and demands of nationalism. See Nguyen Thi Dinh, Jayawardena (196–212), and Marr (190–252). For Hayslip's own, negative attitude toward Western feminism, see her interview in King-Kok Cheung's *Words Matter* (Ho).

11. For details on the public/private split between husband and wife, with the hus-band being called the "Foreign Minister," see Nha-Trang (43–44); the idea that this split can lead to women maintaining the national culture is drawn from Partha Chatterjee, who shows how Indian modernization was accomplished through a bifurcation of gen-der roles (1990). Men, as representatives of the state to the outside world, were in charge of a desirable economic and technological modernization, while women, seen as the bearers of culture, were in charge of protecting the cultural "essence" from Western taint. For Vietnamese women, the belief that their proper place was in the home was re-inforced by the "four virtues" that should characterize their behavior concerning labor, physical appearance, appropriate speech, and proper behavior: "In work, one mastered cooking, sewing, and embroidery, but normally not reading or writing. In physical ap-pearance, one learned to be attractive to one's husband but not enticing to others. In speech, one was self-demeaning and rigidly polite rather than assertive or imaginative. And in behaviour, one was always honest and loyal to one's superiors" (Marr 192).

12. The term "caregivers" and its significance for people of color depicted as such in U.S. narratives are explained in Sau-ling C. Wong ("Diverted Mothering").

13. For more on the representation of Vietnamese women through the figure of Kieu, see Beevi.

14. In terms of power, David Marr notes that family loyalty was sometimes given to the hardworking mother rather than to the father. In larger society, women sometimes could also accrue power; there are several significant women in the pantheon of Vietnamese national heroes, and women played roles in the National Liberation Front and the North Vietnamese war effort. The heroization of women often comes as part and parcel of their categorization as caretakers and sacrificers.

15. Michel Foucault argues that heterosexual relations are a necessary development of capitalism (*The History of Sexuality*); Hayslip's rejection of those relations and her rejection of capitalism therefore resonate with each other.

Chapter Five

1. Another incisive critique of the universalizing tendencies of Western queer politics can be found in Mark Chiang's article on the film *The Wedding Banquet*, where he argues that "the narrative of gay liberation . . . reproduces narratives of universal history that gauge the evolution of western civilization from tradition to modernity," positioning non-Western queer identities and practices on the under- or undeveloped end of this evolutionary model ("Coming Out into the Global System" 387). In a similar fashion, Jasbir K. Puar argues that "queer diasporic discourses often resituate nationalist centerings of the West as the site of sexual liberation, freedom, and visibility" (406). In this chapter, we will see how the Philippines and its domestic queer practices can be the site of this liberation.

2. In Bulosan's *America Is in the Heart*, the brief appearance of gay men who express interest in Carlos is met with his revulsion. In Okada's *No-No Boy*, Ichiro's overbearing mother and passive father are presented in Ichiro's eyes as monstrous and pathetic, respectively, because of their switched gender roles. Earlier in the century, in Sui Sin Far's short story "The Smuggling of Tie Co," from the collection *Mrs. Spring Fragrance*, Tie Co is a woman who dresses as a man in order to be closer to the man she loves; the revelation of her identity is the cause of great consternation.

3. For two very different approaches to colonialism, gender, and the postcolonial woman of color, see Sara Suleri and Trinh (*Woman Native Other*), especially since Suleri makes a point of attacking Trinh's position (and also hooks's) as essentialistic and idealistic.

4. Again, for two different approaches, this time different in their historical and cultural context concerning gender and the public/private division, see Olin on modern Western concepts and Chatterjee (1993) for anticolonial Indian concepts.

5. Rafael also notes that these women are agents who "generate the conditions that make their rescue both possible and desirable. As nurturing mothers and vulnerable lovers, the woman-nation also takes up arms, plans battles, and demands accountability from characters and audiences alike. They are objects of masculine contention, but they are also native interlocutors in the debate over the use of their body politic" (214).

6. Although the Japanese ruled the Philippines for four years (1941–1945), the legacy of their presence in these novels and in contemporary Philippine culture in general seems minute in relation to the impact of Spanish and American colonization.

7. On the historical existence of the concept of a man with a "female heart" or "woman's soul" in the West, see Sedgwick (87) and Silverman (339–388).

8. Bourns headed the 1903–1905 U.S. Census undertaking in the Philippines.

9. It should be noted clearly that what Bhabha documents is the disorienting mimicry and gaze of the colonized, as it is perceived by the colonizer. The colonized themselves may not be affected by the mimicry and the gazing. A scene in *Dogeaters* illustrates this, when the German director Rainer takes the Filipino male prostitute Joey to his borrowed mansion in Manila. Rainer says, "Servants. They end up knowing your secrets, they always end up knowing too much. It's a kind of insidious power," to which the pragmatic Joey replies "Servants can't do shit to you, boss. You're being paranoid" (145). For another take on mimicry and queerness in Filipino culture, see Bascara.

10. In the context of the Philippines, however, we can see that this power needs to be re-articulated, because the transvestite does not occupy a space outside of "proper" discourse, as s/he does in Western society. Transvestism in the Philippines would become explicitly disruptive if it showed not that a man could be a woman but that a man could be "manly" and still prefer other men—something accomplished by the masculine *bakla*, the cassowary.

11. For Boal, "spectator is a bad word," because spectatorship creates passivity and a receptiveness to the coercive aspect of most contemporary theater, based as it is on Aristotelian poetics: that is, drama is supposed to be cathartic, purging the spectator of the type of hubris that brings the downfall of the protagonist. Boal argues that the purging is of characteristics the state doesn't want in its subjects. More than this, though, Boal argues that the real reason that spectatorship is bad is because "the spectator is less than a man" (147), who is reduced to impotence by being passive. This is not an uncommon argument, but it's interesting to see how the transvestites can be seen as both less then men onstage and less than men offstage—until they take the theater into their own hands. Feminist film criticism that addresses the issue of spectatorship has put into question the correlation between activity/passivity and masculinity/femininity, as well as resistance/collusion. See especially the debate between Maureen Turim and Lucie Arbuthnot and Gail Seneca over how to read *Gentlemen Prefer Blondes* and the debate between E. Ann Kaplan and Linda Williams over *Stella Dallas*, both in Erens. For more general discussions of the role of the female spectator and her ability to negotiate meanings in film, see Gledhill; for arguments against automatically aligning activity in the viewer with resistance, see both Mayne and Stacey.

12. For specific accounts of how limitations become advantages, see especially Scott's classic account, which addresses peasants in the industrializing Malaysian context; and for the Philippines, see Guerrero, who discusses how the National People's Army in the Philippines has used the fragmented island geography of the nation to its advantage.

13. For more on the relationship among movie, moviegoer, and marketing, see Jackie Stacey's excellent, empirical account of British female audiences and their reactions to both imported Hollywood film during the 1940s and 1950s and the entire cinematic apparatus of the movie theater, fan clubs, newsletters, etc.; also see Barbara Klinger's account of the marketing of Douglas Sirk's melodramatic films during the 1950s, which shows how our readings of sexuality during the 1950s (as repressed) differ radically from what the marketing strategy shows: sex as a normal method of audience appeal.

14. My highly condensed history of melodrama and its features comes from Marcia Landy's very useful volume on melodrama; for general history and features, see especially the articles by Landy, John G. Cawelti, Peter Brooks, Elsaesser, Daniel Gerould, Thomas Schatz, and Chuck Kleinhans.

15. Douglas Sirk was, of course, one of the most popular Hollywood directors of melodrama during the 1950s, making classics and box-office hits such as *Magnificent Obsession* (also starring Rock Hudson and Jane Wyman) and *Imitation of Life*. More important, Sirk's work has been at the center of the revival of critical interest in melodrama that started in the 1970s. The reasons Sirk becomes crucial to my argument here and to Hagedorn's project are the style and content of 1950s Hollywood melodrama and the subversive innovations that he undertook in melodrama.

16. The second clue that we should do so, as Chiang points out, stems from the German director Rainer Werner Fassbinder, who makes an appearance in the novel as Rainer, a visiting German director who has an affair with Joey. Fassbinder was partially responsible for the revival of interest in Sirk's films in the 1970s and remade *All That Heaven Allows* as *Ali—Fear Eats the Soul* (also alluded to in *Dogeaters* on 133). For the connections between Sirk and Fassbinder, see Mulvey (45–48).

17. According to David Bordwell, classical cinema as a coherent product of the studio system dates from 1917 to 1960 but continues as a style to the present day. Melodrama shared in classical cinema's domination of movie theaters all over the world. For more on classical cinema, see Bordwell's "Classical Hollywood Cinema" and his, Janet Staiger, and Kristin Thompson's *The Classical Hollywood Cinema*.

18. Mulvey's essay is reprinted in her 1989 collection. Stacey vigorously disputes the psychoanalytic feminist position that has derived from Mulvey, arguing that it is too homogenizing (1–48) and homophobic (126–176); Mayne provides a useful introduction to various theories of spectatorship (1–104). Teresa de Lauretis (12–36, 103–157) offers possibly one of the most influential arguments that concern female spectatorship in the post-Mulvey era, although she and Stacey disagree on the question of female identification and desire; Stacey accuses her model of not allowing for lesbian desire.

19. Lee contests E. San Juan Jr.'s dismissal of the prevalence of female stories in *Dogeaters* as a result of an inability on San Juan's part to confront the centrality of female gender and its concerns (81–82). Lee's charge is substantiated by the way in which melodrama has generally been dismissed by critics because of an association between its excesses in plot and mise-en-scène with female sensibilities.

20. The notion of ideological interpellation stems from Louis Althusser, of course. For an account of Althusser's influence in spectatorship theory, see Mayne (13–30) and Rosen (157–159). The subaltern as an "ideal" spectator differs materially, therefore, from Mulvey's abstract and universalizing notion of an ideal spectator who is the subject of the masculine gaze.

21. For an account of how self-sacrificial motherhood has been a central element for Hollywood melodrama, and its conflicted meanings for female audiences as well as patriarchal capitalism, see the Kaplan and Williams debate on *Stella Dallas* in Erens.

22. Sirk's reputation as an ironic manipulator of the melodramatic form, appropriating it to show the contradictions of bourgeois life, especially for women, from the inside out, was established in the 1970s by left-wing British film theorists. His reputation was consolidated by feminist film critics who turned to his melodramas to explore the ways in which gender inequality and sexual desire could be displayed in a conflicted fashion even during the 1950s. For one of the early revivalist articles on Sirk, see Mulvey (39–44); for an influential approach to Sirk's work as ideological attack-in-melodramatic-disguise, see Elsaesser; for an introduction to Sirk's life and films, see Stern; and for a historical recontextualization of Sirk's films and critical reception, see Klinger.

23. As is common with melodramatic plots, our hero is driven hither and thither

by unlikely coincidences that are central to determining that the plot ends up where it should (as in the case of *All That Heaven Allows,* where Ron's timely accident brings Carey to his side).

24. For the relevance of melodrama to an examination of bourgeois family life under capitalism, see Kleinhans.

25. See Schirmer and Shalom for accounts of American racism and atrocities in the Philippines and for statistics on casualty figures. See Kaplan and Pease, especially their respective introductions, for excellent arguments on integrating an anti-imperialist awareness into literary and historical approaches to U.S. culture.

26. For a negative account of pluralism in American studies, see Rogin (272–300). For pluralistic approaches to American literature and history, see Bercovitch and Sollors.

27. This model of the exile comes under attack in San Juan ("In Search of Filipino Writing" 224–225), for what he considers to be its homogenization of diverse diasporic populations with radically different economic possibilities and its romanticization of the privileged aesthetic exile. While San Juan's warnings about homogenization and romanticization are well heeded, Campomanes's model may still very well apply for my purposes in considering writers like Hagedorn and Rosca, who are clearly part of a privileged exilic elite.

Conclusion

1. As I have sought to make clear in the introduction, this book is primarily concerned with the mainstream of the Asian American intellectual class, hence my addressing here a body of readers who are generally predisposed to these goals of social and economic justice. This concern does not overlook the fact that there is *some* ideological diversity in the intellectual class; rather, it recognizes that a *self-identified* Asian American intellectual class—distinct from a population of intellectuals *who happen to be Asian American but who may not recognize or value such an identification*—does, at the present moment, overwhelmingly share a basic consensus concerning the meaning of race and the value of certain kinds of political and intellectual work, which can be articulated around very broadly defined ideas of social and economic justice.

2. The article is reprinted in Amy Tachiki et al., eds., *Roots: An Asian American Reader* (1971).

3. Takaki discusses this use of Chinese laborers (*Strangers* 94–99).

4. Numerous Asian American scholars have written upon the model minority issue. These include Robert S. Chang (53–58), Neil Gotanda, Ruth Y. Hsu, Li (10), Robert G. Lee (180–204), Okihiro (*Margins and Mainstreams* 118–147), Glenn Omatsu, Keith Osajima, Palumbo-Liu (395–418), Natsu Taylor Saito, and Dooboo Shim.

5. The essays by Elaine Kim and Sumi Cho in the anthology *Reading Rodney King, Reading Urban Uprising* illustrate this analysis of the role played by Korean American merchants.

6. Anthony S. Wang is one of the few to have written positively on the topic of Asian American neoconservatism, besides the more well known pundit Arthur Hu, who came to prominence for helping to argue against affirmative action because of its supposed discrimination against Asian American students. Glenn Omatsu sketches a political portrait of Asian American neoconservatives (42–50) and argues that "the emergence of neo-conservatism in our community is a fascinating phenomenon, one

we should analyze and appreciate" (42). Karen Su addresses the role of neoconservatism in relationship to Asian American literature.

7. In his articles "Model Minority Discourse" and "*China Man* Autoeroticism," Tomo Hattori also raises the notion of a model minority discourse that supplements Palumbo-Liu's claims about how the discourse is deployed to interpret and use cultural texts. Hattori argues that model minority discourse "constructs a shadow or parallel majority discourse so that a minor people can enjoy an ethnonationalism of their own" ("*China Man* Autoeroticism" 232); this discourse, which enables assimilation, is "shrewdly and mostly unconsciously camouflaged [by Asian American writers and critics] as opposition to and resistance against dominant culture" ("Model Minority Discourse" 233).

8. The sexism of Chinese patriarchy and the racism of American society are of course inflicted upon the bodies of Chinese men and women, illustrated most vividly in the back-tattooing episode from *The Woman Warrior* (discussed in chapter 3).

9. See Lisa Lowe (*Immigrant Acts*) and Chow.

10. I thank Rachel Lee for referring me to this work.

11. Eric Liu's aptly titled *The Accidental Asian* is probably the best account of how Asian American discourse can hail someone and transform him into an Asian American, almost against his will or intention.

12. Kim notes that "by focusing on the fluidity of the boundaries between inside and outside, sender and receiver, viewer and viewed, Cha insists upon a self that both extends and is contained, like the liquid that is referred to throughout the text" ("Poised on the In-between" 18). Kang describes *Dictee*'s project as a "sincere attempt to inscribe a very fluid and heterogeneous Korean feminist subjectivity" (98), a description that aptly encapsulates the political project of *Writing Self, Writing Nation* as it balances a recognition of heterogeneity with the practical demand of strategic essentialism.

13. The first note refers to F. A. McKenzie's *The Tragedy of Korea*, originally published in 1908 and reprinted in 1969. The book documents the Japanese occupation of Korea and is the source for several quotations in the chapter "History" in *Dictee*. The second note refers to *Story of a Soul: The Autobiography of St. Thérèse of Lisieux*, which provides the source of quotations in the chapter "Love Poetry." The autobiography also is the source of the black-and-white photograph at the beginning of "Love Poetry," which is an image of Saint Thérèse herself playing the role of Joan of Arc. The end of "Love Poetry" has another image of Joan of Arc, from Carl Dreyer's film *The Passion of Joan of Arc* (1928).

14. Following the convention of scholars on Hawai'i such as Brenda Lee Kwon, I use the term "continental" to describe what has habitually been called the mainland because, as they argue, the term "mainland" implies a marginalized stature for Hawai'i in relationship to the rest of the United States. Throughout this book, when I use the word "Hawai'i," I also use the 'okina, which "represents glottal stops in pronunciation" (Kwon 1); as Kwon also notes, the 'okina is not used in Anglicized words like "Hawaiian" and "Hawaii's."

15. For more on this argument, see Fujikane ("Between Nationalisms"), Kwon, Morales, and Sumida ("Sense of Place"). Rodney Morales claims that most writers affiliated with Bamboo Ridge Press, the predominant publisher of local literature, identify themselves as locals; he includes Yamanaka in this count of writers.

16. This brief summary of American colonization in Hawai'i is drawn from Haas ("A Brief History"), Takaki (*Pau Hana*), and Trask.

17. For more on the development and use of Hawai'i Creole English, see Bickerton, Jeff Chang, Fujikane ("Between Nationalisms"), and Sumida ("Postcolonialism").

18. Jonathan Y. Okamura ("Aloha Kanaka") and Stephen Sumida (*And the View from the Shore*) are other scholars who offer definitions and brief histories of local identity and formation.

19. Ironically, local identity, while serving historically to unify an ethnically diverse population against class and racial oppression, can also in the contemporary moment work to perpetuate the political and economic domination of locals over Native Hawaiians. See Fujikane ("Sweeping Racism") and Rosa for further elaborations on this point.

20. Michael Haas (introduction to *Multicultural History*) argues that despite ongoing socioeconomic problems, Hawai'i is characterized by a "harmonious multiculturalism" (xi), and F. James Davis cites extensive racial intermixing as evidence of racial and ethnic tolerance. For a survey of this multicultural approach to Hawai'i, see Jeff Chang.

21. Scholars who express this argument include Ibrahim G. Aoudé, Morales, and Okamura ("Social Stratification" and "Aloha Kanaka").

22. Haunani-Kay Trask (*From a Native Daughter*) and Rob Wilson both offer rigorous attacks upon these stereotypical representations and the actual damaging effects of tourism and the U.S. military presence.

23. The same scholars in note 21 demonstrate these political and economic inequities. Haas also alludes to these problems ("A Brief History").

24. The summary of the development of local literature and its mission is drawn from Fujikane ("Between Nationalisms"), Kwon, and Sumida (*And the View from the Shore*).

25. For an account of the controversies that surround Yamanaka's texts, see Candice Fujikane ("Sweeping Racism"), who also repudiates the validity of the argument that concerns Yamanaka's texts as ironic in their depiction of anti-Filipino racism.

26. Fujikane, Kwon, Morales, and Okamura are other scholars who also express concern over the internal fractures within local culture and the compromised place of locals in relationship to Native Hawaiians and the legacy of colonization.

27. As John P. Rosa points out, however, Yamanaka and other authors in Hawai'i are more concerned with panethnic relations among the wider diversity of populations in Hawai'i than they are with pan-Asian relations. The pan-Asian emphasis in this paragraph is due, of course, to the role in which Yamanaka's work is here cast as an analogy for continental Asian American intrarelations. Personal communication, February 15, 2001.

28. See Ignatiev and Roediger for accounts of the Irish transformation into whiteness.

29. Urvashi Vaid expresses similar sentiments when she argues that "ideology-based movements are more valuable than identity-based ones" (10). Vaid's excellent article concisely identifies the problems and limits of an Asian American coalition implicated with capitalism and identity politics. If Asian Americans think of themselves as part of a progressive coalition or movement, they must confront the fact that because of "the way [they] are structured—issue by issue, or identity by identity—social justice movements cannot boast the kind of ideological or political unity that is found on the conservative right" (13). Hence, the need to organize beyond identity if what we seek is more than visibility and empowerment.

BIBLIOGRAPHY

Ahmad, Aijaz. *In Theory: Classes, Nations, Literatures*. London: Verso, 1992.

Alexander, M. Jacqui. "Redrafting Morality: The Postcolonial State and the Sexual Offences Bill of Trinidad and Tobago." *Third World Women and the Politics of Feminism*. Ed. Chandra Talpade Mohanty, Ann Russo, and Lourdes Torres. Bloomington: Indiana University Press, 1991. 133–152.

Alquizola, Marilyn. "The Fictive Narrator of *America Is in the Heart*." *Frontiers of Asian American Studies: Writing, Research, and Commentary*. Ed. Gail M. Nomura et al. Pullman: Washington State University Press, 1989. 211–217.

———. "Subversion or Affirmation: The Text and Subtext of *America Is in the Heart*." *Asian Americans: Comparative and Global Perspectives*. Ed. Shirley Hune et al. Pullman: Washington State University Press, 1991. 199–210.

Althusser, Louis. "Ideology and Ideological State Apparatuses." Trans. Ben Brewster. *Lenin and Philosophy and Other Essays*. New York: Monthly Review Press, 1971.

Ancheta, Angelo N. *Race, Rights and the Asian American Experience*. New Brunswick, N.J.: Rutgers University Press, 1998.

Anderson, Benedict. *Imagined Communities*. London: Verso, 1991.

Anzaldúa, Gloria. *Borderlands/La Frontera: The New Mestiza*. San Francisco: Aunt Lute Books, 1987.

Aoudé, Ibrahim G. "Political Economy." *Multicultural Hawaii: The Fabric of a Multiethnic Society*. Ed. Michael Haas. New York: Garland, 1998. 267–283.

Appadurai, Arjun. "Disjuncture and Difference in the Global Cultural Economy." *Colonial Discourse and Post-Colonial Theory*. Ed. Patrick Williams and Laura Chrisman. New York: Columbia University Press, 1994. 324–339.

Arbuthnot, Lucie, and Gail Seneca. "Pre-text and Text in *Gentlemen Prefer Blondes.*"
    Issues in Feminist Film Criticism. Ed. Patricia Erens. Bloomington and Indianapo-
    lis: Indiana University Press, 1990. 112–125.

Association for Asian American Studies. "Letter from the AAAS Board." *AAAS
    Newsletter,* September 1998.

Bahri, Deepika. "With Kaleidoscope Eyes: The Potential (Dangers) of Identitarian
    Coalitions." *A Part, yet Apart: South Asians in Asian America.* Ed. Lavina Dhin-
    gra Shankar and Rajini Srikanth. Philadelphia: Temple University Press, 1998.
    25–48.

Balce-Cortes, Nerissa. "Imagining the Neocolony." *Critical Mass* 2.2 (1995): 95–120.

Baldwin, James. *The Fire Next Time.* New York: Vintage, 1962.

Bascara, Victor. "'A Vaudeville against Coconut Trees': Colonialism, Contradiction, and
    Coming Out in Michael Magnaye's *White Christmas.*" *Q&A: Queer in Asian
    America.* Ed. David L. Eng and Alice Y. Hom. Philadelphia: Temple University
    Press, 1998. 95–114.

Baym, Nina. "Melodramas of Beset Manhood: How Theories of Fiction Exclude
    Women Authors." *The New Feminist Criticism: Essay on Women, Literature, and
    Theory.* Ed. Elaine Showalter. New York: Pantheon, 1985. 63–80.

Bederman, Gail. *Manliness and Civilization: A Cultural History of Race in the United
    States, 1880–1917.* Chicago: University of Chicago Press, 1995.

Beevi, Mariam. "The Passing of Literary Traditions: The Figure of the Woman from
    Vietnamese Nationalism to Vietnamese American Transnationalism." *Amerasia
    Journal* 23.2 (1997): 27–53.

Benjamin, Walter. "Critique of Violence." Trans. Edmund Jephcott. *Reflections: Essays,
    Aphorisms, Autobiographical Writings.* Ed. Peter Demetz. New York: Harcourt
    Brace Jovanovich, 1978. 277–300.

Benstock, Shari. "The Female Self Engendered: Autobiographical Writing and Theories
    of Selfhood." *Women and Autobiography.* Ed. Martine Watson Brownley and Al-
    lison B. Kimmich. Wilmington, Del.: Scholarly Resources, 1999. 3–14.

Bercovitch, Sacvan. *The Rites of Assent: Transformations in the Symbolic Construc-
    tion of America.* New York: Routledge, 1993.

Berger, Kenneth. "Rev. of *Child of War, Woman of Peace.*" *Library Journal,* January
    1993:128.

Bhabha, Homi. *The Location of Culture.* London: Routledge, 1994.

Bickerton, Derek. "Language and Language Contact." *Multicultural Hawaii: The Fab-
    ric of a Multiethnic Society.* Ed. Michael Haas. New York: Garland, 1998. 53–66.

Blauner, Robert. *Racial Oppression in America.* New York: Harper and Row, 1972.

Boal, Augusto. *Theatre of the Oppressed.* New York: Theatre Communications Group,
    1979.

Bonacich, Edna. "The Site of Class." *Privileging Positions: The Sites of Asian American
    Studies.* Ed. Gary Y. Okihiro et al. Pullman: Washington State University Press,
    1995. 67–74.

Bordwell, David. "Classical Hollywood Cinema: Narrational Principles and Proce-
    dures." *Narrative, Apparatus, Ideology: A Film Theory Reader.* Ed. Philip Rosen.
    New York: Columbia University Press, 1986. 17–34.

Bordwell, David, Janet Staiger, and Kristin Thompson. *The Classical Hollywood
    Cinema: Film Style and Mode of Production to 1960.* New York: Columbia Uni-
    versity Press, 1985.

Bottomore, Tom. *A Dictionary of Marxist Thought.* 2nd ed. Cambridge: Blackwell,
    1995.

Bourdieu, Pierre. *Distinction: A Social Critique of the Judgement of Taste.* Trans. Richard Nice. Cambridge: Harvard University Press, 1984.

———. *The Field of Cultural Production.* New York: Columbia University Press, 1993.

Brands, H. W. *The Devil We Knew: Americans and the Cold War.* New York: Oxford University Press, 1993.

Brooks, Peter. "The Melodramatic Imagination." *Imitations of Life: A Reader on Film and Television Melodrama.* Ed. Marcia Landy. Detroit: Wayne State University Press, 1991. 50–67.

———. *Body Work: Objects of Desire in Modern Narrative.* Cambridge: Harvard University Press, 1993.

Bulosan, Carlos. *America Is in the Heart.* Seattle: University of Washington Press, 1973.

———. *The Cry and the Dedication.* Ed. E. San Juan Jr. Philadelphia: Temple University Press, 1995.

———. "Labor and Capital: The Coming Catastrophe." *Amerasia Journal* 6 (1979): 134.

Butler, Judith. *Bodies That Matter: On the Discursive Limits of "Sex."* New York: Routledge, 1993.

———. *Excitable Speech: A Politics of the Performative.* New York: Routledge, 1997.

———. *Gender Trouble: Feminism and the Subversion of Identity.* New York: Routledge, 1990.

Cameron, Sharon. *The Corporeal Self: Allegories of the Body in Melville and Hawthorne.* Baltimore: Johns Hopkins University Press, 1981.

Campomanes, Oscar. "Afterword: The New Empire's Forgetful and Forgotten Citizens: Unrepresentability and Unassimilability in Filipino-American Postcolonialities." *Critical Mass* 2.2 (1995): 145–200.

——— "Filipinos in the United States and Their Literature of Exile." *Reading the Literatures of Asian America.* Ed. Shirley Geok-lin Lim and Amy Ling. Philadelphia: Temple University Press, 1992. 49–78.

———. "New Formations of Asian American Studies and the Question of U.S. Imperialism." *positions: east asia cultures critique* 5.2 (1997): 523–550.

Cannell, Fenella. "The Power of Appearances: Beauty, Mimicry, and Transformation in Bicol." *Discrepant Histories: Translocal Essays on Filipino Cultures.* Ed. Vicente L. Rafael. Philadelphia: Temple University Press, 1995. 223–258.

Cawelti, John G. "The Evolution of Social Melodrama." *Imitations of Life: A Reader on Film and Television Melodrama.* Ed. Marcia Landy. Detroit: Wayne State University Press, 1991. 33–49.

Chan, Sucheng. *Asian Americans: An Interpretive History.* Boston: Twayne, 1991.

Chang, Jeff. "Local Knowledge(s): Notes on Race Relations, Panethnicity and History in Hawai'i." *Amerasia Journal* 22.2 (1996): 1–29.

Chang, Robert S. *Disoriented: Asian Americans, Law, and the Nation-State.* New York: New York University Press, 1999.

Chatterjee, Partha. "The Nationalist Resolution of the Woman's Question." *Recasting Women.* Ed. Kumkum Sangari and Sadesh Vaid. New Brunswick, N.J.: Rutgers University Press, 1990.

———. *The Nation and Its Fragments: Colonial and Postcolonial Histories.* Princeton: Princeton University Press, 1993.

Cheung, King-Kok. *Articulate Silences: Hisaye Yamamoto, Maxine Hong Kingston, Joy Kogawa.* Ithaca, NY: Cornell University Press, 1993.

———. "Of Men and Men: Reconstructing Chinese American Masculinity." *Other*

Sisterhoods: Literary Theory and U.S. Women of Color. Ed. Sandra Kumatomo Stanley. Urbana and Chicago: University of Illinois Press, 1998. 173–199.

———. "The Woman Warrior versus the Chinaman Pacific: Must a Chinese American Critic Choose between Feminism and Heroism?" *Conflicts in Feminism.* Ed. Marianne Hirsch and Evelyn Fox Keller. New York: Routledge, 1990. 234–251.

Chiang, Mark. "All That History Allows: Desire and the Phantasmatic Philippines in *Dogeaters.*" Association for Asian American Studies Annual Conference, Oakland, Cal., 1995.

———. "Coming Out into the Global System: Postmodern Patriarchies and Transnational Sexualities in *The Wedding Banquet.*" *Q&A: Queer in Asian America.* Ed. David L. Eng and Alice Y. Hom. Philadelphia: Temple University Press, 1998. 374–395.

Chin, Frank. Afterword. *No-No Boy.* Seattle: University of Washington Press, 1979. 253–260.

———. "Backtalk." *News of the American Place Theater,* May 1972. Reprint in *Counterpoint* 113(1972): 556–557.

———. *The Chickencoop Chinaman and The Year of the Dragon: Two Plays.* Seattle: University of Washington Press, 1981.

———. *The Chinaman Pacific and the Frisco R.R. Co.* Minneapolis: Coffee House Press, 1988.

———. "Come All Ye Asian American Writers of the Real and the Fake." *The Big Aiiieeeee! An Anthology of Chinese American and Japanese American Literature.* Ed. Jeffrey Paul Chan et al. New York: Meridian, 1991. 1–92.

———. *Donald Duk.* Minneapolis: Coffee House Press, 1991.

Chin, Frank, et al., eds. *Aiiieeeee! An Anthology of Asian-American Writers.* New York: Anchor Books, 1975.

Chin, Frank, et al. "Introduction: Fifty Years of Our Whole Voice." *Aiiieeeee! An Anthology of Asian-American Writers.* Ed. Frank Chin et al. New York: Anchor Books, 1975.

Cho, Sumi. "Korean Americans vs. African Americans: Conflict and Construction." *Reading Rodney King, Reading Urban Uprising.* Ed. Robert Gooding-Williams. New York: Routledge, 1993. 196–211.

Chow, Rey. *Ethics after Idealism: Theory-Culture-Ethnicity-Reading.* Bloomington and Indianapolis: Indiana University Press, 1998.

Choy, Philip P., Lorraine Dong, and Marlon K. Hom, eds. *The Coming Man: 19th Century American Perceptions of the Chinese.* Seattle: University of Washington Press, 1994.

Christopher, Renny. *The Viet Nam War/The American War: Images and Representations in Euro-American and Vietnamese Exile Narratives.* Amherst: University of Massachusetts Press, 1995.

Chu, Patricia. *Assimilating Asians: Gendered Strategies of Authorship in Asian America.* Durham: Duke University Press, 2000.

Chuh, Kandice. "Transnationalism and Its Pasts." *Public Culture* 9 (1996): 93–112.

Clifford, James. *The Predicament of Culture: Twentieth-Century Ethnography, Literature, and Art.* Cambridge: Harvard University Press, 1988.

———. "Traveling Cultures." *Cultural Studies.* Ed. Lawrence Grossberg, Cary Nelson and Paula Treichler. New York: Routledge, 1992. 96–116.

Clifford, James, and George E. Marcus, eds. *Writing Culture: The Poetics and Politics of Ethnography.* Berkeley and Los Angeles: University of California Press, 1986.

Connell, R. W. *Masculinities*. Berkeley and Los Angeles: University of California Press, 1995.

Cronin, James E. *The World the Cold War Made: Order, Chaos, and the Return of History*. London: Routledge, 1996.

Daniels, Roger. *Concentration Camps U.S.A.: Japanese Americans and World War II*. New York: Holt, Rinhart, and Winston, 1971.

Daniels, Roger, Sandra C. Taylor, and Harry H. L. Kitano, eds. *Japanese Americans: From Relocation to Redress*. Seattle: University of Washington Press, 1991.

Davis, F. James. "The Hawaiian Alternative to the One-Drop Rule." *American Mixed Race: The Culture of Microdiversity*. Ed. Naomi Zack. Lanham, Md.: Rowland and Littlefield, 1995. 115–131.

de Lauretis, Teresa. *Alice Doesn't: Feminism, Semiotics, Cinema*. Bloomington and Indianapolis: Indiana University Press, 1982.

Debord, Guy. *Society of the Spectacle*. Detroit: Black and Red, 1983

Denning, Michael. *The Cultural Front: The Laboring of American Culture in the Twentieth Century*. London: Verso, 1997.

Doane, Mary Ann. "Film and the Masquerade: Theorizing the Female Spectator." *Issues in Feminist Film Criticism*. Ed. Patricia Erens. Bloomington and Indianapolis: Indiana University Press, 1990. 41–57.

Dong, Lorraine, and Marlon K. Hom. "Defiance or Perpetuation: An Analysis of Characters in *Mrs. Spring Fragrance*." *Chinese America: History and Perspectives*. Ed. Him Mark Lai, Ruthanne Lum McCunn, and Judy Yung. San Francisco: Chinese Historical Society of America, 1987. 139–168.

DuBois, Thomas A. "Constructions Construed: The Representation of Southeast Asian Refugees in Academic, Popular, and Adolescent Discourse." *Amerasia Journal* 19.3 (1993): 1–25.

Eagleton, Terry. *Criticism and Ideology*. London: Verso, 1976.

Eakins, Paul John. Introduction. *American Autobiography: Retrospect and Prospect*. Ed. Paul John Eakins. Madison: University of Wisconsin Press, 1991.

Eaton, Winnifred. *Me: A Book of Remembrance*. Jackson: University of Mississippi Press, 1997.

Elias, Norbert. "Violence and Civilization: The State Monopoly of Physical Violence and Its Infringement." *Civil Society and the State*. Ed. John Keane. London: Verso, 1988. 177–198.

Elsaesser, Thomas. "Tales of Sound and Fury: Observations on the Family Melodrama." *Imitations of Life: A Reader on Film and Television Melodrama*. Ed. Marcia Landy. Detroit: Wayne State University Press, 1991. 68–91.

Eng, David. "In the Shadows of a Diva: Committing Homosexuality in David Henry Hwang's *M. Butterfly*." *Asian American Sexualities: Dimensions of the Gay and Lesbian Experience*. Ed. Russell Leong. New York: Routledge, 1996. 131–152.

Enloe, Cynthia. *Bananas, Beaches, and Bases: Making Feminist Sense of international Politics*. Berkeley and Los Angeles: University of California Press, 1989.

Erens, Patricia, ed. *Issues in Feminist Film Criticism*. Bloomington and Indianapolis: Indiana University Press, 1990.

Espiritu, Yen Le. *Asian American Panethnicity: Bridging Institutions and Identities*. Ed. Sucheng Chan. Philadelphia: Temple University Press, 1992.

———. "From the AAAS President." *Association for Asian American Studies Newsletter*, May 1998: 5–6.

Evangelista, Susan. *Carlos Bulosan and His Poetry: A Biography and Anthology*. Seattle: University of Washington Press, 1985.

Fabian, Johannes. *Time and the Other: How Anthropology Makes Its Object.* New York: Columbia University Press, 1983.

Falk, Pasi. *The Consuming Body.* London: SAGE, 1994.

Fanon, Frantz. *Black Skin, White Masks.* New York: Grove Weidenfeld, 1967.

Foley, Barbara. *Radical Representations: Politics and Form in U.S. Proletarian Fiction, 1929–1941.* Ed. Stanley Fish and Fredric Jameson. Durham: Duke University Press, 1993.

Foucault, Michel. *Discipline and Punish: The Birth of the Prison.* New York: Vintage, 1979.

———. *The History of Sexuality: An Introduction.* Trans. Robert Hurley. Vol. 1. New York: Vintage, 1990.

Frank, Thomas. *The Conquest of Cool: Business Culture, Counterculture, and the Rise of Hip Consumerism.* Chicago: University of Chicago Press, 1997.

Fried, Albert, ed. *McCarthyism, the Great American Red Scare: A Documentary History.* New York: Oxford University Press, 1997.

Fried, Richard M. *Nightmare in Red: the McCarthy Era in Perspective.* New York: Oxford University Press, 1990.

Fujikane, Candice. "Between Nationalisms: Hawaii's Local Nation and Its Troubled Racial Paradise." *Critical Mass* 1.2 (1994): 23–58.

———. "Sweeping Racism under the Rug of 'Censorship': The Controversy over Lois-Ann Yamanaka's *Blu's Hanging.*" *Amerasia Journal* 26.2 (2000): 158–194.

Gans, Herbert. "The Possibility of a New Racial Hierarchy in the Twenty-first-Century United States." *The Cultural Territories of Race: Black and White Boundaries.* Ed. Michele Lamont. Chicago and New York: University of Chicago Press and Russell Sage Foundation, 1999. 371–390.

Garber, Marjorie. *Vested Interests: Cross-Dressing and Cultural Anxiety.* New York: HarperPerennial, 1993.

Gerould, Daniel. "Russian Formalist Theories of Melodrama." *Imitations of Life: A Reader on Film and Television Melodrama.* Ed. Marcia Landy. Detroit: Wayne State University Press, 1991. 118–134.

Gillon, Steven M., and Diane B. Kutz. *America during the Cold War.* New York: Harcourt Brace Jovanovich, 1993.

Glazer, Nathan. "The Emergence of an American Ethnic Pattern." *From Different Shores: Perspectives on Race and Ethnicity in America.* Ed. Ronald Takaki. 2nd ed. New York: Oxford University Press, 1994. 11–23.

Gledhill, Christine. "Pleasurable Negotiations." *Female Spectators: Looking at Film and Television.* Ed. E. Deidre Pribram. London: Verso, 1988. 64–89.

Goldberg, David Theo, ed. *Multiculturalism: A Critical Reader.* Cambridge: Blackwell, 1994.

Goode, Eriche, and Nachman Ben-Yehuda. *Moral Panics: The Social Construction of Deviance.* Oxford: Blackwell, 1994.

Gotanda, Neil. "Re-Producing the Model Minority Stereotype: Judge Joyce Karlin's Sentencing Colloquy in *People v. Soon Ja Du.*" *Reviewing Asian America: Locating Diversity.* Ed. Wendy L. Ng et al. Pullman: Washington State University, 1995. 87–106.

Grosz, Elizabeth. *Volatile Bodies: Toward a Corporeal Feminism.* Bloomington and Indianapolis: Indiana University Press, 1994.

Guerrero, Amado. *Philippine Society and Revolution.* Manila: Pulang Tala, 1971.

Gusdorf, Georges. "Conditions and Limits of Autobiography." *Autobiography: Essays*

Theoretical and Critical. Ed. James Olney. Princeton: Princeton University Press, 1980. 28–48.

Haas, Michael. "A Brief History." *Multicultural Hawaii: The Fabric of a Multiethnic Society.* Ed. Michael Haas. New York: Garland, 1998. 23–52.

———. Introduction. *Multicultural Hawaii: The Fabric of a Multiethnic Society.* Ed. Michael Haas. New York: Garland, 1998. 3–21.

Hagedorn, Jessica. *Dogeaters.* New York: Penguin Books, 1990.

Hall, Stuart, et al. *Policing the Crisis: Mugging, the State, and Law and Order.* New York: Holmes and Meier, 1978.

Haraway, Donna. *Simians, Cyborgs, and Women: The Reinvention of Nature.* New York: Routledge, 1991.

Hart, Donn V. "Homosexuality and Transvestism in the Philippines: The Cebuan Filipino Bayot and Lakin-on." *Behavior Science Notes* 4 (1986) 211–248.

Harvey, David. *The Condition of Postmodernity.* Cambridge: Blackwell, 1989.

Hattori, Tomo. "*China Man* Autoeroticism and the Remains of Asian America." *Novel* 31.2 (1998): 215–236.

———. "Model Minority Discourse and Asian American Jouis-Sense." *differences: A Journal of Feminist Cultural Studies* 11.2 (1999): 228–247.

Hau, Caroline S. "*Dogeaters,* Postmodernism and the 'Worlding' of the Philippines." *Philippines Post-Colonial Studies.* Ed. Cristina Pantoja Hidalgo and Priscelina Patajo-Legasto. Quezon City: University of the Philippines Press, 1993. 113–127.

Hayslip, Le Ly with James Hayslip. *Child of War, Woman of Peace.* New York: Doubleday, 1993.

Hayslip, Le Ly, with James Wurts. *When Heaven and Earth Changed Places.* New York: Doubleday, 1989.

Heilbrun, Carolyn G. "Women's Autobiographical Writings: New Forms." *Women and Autobiography.* Ed. Martine Watson Brownley and Allison B. Kimmich. Wilmington, Del.: Scholarly Resources, 1999. 15–32.

Hennessy, Rosemary. "Queer Theory, Left Politics." *Marxism beyond Marxism.* Ed. Saree Makdisi, Cesare Casarino, and Rebecca E. Karl. New York: Routledge, 1996. 214–242.

Hersh, Seymour. *My Lai 4: A Report on the Massacre and Its Aftermath.* New York: Vintage, 1970.

Hinds, Lynn Boyd, and Theodore Otto Windt Jr. *The Cold War as Rhetoric: The Beginnings, 1945–1950.* New York: Praeger, 1991.

Hing, Bill Ong. *Making and Remaking Asian America through Immigration Policy, 1850–1990.* Stanford: Stanford University Press, 1993.

Ho, Khanh. "Le Ly Hayslip." *Words Matter: Conversations with Asian American Writers.* Ed. King-Kok Cheung. Honolulu: University of Hawai'i Press, 2000. 105–119.

hooks, bell. "Reflections on Race and Sex." *Yearning: Race, Gender, and Cultural Politics.* Boston: South End Press, 1990.

Hsu, Ruth Y. "'Will the Model Minority Please Identify Itself?' American Ethnic Identity and Its Discontents." *Diaspora* 5.1 (1996): 37–63.

Hune, Shirley. "Asian American Studies: Transforming Higher Education." *Reflections on Shattered Windows: Promises and Prospects for Asian American Studies.* Ed. Gary Y. Okihiro, et al. Pullman: Washington State University Press, 1988. 1–4.

Huynh Sanh Thong. Introduction. *The Tale of Kieu.* Nguyen Du. Trans. Huynh Sanh Thong. New Haven: Yale University Press, 1983.

Hyde, Alan. *Bodies of Law*. Princeton: Princeton University Press, 1997.

Ignatiev, Noel. *How the Irish Became White*. New York: Routledge, 1995.

Jameson, Fredric. *Postmodernism, or, The Cultural Logic of Late Capitalism*. Durham, N.C.: Duke University Press, 1991.

Jamieson, Neil. *Understanding Vietnam*. Berkeley: University of California Press, 1993.

JanMohamed, Abdul R., and David Lloyd, eds. *The Nature and Context of Minority Discourse*. New York: Oxford University Press, 1990.

Jayawardena, Kumani. *Feminism and Nationalism in the Third World*. London: Zed Books, 1986.

Jeffords, Susan. *The Remasculinization of America: Gender and the Vietnam War*. Bloomington: University of Indiana Press, 1989.

Jelinek, Estelle C. Introduction. *Women's Autobiography: Essays in Criticism*. Ed. Estelle C. Jelinek. Bloomington: Indiana University Press, 1980. 1–20.

Johnson, James Weldon. *The Autobiography of an Ex-Colored Man*. New York: Penguin, 1990.

Kadohata, Cynthia. *In the Heart of the Valley of Love*. New York: Viking, 1992.

Kang, L. Hyun Yi. "The 'Liberatory Voice' of Theresa Hak Kyung Cha's *Dictee*." *Writing Self, Writing Nation: Essays on Theresa Hak Kyung Cha's Dictee*. Ed. Elaine H. Kim and Norma Alarcón. Berkeley: Third Woman Press, 1994. 73–99.

Kaplan, Amy. "'Left Alone with America': The Absence of Empire in the Study of American Culture." *Cultures of United States Imperialism*. Ed. Amy Kaplan and Donald A. Pease. Durham: Duke University Press, 1993. 3–21.

Kaplan, Amy, and Donald A. Pease, eds. *Cultures of United States Imperialism*. Durham: Duke University Press, 1993.

Kaplan, E. Ann. "The Case of the Missing Mother: Maternal Issues in Vidor's *Stella Dallas*." *Issues in Feminist Film Criticism*. Ed. Patricia Erens. Bloomington and Indianapolis: Indiana University Press, 1990. 126–136.

Kerkvliet, Benedict J. *The Huk Rebellion: A Study of the Peasant Revolt in the Philippines*. Berkeley: University of California Press, 1977.

Kessler, Richard J. *Rebellion and Repression in the Philippines*. New Haven: Yale, 1989.

Kester, Gunilla Theander. *Writing the Subject: Bildung and the African American Text*. New York: Peter Lang, 1995.

Kiang, Peter Nien-chu. "Bringing It All Back Home: New Views of Asian American Studies and the Community." *Frontiers of Asian American Studies: Writing, Research, and Commentary*. Ed. Gail M. Nomura et al. Pullman: Washington State University, 1989. 305–314.

Kibria, Nazli. "The Racial Gap: South Asian American Racial Identity and the Asian American Movement." *A Part, yet Apart: South Asians in Asian America*. Ed. Lavina Dhingra Shankar and Rajini Srikanth. Philadelphia: Temple University Press, 1998. 69–78.

Kim, Daniel Y. "The Strange Love of Frank Chin." *Q&A: Queer in Asian America*. Ed. David L. Eng and Alice Y. Hom. Philadelphia: Temple University Press, 1998. 270–303.

Kim, Elaine. *Asian American Literature: An Introduction to the Writings and Their Social Context*. Philadelphia: Temple University Press, 1982.

———. "Beyond Railroads and Internment: Comments on the Past, Present, and Future of Asian American Studies." *Privileging Positions: The Sites of Asian American Studies*. Ed. Gary Y. Okihiro et al. Pullman: Washington State University, 1995. 1–9.

————. "A Critique of *Strangers from a Different Shore.*" *Amerasia Journal* 16.2 (1990): 101–111.

————. "Home Is Where the *Han* Is." *Reading Rodney King, Reading Urban Uprising.* Ed. Robert Gooding-Williams. New York: Routledge, 1993. 219–235.

————. "Poised on the In-between: A Korean American's Reflections on Theresa Hak Kyung Cha's *Dictee.*" *Writing Self, Writing Nation: Essays on Theresa Hak Kyung Cha's Dictee.* Ed. Elaine H. Kim and Norma Alarcón. Berkeley: Third Woman Press, 1994. 3–30.

Kim, Elaine H., and Norma Alarcón, eds. *Writing Self, Writing Nation: Essays on Theresa Hak Kyung Cha's Dictee.* Berkeley: Third Woman Press, 1994.

Kim, Elaine H., and Lisa Lowe, eds. *positions: east asia cultures critique* 5.2 (1997).

Kimmel, Michael. *Manhood in America: A Cultural History.* New York: Free Press, 1996.

Kingston, Maxine Hong. *The Woman Warrior.* New York: Vintage International, 1989.

Kitano, Harry H. L. "The Effects of the Evacuation on the Japanese Americans." *Japanese Americans: From Relocation to Redress.* Ed. Roger Daniels, Sandra C. Taylor and Harry H. L. Kitano. Seattle: University of Washington Press, 1991. 151–158.

Kleinhans, Chuck. "Notes on Melodrama and the Family under Capitalism." *Imitations of Life: A Reader on Film and Television Melodrama.* Ed. Marcia Landy. Detroit: Wayne State University Press, 1991. 197–204.

Klinger, Barbara. *Melodrama and Meaning: History, Culture, and the Films of Douglas Sirk.* Bloomington and Indianapolis: Indiana University Press, 1994.

Kogawa, Joy. *Obasan.* Boston: David R. Godine, 1982.

Kolodny, Annette. *The Lay of the Land: Metaphor as Experience and History in American Life and Letters.* Chapel Hill: University of North Carolina Press, 1975.

Kondo, Dorinne. *About Face: Performing Race in Fashion and Theater.* New York: Routledge, 1997.

Koshy, Susan. "The Fiction of Asian American Literature." *Yale Journal of Criticism* 9.2 (1996). 315–346.

Kovel, Joel. *Red Hunting in the Promised Land: Anticommunism and the Making of America.* New York: Basic Books, 1994.

Kwon, Brenda Lee. "Beyond Keeamoku: Koreans, Nationalism, and Local Culture in Hawai'i." Dissertation. University of California, Los Angeles, 1997.

Kwong, Peter. "Asian American Studies Needs Class Analysis." *Privileging Positions: The Sites of Asian American Studies.* Ed. Gary Y. Okihiro et al. Pullman: Washington State University Press, 1995. 75–81.

Landy, Marcia, ed. *Imitations of Life: A Reader on Film and Television Melodrama.* Detroit: Wayne State University Press, 1991.

————. Introduction. *Imitations of Life: A Reader on Film and Television Melodrama.* Ed. Marcia Landy. Detroit: Wayne State University Press, 1991. 13–30.

Lee, Gus. *China Boy.* New York: Dutton, 1991.

————. *Honor and Duty.* New York: Alfred A. Knopf, 1994.

Lee, Rachel. *The Americas of Asian American Literature.* Princeton: Princeton University Press, 1999.

————. "Asian American Cultural Production in Asian-Pacific Perspective." *boundary 2* 26.2 (1999): 231–254.

Lee, Robert G. *Orientals: Asian Americans in Popular Culture.* Philadelphia: Temple University Press, 1999.

Leffler, Melvyn P. *The Specter of Communism: The United States and the Origins of the Cold War, 1947–1953.* New York: Hill and Wang, 1994.

Leong, Russell, ed. *Asian American Sexualities: Dimensions of the Gay and Lesbian Experience*. New York: Routledge, 1996.

Li, David. *Imagining the Nation: Asian American Literature and Cultural Consent*. Stanford: Stanford University Press, 1998.

Lim, Shirley Geok-lin. "Immigration and Diaspora." *An Interethnic Companion to Asian American Literature*. Ed. King-Kok Cheung. New York: Cambridge University Press, 1997. 289–311.

Ling, Amy. *Between Worlds: Women Writers of Chinese Ancestry*. Elmsford, N.Y.: Pergamon, 1990.

———. "Edith Eaton: Pioneer Chinamerican Writer and Feminist." *American Literary Realism* 16.2 (1983): 287–298.

Ling, Jinqi. "Identity Crisis and Gender Politics: Reappropriating Asian American Masculinity." *An Interethnic Companion to Asian American Literature*. Ed. King-Kok Cheung. New York: Cambridge University Press, 1997. 312–337.

———. *Narrating Nationalisms: Ideology and Form in Asian American Literature*. New York: Oxford University Press, 1998.

———. "Race, Power, and Cultural Politics in John Okada's *No-No Boy*." *American Literature* 67.2 (1995): 359–381.

Lisieux, St. Thérèse of. *Story of a Soul: The Autobiography of St. Thérèse of Lisieux*. Trans. John Washington Clarke. Washington, D.C.: ICS, 1972.

Liu, Eric. *The Accidental Asian: Notes of a Native Speaker*. New York: Random House, 1999.

Lloyd, David. *Anomalous States*. Durham: Duke University Press, 1993.

———. *Nationalism and Minor Literature: James Clarence Mangan and the Emergence of Irish Cultural Nationalism*. Berkeley: University of California Press, 1987.

Lomperis, Timothy. *"Reading the Wind": The Literature of the Vietnam War*. Durham: Duke University Press, 1987.

Lowe, Donald M. *The Body in Late-Capitalist USA*. Durham: Duke University Press, 1995.

Lowe, Lisa. *Immigrant Acts: On Asian American Cultural Politics*. Durham: Duke University Press, 1996.

———. "Unfaithful to the Original: The Subject of *Dictee*." *Writing Self, Writing Nation: Essays on Theresa Hak Kyung Cha's Dictee*. Eds. Elaine H. Kim and Norma Alarcón. Berkeley: Third Woman Press, 1994. 35–69.

Luibhéid, Eithne. "The 1965 Immigration and Nationality Act: An 'End' to Exclusion?" *positions: east asia cultures critique* 5.2 (1997): 501–522.

Lukács, Georg. *History and Class Consciousness*. Trans. Rodney Livingstone. Cambridge: MIT Press, 1968.

Lummis, Charles. "Profile of Sui Sin Far." *Land of Sunshine* 13.5 (1900): 336.

Lye, Colleen. "Toward an Asian (American) Cultural Studies: Postmodernism and the 'Peril of Yellow Capital and Labor.'" *Privileging Positions: The Sites of Asian American Studies*. Ed. Gary Y. Okihiro, et al. Pullman: Washington State University Press, 1995. 47–56.

Ma, Sheng-Mei. *Immigrant Subjectivities in Asian American and Asian Diaspora Literatures*. Albany: State University of New York Press, 1998.

Macherey, Pierre. *A Theory of Literary Production*. London: Routledge, 1978.

Manalansan, Martin. "In the Shadows of Stonewall: Examining Gay Transnational Politics and the Diasporic Dilemma." *The Politics of Culture in the Shadow of Capital*. Ed. Lisa Lowe and David Lloyd. Durham: Duke University Press, 1997. 485–505.

——. "Speaking of AIDS: Language and the Filipino 'Gay' Experience in America." *Discrepant Histories: Translocal Essays on Filipino Cultures*. Ed. Vicente L. Rafael. Philadelphia: Temple University Press, 1995. 193–220.

Mar, Donald. "The Lost Second Generation of Asian American Scholars." *Reflections on Shattered Windows: Promises and Prospects for Asian American Studies*. Ed. Gary Y. Okihiro, et al. Pullman: Washington State University Press, 1988. 37–42.

Marchetti, Gina. *Romance and the "Yellow Peril": Race, Sex, and Discursive Strategies in Hollywood Fiction*. Berkeley: University of California Press, 1993.

Marr, David. *Vietnamese Tradition on Trial, 1920–1945*. Berkeley: University of California Press, 1981.

Martini, Fritz. "Bildungsroman—Term and Theory." *Reflection and Action: Essays on the Bildungsroman*. Ed. James Hardin. Columbia: University of South Carolina Press, 1991. 1–25.

Marx, Karl. *Capital*. Vol. 1. New York: Penguin, 1976.

Mason, John W. *The Cold War: 1945–1991*. London: Routledge, 1996.

Matsuda, Mari. *Where Is Your Body? and Other Essays on Race, Gender, and the Law*. Boston: Beacon Press, 1996.

Matsukawa, Yuko. "Cross-Dressing and Cross-Naming: Decoding Onoto Watanna." *Tricksterism in Turn-of-the-Century American Literature: A Multicultural Perspective*. Ed. Elizabeth Ammons and Annette White-Parks. Hanover: University Press of New England, 1994. 106–125.

Mayne, Judith. *Cinema and Spectatorship*. London: Routledge, 1993.

McClain, Charles J. *In Search of Equality: The Chinese Struggle against Discrimination in Nineteenth-Century America*. Berkeley: University of California Press, 1994.

Mohanty, Chandra Talpade. "Cartographies of Struggle: Third World Women and the Politics of Feminism." *Third World Women and the Politics of Feminism*. Ed. Chandra Talpade Mohanty, Ann Russo, and Lourdes Torres. Bloomington: Indiana University Press, 1991. 1–47.

Morales, Rodney. "Literature." *Multicultural Hawaii: The Fabric of a Multiethnic Society*. Ed. Michael Haas. New York: Garland, 1998. 107–129.

Morrante, P. C. *Remembering Carlos Bulosan: His Heart Affair with America*. Quezon City: New Day, 1984.

Moy, James S. *Marginal Sights: Staging the Chinese in America*. Iowa City: University of Iowa Press, 1993.

Mulvey, Laura. *Visual and Other Pleasures*. Bloomington and Indianapolis: Indiana University Press, 1989.

Mura, David. *Turning Japanese: Memoirs of a Sansei*. New York: Atlantic Monthly Press, 1991.

Nackenoff, Carol. *The Fictional Republic: Horatio Alger and American Political Discourse*. New York: Oxford University Press, 1994.

Najmi, Samina. Introduction. *The Heart of Hyacinth*. Onoto Wtanna. Seattle: University of Washington Press, 2000. v–xlvi.

Nguyen Du. *The Tale of Kieu*. Trans. Huynh Sanh Thong. New Haven: Yale University Press, 1983.

Nguyen Thi Dinh. *No Other Road to Take*. Trans. Mai Elliot. Ithaca, N.Y.: Cornell University, Dept. of Asian Studies, 1976.

Nha-Trang Cong-Huyen-Ton-Nu-Thi. "The Traditional Roles of Women as Reflected in Oral and Written Vietnamese Literature." Dissertation. University of California, Berkeley, 1973.

Niranjana, Tejaswini. *Siting Translation: History, Post-Structuralism, and the Colonial Context*. Berkeley and Los Angeles: University of California Press, 1992.

Oishi, Eve. Introduction. *Miss Numè of Japan*. Onoto Watanna. Baltimore: Johns Hopkins University Press, 1999. xi–xxxii.

Okada, John. *No-No Boy*. Seattle: University of Washington Press, 1976.

Okamura, Jonathan. "Social Stratification." *Multicultural Hawaii: The Fabric of a Multiethnic Society*. Ed. Michael Haas. New York: Garland, 1998. 185–204.

Okamura, Jonathan Y. "Aloha Kanaka Me Ke Aloha 'Aina: Local Culture and Society in Hawai'i." *Amerasia Journal* 7.2 (1980): 119–137.

———. "When Will It End?" *Association for Asian American Studies Newsletter*, May 1998: 9.

Okazaki, Steven. *American Sons*. San Francisco: Farallon Films, 1995.

Okihiro, Gary. Introduction. *Reflections on Shattered Windows: Promises and Prospects for Asian American Studies*. Ed. Gary Y. Okihiro et al. Pullman: Washington State University Press, 1988. xvii–xviii.

———. *Margins and Mainstreams: Asians in American History and Culture*. Seattle: University of Washington Press, 1994.

Olin, Susan Moller. "Gender, the Public and the Private." *Political Theory Today*. Ed. David Held. Stanford: Stanford University Press, 1991.

Omatsu, Glenn. "The 'Four Prisons' and the Movements of Liberation: Asian American Activism from the 1960s to the 1990s." *The State of Asian America: Activism and Resistance in the 1990s*. Ed. Karen Aguilar–San Juan. Boston: South End Press, 1994. 19–69.

Omi, Michael. "It Just Ain't the Sixties No More: The Contemporary Dilemmas of Asian American Studies." *Reflections on Shattered Windows: Promises and Prospects for Asian American Studies*. Ed. Gary Y. Okihiro, et al. Pullman: Washington State University Press, 1988. 31–36.

Omi, Michael, and Howard Winant. *Racial Formation in the United States*. 2nd ed. New York: Routledge, 1994.

Ong, Aihwa. *Flexible Citizenship: The Cultural Logics of Transnationality*. Durham: Duke University Press, 1999.

———. *Spirits of Resistance and Capitalist Discipline: Factory Women in Malaysia*. Albany: State University of New York Press, 1987.

Ong, Paul, Edna Bonacich, and Lucie Cheng, eds. *The New Asian Immigration in Los Angeles and Global Restructuring*. Philadelphia: Temple University Press, 1994.

Osajima, Keith. "Asian Americans as the Model Minority: An Analysis of the Popular Press Image in the 1960s and 1980s." *Reflections on Shattered Windows: Promises and Prospects for Asian American Studies*. Ed. Gary Y. Okihiro et al. Pullman: Washington State University Press, 1988. 165–174.

Palumbo-Liu, David. *Asian/American: Historical Crossings of a Racial Frontier*. Stanford: Stanford University Press, 1999.

Parreñas, Rhacel Salazar. ""White Trash' Meets the 'Little Brown Monkeys': The Taxi Dance Hall as a Site of Interracial and Gender Alliances between White Working Class Women and Filipino Immigrant Men in the 1920s and 30s." *Amerasia Journal* 24.2 (1998): 115–134.

Pennybacker, Mindy. "What Boddah You?: The Authenticity Debate." *Nation*, March 1, 1999. http://www.thenation.com/issue/990301/0301pennybacker.shtml (20 January 2001).

Percival, Olive. "An Afternoon in Chinatown." *Land of Sunshine* 11.1 (1899): 50–52.

Pomeroy, William J. *The Philippines: Colonialism, Collaboration, and Resistance!* New York: International Publishers, 1992.

Porter, Carolyn. *Seeing and Being: The Plight of the Participant Observer in Emerson, James, Adams, and Faulkner.* Middletown, Conn.: Wesleyan University Press, 1981.

Prashad, Vijay. "Crafting Solidarities." *A Part, yet Apart: South Asians in Asian America.* Ed. Lavina Dhingra Shankar and Rajini Srikanth. Philadelphia: Temple University Press, 1998. 105–126.

———. *The Karma of Brown Folk.* Minneapolis: University of Minnesota Press, 2000.

Puar, Jasbir K. "Transnational Sexualities: South Asian (Trans)nation(alism)s and Queer Diasporas." *Q&A: Queer in Asian America.* Ed. David L. Eng and Alice Y. Hom. Philadelphia: Temple University Press, 1998. 405–422.

Radway, Janice. *Reading the Romance: Women, Patriarchy, and Popular Literature.* Chapel Hill: University of North Carolina Press, 1991.

Rafael, Vicente. "White Love: Surveillance and Nationalist Resistance in the U.S. Colonization of the Philippines." *Cultures of United States Imperialism.* Ed. Amy Kaplan and Donald A. Pease. Durham: Duke University Press, 1993. 185–218.

Revilla, Linda. "Our History, Our Future." *Association for Asian American Studies Newsletter,* May 1998: 8.

Rideout, Walter. *The Radical Novel in the United States 1900–1954.* New York: Columbia University Press, 1992.

Roediger, David R. *The Wages of Whiteness: Race and the Making of the American Working Class.* New York: Verso, 1991.

Rogin, Michael Paul. *"Ronald Reagan," the Movie, and Other Episodes in Political Demonology.* Berkeley: University of California Press, 1987.

Rosa, John P. "Local Story: The Massie Case Narrative and the Cultural Production of Local Identity in Hawai'i." *Amerasia Journal* 26.2 (2000): 93–115.

Rosca, Ninotchka. *State of War.* New York: W. W. Norton, 1988.

Rosen, Philip, ed. *Narrative, Apparatus, Ideology: A Film Theory Reader.* New York: Columbia University Press, 1986.

Rotundo, E. Anthony. *American Manhood: Transformations in Masculinity from the Revolution to the Modern Era.* New York: Basic Books, 1993.

Rowe, John Carlos. "'Bringing It All Back Home': American Recyclings of the Vietnam War." *The Violence of Representation.* Ed. Nancy Armstrong and Leonard Tennenhouse. London: Routledge, 1989. 197–218.

Said, Edward. *Orientalism.* New York: Vintage, 1979.

Saito, Natsu Taylor. "Model Minority, Yellow Peril: Functions of 'Foreignness' in the Constructions of Asian American Legal Identity." *Asian Law Journal* 4.71 (1997): 71–95.

Sammons, Jeffrey L. "The Bildungsroman for Nonspecialists: An Attempt at a Clarification." *Reflection and Action: Essays on the Bildungsroman.* Ed. James Hardin. Columbia: University of South Carolina Press, 1991. 26–45.

San Juan, E., Jr. "In Search of Filipino Writing: Reclaiming Whose 'America'?" *The Ethnic Canon: Histories, Institutions, and Interventions.* Ed. David Palumbo-Liu. Minneapolis: University of Minneapolis Press, 1995. 213–240.

———. Introduction. *The Cry and the Dedication.* Carlos Bulosan. Philadelphia: Temple University Press, 1995. ix–xxxvi.

———. Introduction. *On Becoming Filipino: Selected Writings of Carlos Bulosan.* Carlos Bulosan. Philadelphia: Temple University Press, 1995. 1–44.

————. *Racial Formations/Critical Transformations: Articulations of Power in Ethnic and Racial Studies in the United States.* Atlantic Highland, N.J.: Humanities Press, 1992.

Sánchez-Eppler, Karen. *Touching Liberty: Abolition, Feminism, and the Politics of the Body.* Berkeley: University of California Press, 1993.

Scarry, Elaine. *The Body in Pain.* New York: Oxford University Press, 1985.

Schatz, Thomas. "The Family Melodrama." *Imitations of Life: A Reader on Film and Television Melodrama.* Ed. Marcia Landy. Detroit: Wayne State University Press, 1991. 148–167.

Schatzki, Theodore R., and Wolfgang Natter. "Sociocultural Bodies, Bodies Sociopolitical." *The Social and Political Body.* Ed. Theodore R. Schatzki and Wolfgang Natter. New York: Guilford, 1996. 1–25.

Schaub, Thomas Hill. *American Fiction in the Cold War.* Madison: University of Wisconsin Press, 1991.

Schilling, Chris. *The Body and Social Theory.* London: SAGE, 1993.

Schirmer, Daniel B., and Stephen Rosskamm Shalom, eds. *The Philippines Reader: A History of Colonialism, Neocolonialism, Dictatorship, and Resistance.* Boston: South End Press, 1987.

Schueller, Malini Johar. *U.S. Orientalisms: Race, Nation, and Gender in Literature, 1790–1890.* Ann Arbor: University of Michigan Press, 1998.

Scott, James C. *Weapons of the Weak: Everyday Forms of Peasant Resistance.* New Haven: Yale University Press, 1985.

Scott, Joan W. "The Evidence of Experience." *The Lesbian and Gay Studies Reader.* Eds. Henry Abelove, Michèle Aina Berale, and David M. Halperin. New York: Routledge, 1993.

Sedgwick, Eve Kosofsky. *Epistemology of the Closet.* Berkeley and Los Angeles: University of California Press, 1990.

Shah, Sonia, ed. *Dragon Ladies: Asian American Feminists Breathe Fire.* Boston: South End Press, 1997.

Shankar, Lavina Dhingra. "The Limits of (South Asian) Names and Labels: Postcolonial or Asian American?" *A Part, yet Apart: South Asians in Asian America.* Ed. Lavina Dhingra Shankar and Rajini Srikanth. Philadelphia: Temple University Press, 1998. 49–66.

Shankar, Lavina Dhingra, and Rajini Srikanth. "Introduction: Closing the Gap? South Asians Challenge Asian American Studies." *A Part, yet Apart: South Asians in Asian America.* Ed. Lavina Dhingra Shankar and Rajini Srikanth. Philadelphia: Temple University Press, 1998. 1–22.

————, eds. *A Part, yet Apart: South Asians in Asian America.* Philadelphia: Temple University Press, 1998.

Shim, Doobo. "From Yellow Peril through Model Minority to Renewed Yellow Peril." *Journal of Communication Inquiry* 22.4 (1998): 385–409.

Shinagawa, Larry, and Gin Pang. "Asian American Panethnicity and Intermarriage." *Amerasia Journal* 22.2 (1996): 127–152.

Shipler, David K. "A Child's Tour of Duty: Rev. of *When Heaven and Earth Changed Places.*" *New York Times Book Review* 25 (June 1990): 1, 37.

Silverman, Kaja. *Male Subjectivity at the Margins.* New York: Routledge, 1992.

Simpson, Caroline Chung, David Eng, and Wendy Ho. "Response by the Fiction Award Committee." *Association for Asian American Studies Newsletter,* May 1998: 6–7.

Slotkin, Richard. *Regeneration through Violence.* Middletown: Wesleyan University Press, 1973.

Smith, Sidonie. *A Poetics of Women's Autobiography*. Bloomington and Indianapolis: Indiana University Press, 1987.

———. "Resisting the Gaze of Embodiment: Women's Autobiography in the Nineteenth Century." *American Women's Autobiography: Fea(s)ts of Memory*. Ed. Margo Culley. Madison: University of Wisconsin Press, 1992. 75–110.

So, Christine. "Delivering the Punch Line: Racial Combat as Comedy in Gus Lee's *China Boy*." *MELUS* 21.4 (1996): 141-155.

Solberg, S. E. "Sui Sin Far/Edith Eaton: First Chinese-American Fictionalist." *MELUS* 8.1 (1981): 27–40.

Sollors, Werner. *Beyond Ethnicity: Consent and Descent in American Culture*. New York: Oxford University Press, 1986.

Sone, Monica. *Nisei Daughter*. Seattle: University of Washington Press, 1979.

Song, Min. "The Unknowable and Sui Sin Far: The Epistemological Limits of 'Oriental' Sexuality." *Q&A: Queer in Asian America*. Ed. David L. Eng and Alice Y. Hom. Philadelphia: Temple University Press, 1998. 304–322.

Spivak, Gayatri Chakravorty. "Can the Subaltern Speak?" *Colonial Discourse and Post-Colonial Theory*. Ed. Patrick Williams and Laura Chrisman. New York: Columbia University Press, 1994. 66–111.

Stacey, Jackie. *Star Gazing: Hollywood Cinema and Female Spectatorship*. London: Routledge, 1994.

Stern, Michael. *Douglas Sirk*. Boston: Twayne, 1979.

Stone, Oliver. *Heaven and Earth*. Burbank, Calif.: Warner Brothers, 1994.

Su, Karen. "Jade Snow Wong's Badge of Distinction in the 1990s." *Hitting Critical Mass* 2.1 (1994). http://ist-socrates.berkeley.edu/~critmass/v2n1/su1.html (August 2001).

Sui Sin Far. "Leaves from the Mental Portfolio of an Eurasian." *The Big Aiiieeeee! An Anthology of Chinese American and Japanese American Literature*. Ed. Jeffrey Paul Chan et al. New York: Meridian, 1991. 125–132.

———. *Mrs. Spring Fragrance*. Chicago: A. C. McClurg, 1912.

Suleri, Sara. "Woman Skin Deep: Feminism and the Postcolonial Condition." *Colonial Discourse and Post-Colonial Theory*. Ed. Patrick Williams and Laura Chrisman. New York: Columbia University Press, 1994. 244–256.

Sumida, Stephen. *And the View from the Shore: Literary Traditions of Hawai'i*. Seattle: University of Washington Press, 1991.

———. "Postcolonialism, Nationalism, and the Emergence of Asian/Pacific Literatures." *An Interethnic Companion to Asian American Literature*. Ed. King-Kok Cheung. New York: Cambridge University Press, 1997. 274–288.

———. "Sense of Place, History, and the Concept of the 'Local' in Hawaii's Asian/Pacific American Literatures." *Reading the Literature of Asian America*. Ed. Shirley Geok-Lin Lim and Amy Ling. Philadelphia: Temple University Press, 1992. 215–238.

Synnott, Anthony. *The Body Social: Symbolism, Self and Society*. London: Routledge, 1993.

Tachiki, Amy, et al., eds. *Roots: An Asian American Reader*. Los Angeles: UCLA Asian American Studies Center, 1971.

Tadiar, Neferti Xina M. "Manila's New Metropolitan Form." *differences: A Journal of Feminist Criticism* 5.3 (1993): 154–177.

Takagi, Dana. *The Retreat from Race: Asian-American Admissions and Racial Politics*. New Brunswick, N.J.: Rutgers University Press, 1992.

Takaki, Ronald. *Iron Cages: Race and Culture in 19th-Century America.* New York: Oxford University Press, 1990.

———. *Pau Hana: Plantation Life and Labor in Hawaii.* Honolulu: University of Hawai'i Press, 1983.

———. "Reflections on Racial Patterns in America." *From Different Shores: Perspectives on Race and Ethnicity in America.* Ed. Ronald Takaki. 2nd ed. New York: Oxford University Press, 1994. 24–35.

———. *Strangers from a Different Shore: A History of Asian Americans.* Boston: Little, Brown, 1989.

Thompson, Richard Austin. *The Yellow Peril, 1890–1924.* New York: Arno, 1978.

Trask, Haunani-Kay. *From a Native Daughter: Colonialism and Sovereignty in Hawai'i.* Honolulu: University of Hawai'i Press, 1999.

———. "Settlers of Color and 'Immigrant' Hegemony: 'Locals' in Hawai'i." *Amerasia Journal* 26.2 (2000): 1–24.

Trinh T. Minh-ha. "All-Owning Spectatorship." *When the Moon Waxes Red: Representation, Gender, and Cultural Politics.* New York: Routledge, 1991. 81–105.

———. *Woman Native Other.* Bloomington: Indiana University Press, 1989.

Truong, Monique Thuy-Dung. "The Emergence of Voices: Vietnamese American Literature 1975–1990." *Amerasia Journal* 19.3 (1993): 27–50.

Tuan, Mia. *Forever Foreigners or Honorary Whites?: The Asian Ethnic Experience Today.* New Brunswick, N.J.: Rutgers University Press, 1998.

Turim, Maureen. "Gentlemen Consume Blondes." *Issues in Feminist Film Criticism.* Ed. Patricia Erens. Bloomington and Indianapolis: Indiana University Press, 1990. 101–111.

Turner, Bryan S. *The Body and Society.* New York: Blackwell, 1984.

U.S. News & World Report. "Success Story of One Minority Group in U.S." *Roots: An Asian American Reader.* Ed. Amy Tachiki et al. Los Angeles: UCLA Asian American Studies Center, 1971. 6–9.

Vaid, Urvashi. "Inclusion, Exclusion and Occlusion: The Queer Idea of Asian Pacific American-ness." *Amerasia Journal* 25.3 (1999/2000): 1–16.

Wang, Anthony S. "Demystifying the Asian American Neo-Conservative: A Strange and New Political Animal?" *Asian Law Journal* 5.213 (1998): 213–246.

Watanna, Onoto. *Miss Numè of Japan.* Chicago: Rand, McNally, 1899.

———. *Miss Numè of Japan.* Baltimore: Johns Hopkins University Press, 1999.

———. *Sunny-San.* Toronto: McClelland and Stewart, 1922.

———. *The Wooing of Wistaria.* New York: Harper, 1902.

Weeks, Kathi. "Subject for a Feminist Standpoint." *Marxism beyond Marxism.* Ed. Saree Makdisi, Cesare Casarino, and Rebecca E. Karl. New York: Routledge, 1996. 89–118.

Weglyn, Michi. *Years of Infamy.* New York: William Morrow, 1976.

Wei, William. *The Asian American Movement.* Philadelphia: Temple University Press, 1993.

Whitam, Frederick L., and Robin M. Mathy. *Male Homosexuality in Four Societies: Brazil, Guatemala, the Philippines, and the United States.* New York: Praeger, 1986.

White-Parks, Annette. ""We Wear the Mask': Sui Sin Far as One Example of Trickster Authorship." *Tricksterism in Turn-of-the-Century American Literature: A Multicultural Perspective.* Ed. Elizabeth Ammons and Annette White-Parks. Hanover: University Press of New England, 1994. 1–20.

————. *Sui Sin Far/Edith Maude Eaton: A Literary Biography*. Urbana and Chicago: University of Illinois Press, 1995.

Whitfield, Stephen J. *The Culture of the Cold War*. Baltimore: Johns Hopkins University Press, 1991.

Wiegman, Robyn. *American Anatomies: Theorizing Race and Gender*. Durham, N.C.: Duke University Press, 1995.

Williams, Linda. "'Something Else besides a Mother': *Stella Dallas* and the Maternal Melodrama." *Issues in Feminist Film Criticism*. Ed. Patricia Erens. Bloomington and Indianapolis: Indiana University Press, 1990. 137–162.

Wilson, Rob. "Bloody Mary Meets Lois-Ann Yamanaka: Imagining Hawaiian Locality from *South Pacific* to Bamboo Ridge." *Public Culture* 8 (1995): 127–158.

Wong, Sau-ling C. "Denationalization Reconsidered: Asian American Cultural Criticism at a Theoretical Crossroads." *Amerasia Journal* 21.1 & 2 (1995): 1–28.

————. "Diverted Mothering: Representations of Caregivers of Color in the Age of 'Multiculturalism.'" *Mothering: Ideology, Experience, and Agency*. Ed. Grace Chang, Evelyn Nakano-Glenn, and Linda Rennie-Forcey. New York: Routledge, 1994.

————. "Ethnicizing Gender: An Exploration of Sexuality as Sign in Chinese Immigrant Literature." *Reading the Literatures of Asian America*. Ed. Shirley Geok-lin Lim and Amy Ling. Philadelphia: Temple University Press, 1992. 111–129.

————. "Kingston's Handling of Traditional Chinese Sources." *Approaches to Teaching Kingston's The Woman Warrior*. Ed. Shirley Geok-lin Lim. New York: Modern Language Assocation, 1991. 29–36.

————. *Reading Asian American Literature*. Princeton: Princeton University Press, 1993.

Wong, Shelley Sunn. "Unnaming the Same: Theresa Hak Kyung Cha's *Dictee*." *Writing Self, Writing Nation: Essays on Theresa Hak Kyung Cha's Dictee*. Ed. Elaine H. Kim and Norma Alarcón. Berkeley: Third Woman Press, 1994. 103–140.

Wu, William F. *The Yellow Peril: Chinese Americans in American Fiction, 1850–1940*. Hamden, Conn.: Archon, 1982.

Yamamoto, Traise. *Masking Selves, Making Subjects: Japanese American Women, Identity, and the Body*. Berkeley and Los Angeles: University of California Press, 1999.

Yamanaka, Lois-Ann. *Blu's Hanging*. New York: Farrar, Straus, and Giroux, 1997.

————. *Heads by Harry*. New York: Farrar, Straus, anmd Giroux, 1999.

————. *Wild Meat and the Bully Burgers*. New York: Harvest Books, 1997.

Yin, Xiao-Huang. "Between the East and West: Sui Sin Far—the First Chinese-American Woman Writer." *Arizona Quarterly* 47.4 (1991): 49–84.

Yung, Judy. *Unbound Feet: A Social History of Chinese Women in San Francisco*. Berkeley and Los Angeles: University of California Press, 1995.

Zia, Helen. *Asian American Dreams: The Emergence of an American People*. New York: Farrar, Straus, and Giroux, 2000.

Zizek, Slavoj. "Multiculturalism, or the Cultural Logic of Multinational Capitalism." *New Left Review* 225 (1997): 28–51.

INDEX